The Holo

Model for the proposed Shoah Centre, Manchester, by Daniel Libeskind. Photo: James Manning, reproduced with permission.

The Holocaust

Critical historical approaches

Donald Bloxham and Tony Kushner

Manchester University Press
Manchester and New York

distributed exclusively in the USA by Palgrave

Published by Manchester University Press
Oxford Road, Manchester M13 9NR, UK
and Room 400, 175 Fifth Avenue, New York, NY 10010, USA
www.manchesteruniversitypress.co.uk

Distributed exclusively in the USA by
Palgrave, 175 Fifth Avenue, New York,
NY 10010, USA

Distributed exclusively in Canada by
UBC Press, University of British Columbia, 2029 West Mall,
Vancouver, BC, Canada V6T 1Z2

British Library Cataloguing-in-Publication Data
A catalogue record for this book is available from the British Library

Library of Congress Cataloging-in-Publication Data applied for

ISBN   0 7190 3778 6 *hardback*
EAN   978 0 7190 3778 8
ISBN   0 7190 3779 4 *paperback*
EAN   978 0 7190 3779 5

First published 2004

13 12 11 10 09 08 07 06 05 04   10 9 8 7 6 5 4 3 2 1

Printed in Great Britain
by Bell & Bain Limited, Glasgow

To Jo Reilly, for her contribution to the study of the
Holocaust in Britain, and to Colin Richmond, fellow non-
driver who has taught us all to think more carefully

Contents

Preface

This book was originally due for publication in the early 1990s. Its delay, by up to ten years, has been in many ways fortunate, although we doubt that our publisher has necessarily seen it in such a positive light. In these years Holocaust studies has developed substantially. Empirical work has intensified, aided by the availability of new sources, especially from the former eastern bloc. Theoretical sophistication has also evolved in a range of disciplines. No longer is the Holocaust specialist regarded as someone quirky or obsessive. Public interest in the Holocaust has been illustrated by the success of Holocaust museums in many western countries and in films such as *Schindler's List*. Genocide in Africa has increased awareness of its relevance outside Europe, North America, Israel and the Jewish diaspora.

Whether the intensity of interest will be maintained – somewhat bizarrely, it has grown exponentially the further we have moved chronologically from the events themselves – is impossible to predict. In a further ten years this book may appear a dinosaur or a museum piece either because scholarship has continued to develop so quickly or because interest in the Holocaust subsequently peaked. The book is designed to provide its readers with the apparatus necessary to confront and engage critically with the complexity of Holocaust historiography and some of its players and primary sources, as well as with the shaping and re-shaping of Holocaust memory. Indeed, it may be deemed to have succeeded if it provides the tools for later scholars to investigate the subject matter further, thereby making it obsolete.

Preface

Many thanks are in order. First, to Alison Welsby, for her patience, good humour and genuine enthusiasm for this project. She has stayed with it when many of our friends and colleagues, especially those in the Cavaliers cricket team, were in total disbelief that it would ever see the light of day. Inspiration was found in its initial stages from the Jackpot Café in the Portswood suburb of Southampton. Never has so much high cholesterol food been consumed for the greater good of scholarship. Thanks are also due to A. Dirk Moses and Tom Lawson for reading draft chapters of this work. We would also like to pay tribute to two individuals who within Britain have made an enormous but rarely acknowledged contribution to Holocaust studies. The first is Colin Richmond, formerly Professor of Medieval History at the University of Keele, and the first to teach a special subject on the Holocaust in this country. His early retirement from academia is an indictment of all that has gone wrong with British higher education in recent years. On this special subject he taught and motivated one of the authors of this book, as well as Dr Jo Reilly. At the Wiener Library in London and at the Parkes Institute at the University of Southampton Jo Reilly has researched, taught, published and inspired people from school kids to students of the third age. This book is dedicated to these two remarkable and impossible people with love and affection.

TK, Southampton
DB, Edinburgh

Introduction

At the beginning of their penetrating analysis of the Third Reich, *The Racial State*, Michael Burleigh and Wolfgang Wippermann asked why was another book on Nazi Germany needed?[1] The same question could be posed about the genocide of the Jews. Our reasons for producing this book are twofold, and are connected. The first, more straightforward reason is that in one of the most rapidly expanding areas of historical enquiry there is ample scope for occasional footnotes detailing and contextualising additions to the existing body of knowledge. The need for an update is particularly pressing given the volume of intensive research conducted since the fall of the iron curtain allowed access to eastern European archives, research which has shed much new light specifically on the development of the 'final solution of the Jewish question'.

The second and greater of our aims will hopefully produce something of more enduring utility than a survey work with an in-built expiry date. 'Problematisation' is the keyword: the dissection and re-examination of accepted concepts and 'knowledge'. The Holocaust, like Nazism, has become ubiquitous, and not just within a mass media that appears obsessed with the subject. Besides the vast and growing body of academic scholarship, a large number of introductory texts of varying standards is available to feed the demand in the proliferating university courses focusing on the period. As for school education, in Britain study of the Holocaust is now on the national curriculum, an educational imperative complemented by the establishment of a national museum exhibition and 'Holocaust memorial day', and by deployment of the subject in the Labour government's 'citizenship initiative'. This book is a plea for the application of the standard historical tools of contextualisation and nuance so students forming an acquaintance with the Holocaust develop the intellectual faculties necessary to dissect an increasingly large component of their formal and 'moral' education.

As with any subject that achieves iconic dimensions, the Holocaust has done so because it has touched a nerve in society. However – and again like other icons – that very resonance brings with it a host of received wisdoms and canonical 'truths' that have only an imprecise resemblance to the history they invoke. Put slightly differently, all history is viewed through prisms imposed after the fact. But this is of particular significance in the study of the Holocaust because of the extreme and emotive nature of the events in question, where reason is sometimes challenged as a mode of analysis and where popular 'ownership' discourages interpretative leadership by the scholarly profession.

Symbolism is a problematic issue for the modern student, especially as the Holocaust has come to represent ultimate 'evil', however one interprets that concept. Here we might pause to think about Auschwitz, the largest Nazi extermination centre. Auschwitz has for many come to represent the Holocaust as a whole, and yet its complex function is little understood: Auschwitz I was primarily a concentration camp for the local population, and Auschwitz II, Birkenau, approximately 2 km away, had been designated a prisoner-of-war camp and a slave labour reservoir before it became the major killing centre for western, central and southern European Jewry. Might not those tour-groups who visit the present-day Auschwitz site, and the morally outraged in Britain and the USA, be rather more understanding of the presence of symbolic crosses immediately outside Auschwitz I if they realised that more Polish non-Jews died at that part of the complex than did Jews?

At an even more general historical level, what do we mean by the very term 'Holocaust' itself? Clearly this was not an expression used by the Nazis to describe what they were inflicting upon the Jews, nor was it used at the time by their victims. The word achieved popularity well into the post-war era and has since become a jealously guarded label for what Raul Hilberg called, more precisely, *The Destruction of the European Jews*.[2] An obvious difficulty with the application of the all-encompassing epithet is the chronology of the murder of the Jews, which varied from country to country, region to region, and even district to district. Does 'the Holocaust' begin with the invasion of Poland, or the Soviet Union, or should we take Hitler's ascension to power to be the starting point, or the first legalised 'racial' definition of the Jews, neither of which led inevitably to the point of killing? Moreover, the fate of the Jews under various of the German client regimes often stemmed from causes that were different from the German–Jewish dynamic and resulted in different patterns of persecution and murder, thus 'the Holocaust' is scarcely useful analytically in terms of the perpetration process.

From the opposite point of view to that of the perpetrators, 'the Holocaust' can stand as shorthand for the Jewish experience during the Second World War and/or the Nazi period. Yet the experience of victimhood was not a standard one either: it had no set beginning or end point. Here, it is worth noting that the most sophisticated scholars of Nazi policy have chosen not to use the unscientific 'Holocaust'. Raul Hilberg's massive study preceded the popular usage of the term, but the foremost authority over the last two decades, Christopher Browning, has referred consistently to the more specific Nazi term the 'final solution',[3] while the cohort of German historians who have made a great recent impact with detailed studies of the occupation of eastern Europe have preferred to employ simple descriptive terminology such as Nazi 'Jewish policy' (*Judenpolitik*) or the 'policy/policies of annihilation' (*Vernichtungspolitik*).[4]

The prisms through which we as a society now view the murder of the Jews are legion, but there are some of obvious and widespread relevance. We have selected three as the basis for our examination – the 'victims' and their experience (chapter 1), the 'perpetrators' and their deeds (chapters 2 and 3) and the 'bystanders' and their responses (chapter 4) – while seeking whenever necessary to question the validity of these popular categories.

None of the questions raised here is examined exhaustively. That is not the function of an introductory volume, and besides, more detailed studies are referred to in both the notes and the bibliography. Neither will the book provide a chronology of im-

3

portant events, nor a 'history' of the Holocaust in any conventional sense. Nor will it re-stage set-piece historiographical debates, some of which are now obsolete, for the convenience of student examination preparation. Rather, we hope to equip the reader with the means to approach a central event of the twentieth century from a number of directions, and unencumbered by some of the baggage that has become attached to the study of it. We have entitled the study *The Holocaust: Critical Historical Approaches*. Within the space available, and given the hugeness of the task, it would be impossible here to produce a full 'counter-history'. Nevertheless, the aim is to move beyond a mere critique of the existing literature and to suggest, if sometimes only tentatively, fresh directions, approaches and opportunities for the future development of what has become known as Holocaust studies.

Our three prisms are placed in no rank of importance to the reader, but there is a logic to their order of presentation. First, in chapter 1, we examine the experience of the survivor, as illustrated primarily through memoirs but also through live, recorded or transcribed oral testimony. In rarer cases also we have the writings of those who did not survive the murder process, generally in the form of diaries, and generally describing the world of the ghettos rather than the extermination camps and other killing grounds.

Jeshajahu Weinberg (founding director) and Rina Elieli (his consultant) relate how the United States Holocaust Memorial Museum in Washington, which opened in April 1993, 'describes the roles of the actors who were involved in the Holocaust: the perpetrators, the victims, the bystanders, the rescuers, and the liberators. The victims wanted the world to know. The perpetrators wanted the world not to know. The bystanders wanted the world not to know that they knew.'[5] If the victims' purpose was to inform the world then the fast diminishing number of survivors can take comfort in the fact that they have succeeded. The Holocaust is now firmly established as the most remembered and engaged-with act of genocide or persecution in history. In contrast to earlier marginalisation, survivors such as Wiesel are now treated with the greatest respect, even awe.[6] It has been written of Simon Wiesenthal, survivor of Buchenwald and Mauthausen turned Nazi hunter, that '[l]ike all Holocaust survivors, years of neglect and even contempt were followed by the other side of the coin – sanctification'.[7]

There is no problem in focusing on the perpetrators *per se*, as indeed we do for half of this book, but several caveats are in order. First, there is the danger of titillation: like it or not, National Socialism has become eroticised and the sado-masochistic potential of representing the killers has to be kept in mind and minimised. Daniel Goldhagen's *Hitler's Willing Executioners*, in its desire to show the horrors committed by 'ordinary Germans', ultimately falls into the trap of providing titillation through the horrors inflicted on its victims.[8] Second, and linked to the first, the representation of the victims also requires care and thought. Jews and others persecuted by the Third Reich were largely powerless to stop the onslaught and in this sense are irrelevant to how the perpetrators carried out the destruction process. And yet historians of the huge traumas of the modern age – whether in the form of genocide, war, slavery, imperialism (or a combination of these forms) – have still to find the appropriate voice to communicate the horror of these experiences. When few in the historical or heritage world want to face humankind's potential for destructiveness and cruelty, it may seem churlish to criticise those that do for their mode of representation. Hilberg relates how he argued for the inclusion of a wall devoted to the 'photographic portraits of sixteen or twenty perpetrators, known and unknown, to represent the civil service, the military, industry, and the party' at the United States Holocaust Memorial Museum. The concept of the 'Hilberg wall', however, was never really accepted. The very ordinariness of many of the perpetrators, and the positions they occupied, perhaps raised too many uncomfortable questions. As Hilberg states in relation to the Washington museum, the 'fadeout of the perpetrator [was] no accident'.[9]

There is the potential, however, for replicating the perpetrators' view of their victims as mere objects, numbers and categories to be abused and disposed of – as essentially 'other' to 'us'. Hilberg rightly points out the danger of presenting the victims as simply heroic. Yet he neither suggests alternative forms of representation, nor confronts the dilemmas of using German documents where, as he somewhat understates it, the 'victims do not have much individuality'.[10] Moreover, rather than emerge as heroic, the victims have often been portrayed in a state of utter degradation. For example, images from the liberated western concentration camps of dead and decomposing bodies are used freely to illustrate the horrors of Nazism or more generally man's capacity for evil without any care given to who those are in the photographs.[11] Likewise, Marcus Wood has criticised representations of slavery in British museums: 'Museum parodies of the middle passage, which claim to "put us there", may well do more harm than good. You cannot merchandise, advertise and package the middle passage.'[12] Wood adds that in Liverpool in the 'Transatlantic Slavery' gallery of the Merseyside Maritime Museum a tension exists between the

> presentation of European and African cultures. The Liverpool we are shown looks foreign because of time, but its foreignness is mediated by the familiarity of historical displays in museums; the Africa we are shown looks foreign because it is foreign. The European side of things is comfortably aged ... Despite their horrible functions the branding irons and slave collars on display are almost reassuring ... The presentation of African cultures is altogether different [conforming] to the conventions of anthropological and ethnographical exhibits ... The assumption here is that the audience is being brought before something alien and exotic, another style of life, another way of living.[13]

Critical analysis is required to explain processes of destruction and how ordinary people can so easily become murderers. Part of such processes, however, is to disregard the shared humanity of those to be killed. The history and sociology of perpetrators that dismisses the victims will become part of the problem rather than the solution.

Victim evidence needs to be taken seriously in its own right, which means moving beyond the focus purely on the years of persecution. A life story approach is required, examining the years before the Holocaust impacted on the individual, as well as during it, and, for the survivors, their life beyond liberation and the end of the war. Such testimony can be, and frequently is, used with sensitivity as an illustrative device to show the impact of Nazi policies. More important, however, is its potential, given the scale and variety of materials available, as a form of social history in which ordinary people have constructed and re-constructed their lives through the impact of the most traumatic experiences. Never before have historians and others been given the opportunity to confront the experience of persecution through such an abundance of testimony. Furthermore, in contrast to forced confessions and legal evidence that is often all that is available to those working with persecutions of the past, such as witchcraft mania or the Spanish Inquisition, this testimony has been given and continues to be given with relative freedom. Nevertheless, the emphasis must be on the word relative. It has to be remembered, for example, that the ghetto diarists were mindful of their writings falling into the wrong hands and incriminating friends and associates. They are often discreet, therefore, on issues such as resistance. More starkly, those in the death camps who survived the initial selections rarely had access to pen and paper.[14] In more recent times, some survivors have submitted to oral and video interviewing because they think it is important to do so, rather than out of any major impulse towards autobiography. Most importantly, we accept Henry Greenspan's comments, that 'survivors have come to anticipate listeners' expectations'.[15]

Returning to the concept of the 'victim', the early historiography on the Holocaust in the 1950s, culminating in Hilberg's monumental work published in 1961, continued the focus of the war trials and rarely moved beyond the perpetrators. Claims in the later 1950s and early 1960s of Jewish passivity or collusion of the Jewish leadership in the ghettos, however, stimulated much work on resistance, and particularly armed resistance. This built on earlier commemoration of the Warsaw ghetto rebellion of April 1943 and broadened the scope to include revolts in other ghettos and the death camps, the work of the Jewish partisans and non-violent forms of resistance.[16] The victims were, by the 1960s, no longer silent or faceless but it still took several decades before they were to be regarded as, as has been said of Elie Wiesel, a 'messenger to all humanity'.[17] The huge number of Holocaust memoirs that have appeared since the late 1980s reflects undoubtedly a generational development within the survivors themselves as well as their growing fears of Holocaust denial, a repeat, to them, of their camp nightmare of post-war disbelief. It also reflects a demand, commercial and otherwise, for their work. In a western world where many seek to be seen and treated as victims, the murder of European Jewry has developed an iconic status. There is a danger that we have moved from one extreme to another – from the absence of reflection on victims in 1945 through to the situation in a postmodern world where we are, as the French student protest movement in 1968 sloganised, 'all German Jews'.[18] Rather than accepting simply that the 'victims wanted the world to know', it is necessary now to pursue a more inclusive position where we know about the victims – their particularity and individuality – and develop a critical understanding of them, both theoretically and through their testimony. That is the purpose of the first chapter of this study, penned by Tony Kushner.

Next, Donald Bloxham considers the perpetration of the 'final solution' over the second and third chapters. This is the area over which most ink has been spilt, and of our three prisms it is the only one that casts light on the inner mechanics of genocide and illuminates causality. It has spawned the most globally controversial explanations and the greatest generalisations, and must be at the heart of any assessment of the Holocaust and its historiography, as it is here. The question of why Germans and others killed Jews (and others) is the fundamental one. This implies examinations on a number of levels: how a party-state came to propagate an ideology of virulent racism; how that theoretical racism was translated into a policy of murder and then increasingly total murder; and how that policy was accepted, contributed to and implemented by a wide variety of individuals and institutions.

In metaphysical terms comprehension of the 'final solution' may be impossible, as various theologians and survivors have contended.[19] Perhaps the same conclusion would be drawn from theological attempts to come to terms with other genocides and man-made catastrophes, yet such attempts have tellingly never been made in the mainstream. But this is in any case to follow the dead-end path described earlier, and to address the Holocaust from the popular perspective of today as a monumental, unitary, epoch-making event before which human analytical techniques must be doomed to failure. Regardless of the nature of the genocide as a whole, as Christopher Browning has written, its contingent parts are anything but 'unique',[20] and they are certainly explicable. 'Auschwitz' as a symbol may be unapproachable, but Auschwitz-Birkenau, the killing centre uncovered by Soviet forces on 27 January 1945, is not. Like any historical episode, 'The Holocaust' can be broken down and rendered more understandable.

How often, for instance, is it heard said that the 'uniqueness' (a singularly unscholarly term) of the genocide of the Jews relies upon the totality of the Nazis' intentions towards their victims, upon the fact that every single one was to be pursued relentlessly and without regard to the damage that this might do to the rest of the German war effort? Indeed, this assertion is not only the product of popular wisdom. Several historians have made similar claims in comparative analyses that seek to establish the 'final solution' as unique amongst genocides.[21] Yet a cursory examination of German history between 1933 and 1945 shows that totality in murderous intention developed out of a number of different and sometimes conflicting strands of Nazi policy, the most obvious being the prevailing desire in the second half of the 1930s to encourage and force Jews to emigrate from the Reich. In terms of the more-or-less immediate murder of every Jew within German influence, policy was probably still developing until late spring 1942, long after the killing process itself began.[22]

As to the idea of the Jews being murdered irrespective of economic and logistical implications, a look at specifics shows that the railway traffic of Jews to the killing grounds was not at the expense of the war effort; the proportion of trains transporting Jews was minute, and these deportation trains were assigned priority well below the requirements of the German military.[23] Equally, even committed Nazis pressed with some success for the temporary exemption of certain Jewish workers and workforces at certain times.[24] Further to the notion of every single Jew anywhere being scheduled for death, we might consider the programme of exchange for which the Bergen-Belsen concentration camp was erected early in 1943. Given that for the British people in particular Belsen was promoted as *the* symbol of the depravity of Nazism after its 'liberation' in 1945,[25] it is somewhat ironic that the camp was originally intended to serve as a holding centre for Jewish citizens of non-Nazi, non-occupied countries, who might be given safe passage out of German hands in return for the transfer into the Reich of Germans living outside the German sphere of power.[26]

That murder held sway in Nazi Jewish policy from mid-1941 is clear evidence of the pathological antisemitism of key orchestrators of the destruction process, and of the situation of radicalisation that the Nazi state had by then reached. Yet it would be wrong to extrapolate from that to claim that everyone involved in the development of Jewish policy subscribed to the same fanatically held, fantastic beliefs, or to deny the role of prosaic motives for participation in extraordinary acts.

Goldhagen's bestseller *Hitler's Willing Executioners* provides a straw man that can easily be knocked down.[27] Essentially, Goldhagen attempts to locate the genesis of genocide solely in an ingrained and pathological German hatred of Jews. However, in his focus upon the 'exterminatory' will of the average German he ignores much research on the unexceptional nature of German antisemitism prior to 1933, on the absence of a plan of murder before the summer of 1941 at the earliest, and on the complexity of policy-making in the 'Third Reich'. Nor does his analysis allow for the fact that the Nazis murdered huge numbers of non-Jews in killing campaigns running alongside the 'final solution of the Jewish question'. These murders may not have been carried out as a result of precisely the same thought processes that led to the 'final solution', but it is impossible to understand the killing of the Jews without apprehending the previous killing of Germany's 'disabled', or the simultaneous killing of huge numbers of Romanies and Slavs (and Goldhagen is by no means alone in ignoring them).

Breaking down monolithic 'explanations' like Goldhagen's is as important as breaking down the monolithic concept of the Holocaust. But the process of historical investigation cannot just be the negative one of ascertaining what cannot be said. This book is far from a postmodern critique of the very art of the historian; it aspires in these central chapters to provide some explanatory contexts and concepts. Constructive endeavour is the most difficult, owing to the ever-increasing breadth and depth of our knowledge of the Nazi system and its control of Europe. Thus, for instance, a wave of scholarship is certainly right to identify the 'blood and guts' indoctrination and brutalisation of German soldiers who contributed impetus and scope to the killing in eastern Europe,[28] but how is this to be squared with the model of a modern, impersonal 'machinery of destruction' created and endorsed by Hilberg[29] and Zygmunt Bauman[30] respectively. And can either interpretation stand up in the face of the new research findings since the end of the Cold War which emphasise simultaneously the complexity of the Nazi decision-making process and the degree of ideological consensus underpinning it *and* regional variations in the murder process? Chapter 3 in particular seeks ways in which these different visions might be reconciled.

The attempt to piece together some of the mosaic inevitably means that we are engaged in an interpretative exercise which the reader may find it useful to break down in turn. Clearly no book is a set of blank pages onto which the sources inscribe themselves 'objectively', and this point has been illustrated particularly vividly in Holocaust historiography. We should not be surprised, for instance, when 'conservative' historians, stressing the role in history of great men and great ideas, contend, as so-called intentionalists such as Lucy Dawidowicz or Gerald Fleming have done, that the Holocaust was the outcome of the long-standing 'intention' or blueprint of Hitler.[31] Nor, conversely, should we be surprised when social historians schooled in the study of modern society and its complex structures emerge from their studies concluding, like 'functionalists' such as Hans Mommsen and Martin Broszat, that mass murder sprang from a bureaucratic solution to a policy problem created by radical but short-sighted Nazi leaders.[32]

Even leaving aside the question of rigour in research, a scholar's experience, predisposition, training and ideology all work to influence the selection and interpretation of evidence. The outcome of such considerations must be self-awareness and circumscription on our parts in terms of re-presenting aspects of the past here. Part of such caution is the acknowledgement of partiality in our writing, and the anticipation of partiality in the reader. We must as a basic minimum recognise that we are writing as and for the inhabitants of a liberal democracy at the start of the twenty-first century, with all the predispositions that that identity entails. Thus the writing will be differently angled than would an equivalent authored in and for Britain, or for West Germany, or indeed for East Germany, in the decades following the Second World War. This point is of particular relevance to the fourth and final chapter, which considers one of the supposedly most relevant moral 'lessons' of the Holocaust for the modern, western world.

In the final chapter, Kushner examines the relationship between the Holocaust and the so-called bystanders, the third of the classic triumvirate of parties to the genocide. This study does not include a detailed study of every sub-group of the very broad collective of bystanders: some of those complicit in the murder

process are studied in chapter 2. While occupied countries such as
Poland and Denmark are referred to, the focus is upon the role of
the 'free world', particularly the liberal democracies and especially Britain and the United States, the leading western Allies
during the war. The intention of this chapter is to go beyond the
easy moral critique of bystanders which is increasingly coming to
the fore. It aims to understand what they did and did not do, and,
through careful comparisons, to examine the choices available to
contemporaries. The emphasis of this chapter is, following the
work of Michael Marrus, to avoid the tendency 'to condemn,
rather than to explain'.[33] It places, for example, policy towards the
entry of those fleeing from the Nazi regime in the context of
longer-term refugee and immigration policies of the British and
American state structures. In particular, it examines the ideological and cultural factors behind Anglo-American reactions and responses to the Jewish plight, avoiding simplistic explanations
such as 'antisemitism', but at the same time analysing when, and
when not, the Jewishness of the victims became relevant.

A source that became available as this book was going to press
exposes the dangers of reductive approaches to this controversial
area in which there are many vested emotional interests. In the
summer of 2003 the 1947 diary of Harry S. Truman, President of
the United States from 1945 to 1953, was discovered. In July 1947 a
ship carrying Jewish survivors of the Holocaust coming from the
Displaced Persons (DP) camps in Europe was turned back, having
reached Palestine, by the British authorities. Former Treasury
Secretary Henry Morgenthau, who was Jewish, approached the
President to seek his intervention. Truman was furious, writing in
his diary that

> The Jews, I find, are very, very selfish. They care not how many
> Estonians, Latvians, Finns, Poles, Yugoslavs or Greeks get mur-
> dered or mistreated as DPs as long as the Jews get special treat-
> ment. Yet when they have power, physical, financial or political,
> neither Hitler nor Stalin has anything on them for cruelty or mis-
> treatment of the underdog.[34]

Reactions to the diary disclosure have been predictable – shock at
Truman's apparent antisemitism followed by denials that he was
prejudiced against the Jews. Truman previously had been seen as
a friend of the Jews and especially as a supporter of the creation of

the state of Israel in 1948.[35] What the diary entry suggests is the limitations of concepts such as antisemitism or pro-Jewishness. It shows that Truman was capable of buying into a negative discourse about Jews as self-centred, exclusive and powerful, as well as, at different times, much more positive attitudes and responses. Such ambivalence, which was capable of driving government policy, was, as chapter 4 will highlight, the norm rather than the exception within the liberal democracies.

A sense of balance and proportion is particularly required in studying bystanders, especially when they were as remote from the killing fields as were Britain and the United States. On the one hand, the chapter does not assume that making the 'right' choices would have necessarily changed the cause of the Holocaust. On the other, it recognises that the Holocaust was not inevitable – it is possible to become mesmerised by the horrible, huge fact that it happened and was not stopped, and to accept, in a perverse way, the warped internal logic of the Nazis themselves that it needed to happen. Instead, it needs to be recognised that the Holocaust was made possible by both the action of the scores of thousands of perpetrators and the inaction of millions of bystanders. Ultimately, for many on the continent, what Primo Levi referred to as the 'grey zone'[36] operated between perpetrators and bystanders, further complicated by those who were also, in different ways, victims of the Nazis. The status of those in the Anglo-American world, inside and outside of government, was in this sense less compromised as they were spared the possibility of becoming perpetrators. While they suffered from the Nazis' military might, they were in no way victims of the racial state. Theirs, then, was a purer, more remote, but certainly not powerless form of bystanding. And as will be shown here, their issues were no less complex.

Notes

1   Michael Burleigh and Wolfgang Wippermann, *The Racial State: Germany 1933–1945* (Cambridge, Cambridge University Press, 1991).

2   Raul Hilberg, *The Destruction of the European Jews*, 3 vols (New York, Holmes and Meier, 1985).

3   For example, Christopher Browning, *Fateful Months: Essays on the Emergence of the Final Solution* (New York, Holmes and Meier, 1991); Christopher Browning, *The Path to Genocide: Essays on Launching the Final*

Solution (Cambridge, Cambridge University Press, 1992).

4   Ulrich Herbert (ed.), *Nationalsozialistische Vernichtungspolitik: Neue Forschungen und Kontroversen* (Frankfurt am Main, Fischer, 1997); Dieter Pohl, *Von der 'Judenpolitik' zum Judenmord: Der Distrikt Lublin des Generalgouvernements 1939–1944* (Frankfurt am Main, Lang, 1993); Peter Longerich, *Politik der Vernichtung: Eine Gesamtdarstellung der nationalsozialistischen Judenverfolgung* (Munich, Piper, 1998). For an early conceptualisation of 'Jewish policy', see Uwe Dietrich Adam, *Judenpolitik im dritten Reich* (Düsseldorf, Droste, 1972).

5   Jeshajahu Weinberg and Rina Elieli, *The Holocaust Museum in Washington* (New York, Rizzoli, 1995), p. 17.

6   Elie Wiesel, *All Rivers Run to the Sea: Memoirs* (New York, Alfred Knopf, 1996).

7   Anne Karpf, 'The Hunter Who Lost His Way', *Guardian*, 1 May 2003.

8   Joseph Slade, 'Nazi Imagery in Contemporary Culture: The Limits of Representation', *Dimensions*, vol. 11, no. 2 (1997), pp. 9–15.

9   Raul Hilberg, *The Politics of Memory: The Journey of a Holocaust Historian* (Chicago, Ivan R. Dee, 1996), pp. 130–1.

10   Ibid., p. 132.

11   Tony Kushner, 'The Holocaust and the Museum World in Britain: A Study of Ethnography', in Sue Vice (ed.), *Representing the Holocaust* (London, Frank Cass, 2003), pp. 27–30.

12   Marcus Wood, *Blind Memory: Visual Representations of Slavery in England and America 1780–1865* (Manchester, Manchester University Press, 2000), p. 300.

13   Ibid., pp. 298–9.

14   Primo Levi, for example, was in a 'privileged' position in the Buna chemical works in the Monowitz camp in the Auschwitz complex, and thus could write notes towards his first autobiographical account of the *lager*.

15   Henry Greenspan, *On Listening to Holocaust Survivors: Recounting and Life History* (New York, Praeger, 1998), p. 170.

16   See, for example, Reuben Ainsztein, *Jewish Resistance in Nazi-Occupied Eastern Europe* (London, Elek, 1974); S. Krakowski, *The War of the Doomed: Jewish Armed Resistance in Poland, 1942–1944* (New York, Holmes and Meier, 1984).

17   Robert McAfee Brown, *Elie Wiesel: Messenger to All Humanity* (Notre Dame, Ind., University of Notre Dame Press, 1989).

18   Alain Finkielkraut, 'All German Jews?', in idem, *The Imaginary Jew* (Lincoln, University of Nebraska Press, 1994), pp. 17–34.

19   See chapter 2, p. 68 below.

20   Christopher Browning, 'Ordinary Germans or Ordinary Men?',

Introduction

address at the inauguration of the Dorot chair of modern Jewish and Holocaust studies (Atlanta, Ga., Emory University, 1994), p. 9.

21   See chapter 2, pp. 66–9 below.

22   See, for example, Longerich, *Politik der Vernichtung*.

23   Alfred C. Mierzejewski, 'A Public Enterprise in the Service of Mass Murder: The Deutsche Reichsbahn and the Holocaust', *Holocaust and Genocide Studies*, vol. 15, no. 1 (2001), pp. 33–46.

24   Donald Bloxham, 'Jewish Slave Labour and its Relationship to the "Final Solution"', in John Roth and Elizabeth Maxwell (eds), *Remembering for the Future: The Holocaust in an Age of Genocide* (Basingstoke, Macmillan, 2001), vol. 1, pp. 163–86.

25   Joanne Reilly, *Belsen: The Liberation of a Concentration Camp* (London, Routledge, 1998).

26   Alexandra-Eileen Wenck, *Zwischwen Menschenhandel und 'Endlösung': Das Konzentrationslager Bergen-Belsen* (Paderborn, Ferdinand Schöningh, 2000).

27   Daniel Jonah Goldhagen, *Hitler's Willing Executioners: Ordinary Germans and the Holocaust* (London, Little, Brown & Co., 1996).

28   Hannes Heer and Klaus Naumann (eds), *Vernichtungskrieg: Verbrechen der Wehrmacht 1941 bis 1944* (Hamburg, HIS, 1995); Omer Bartov, *Hitler's Army: Soldiers, Nazis and War in the Third Reich* (Oxford, Oxford University Press, 1992).

29   Hilberg, *Destruction*.

30   Zygmunt Bauman, *Modernity and the Holocaust* (New York, Cornell University Press, 1992).

31   Lucy Dawidowicz, *The War Against the Jews, 1933–1945* (London, Penguin, 1987); Gerlad Fleming, *Hitler and the Final Solution* (Berkeley, University of California Press, 1984).

32   Martin Broszat, 'Hitler und die Genesis der "Endlösung": Aus Anlass der Thesen von David Irving', *Vierteljahreshefte für Zeitgeschichte*, vol. 25 (1977), pp. 737–75; Hans Mommsen, 'The Realisation of the Unthinkable: The "Final Solution of the Jewish Question" in the Third Reich', in Gerhard Hirschfeld (ed.), *The Policies of Genocide* (London, German Historical Institute, 1986), pp. 93–144. For a more detailed summary of the intentionalist–functionalist debate, see Michael Marrus, *The Holocaust in History* (London, Weidenfeld and Nicolson, 1988), ch. 3.

33   Marrus, *The Holocaust in History*, p. 157.

34   The diary is available on www.trumanlibrary.org. The particular entry is reproduced in the *Guardian*, 12 July 2003.

35   See the comments reproduced in the *Guardian*, 12 July 2003, and *Jewish Chronicle*, 18 July 2003.

36   Primo Levi, *The Drowned and the Saved* (London, Michael Joseph, 1988), ch. 2.

1

The victims: dealing
with testimony

This chapter provides an overview of the different genres of victim testimony, both contemporary and post-1945, including
ghetto diaries, post-war memoirs and autobiographies, oral and
video histories. It employs a critical approach to such testimony.
Such an approach may appear dubious, potentially undermining
those who suffered so much, and devaluing people who often
took great risks during the war or suffered personal pain after it in
the act of creating their testimony. On the contrary, the purpose is
to take seriously the testimony, recognising its intrinsic importance, and through it to explore the category of victim and how
this fits into Holocaust historiography and, more widely, the
study of the contemporary world. Whilst enormous progress has
been made in recent years in both the collecting and the respect
paid to survivor testimony, the use that is to be made of this material has hardly been subject to debate. This lacuna is especially
striking as, adding together the written, oral and video testimony,
it is the largest body of material on one event produced by those
who experienced it, perhaps already totalling some 100,000 individual accounts.[1]

The Italian survivor Primo Levi related in his last book, *The
Drowned and the Saved*, how many in the camps had the nightmare
that should they survive, they would not be believed or 'indeed
were not even listened to'.[2] For some, in the immediate post-war
period, this nightmare was realised.[3] Now the survivors' words,
in text and speech, are cherished. And yet, as Henry Greenspan
suggests, despite all this surface respect we have still not learned

how to listen to survivors properly: 'It takes time to get to know recounters, not as abstract "witnesses", but as particular people who bring to retelling their specific concerns, identities and styles … It also takes time to discover one's role as a listener, both in its particularity and as survivors have come to anticipate listeners' expectations in general.'[4]

Historians have been prone to approach Holocaust testimony largely with the wrong expectations. Raul Hilberg, particularly, for many decades the most important student of the destruction process, has been dismissive of the 'reliability' of post-war written and oral testimony and its 'limits and limitations'.[5] He writes in his autobiography that he has 'read countless accounts of survivors. I looked for missing links in my jigsaw puzzle. I tried to glimpse the Jewish community. I searched for the dead. Most often, however, I had to remind myself that what I wanted from them they could not give me, no matter what they said.'[6]

Hilberg, however, describes the diary of Adam Czerniakow, head of the Warsaw Jewish Council or Judenrat, as 'the most important Jewish record of that time'.[7] But why is Czerniakow's diary so significant for Hilberg? The answer is that it gives a unique insight into the mechanics of how the Jews in the Nazis' largest ghetto were organised from initial concentration through to deportation. For Hilberg, the Jewish councils were an integral part of the destruction process, without which the 'final solution' would not have run so smoothly. Hilberg has rightly been criticised for the crudity of his analysis and for the lack of understanding and knowledge he shows of Jewish history. Certainly as literature, and even as an insight into the impact of persecution on an individual and collective level, it is hard to make the case that Czerniakow's is any more important than the many other remarkable diaries written in the ghettos. Whilst Hilberg's work has subsequently become more balanced, it remains the case that his interest lies outside the Jewish experience of persecution.[8] As he wrote in the preface to *The Destruction of the European Jews*, the book was not 'about the Jews. It is a book about the people who destroyed the Jews. Not much will be read here about the victims. The focus is placed on the perpetrators.'[9]

Levi wrote in his last book that

17

we, the survivors, are not the true witnesses. This is an uncomfortable notion, of which I have become conscious little by little, reading the memoirs of others and reading mine at a distance of years. We survivors are not only an exiguous but also an anomolous minority: we are those who by their prevarications or abilities or good luck did not touch bottom. Those who did so ... are ... the complete witnesses, the ones whose deposition would have a general significance.

Levi added that in relation to the Holocaust the 'submerged' are 'the rule' and those who survived and gave their testimony are 'the exception'.[10] There will always be, as Levi was forced to recognise, an ultimate barrier to bearing witness. His fellow survivor, Elie Wiesel, has gone even further: 'Auschwitz is something else, always something else. It is a universe outside the universe, a creation that exists parallel to creation ... The truth of Auschwitz remains hidden in its ashes.'[11]

It is essential not to expect the impossible from survivor testimony: one does not have to mystify the Holocaust,[12] as does Wiesel, to accept that we will and can never know the horror experienced by the six million Jews and others, the vast majority of whom left no form of testimony; for many, there are no traces of existence whatsoever. Gayatri Chakravorty Spivak has asked, in the context of Indian women in British colonial India and especially the practice of *sati*, or widow self-immolation: 'Can the subaltan speak?' Her answer is categorical: due to the political, economic and ideological power of British colonial rule, the 'othering' process is such that the unproblematic representation of the Indian woman, under the triple burden of being 'poor, black, and female', is impossible. In short, argues Spivak, '[t]he subaltan cannot speak'.[13] The situation with Holocaust testimony cannot be classified so starkly. Even taking into account survivors' experiential limitation and inherent marginality in power relations, as well as their untypicality, the potential of this staggeringly large resource of autobiographical acts is remarkable, if so far largely unrealised. In contrast, American slave narratives run into the scores,[14] and there are similarly small numbers of Nazi era testimonies from Gypsies, those deemed 'physically and mentally unfit', and Soviet prisoners of war. Indeed, the scale of Holocaust victim testimonies is the exception rather than the norm in the history of the persecuted and exploited.

The nature of contemporary testimony

In October 1943 Himmler infamously told a group of SS leaders that the 'annihilation of the Jewish people' was to be 'an unwritten and never-to-be-written page of glory' in German history. It was glorious not only through the service rendered to the well-being of 'the body of the German nation' but also because the 'final solution' had been executed without those carrying it out compromising their morality. It had been a triumph '[t]o have stuck this out and ... to have kept our integrity ... our inward being, our soul, our character'.[15] There is bitter irony in the fact that, although the Nazis came close to realising their dystopian dream, few historical events have subsequently achieved such historical attention. It is intensified when the quantity and quality of Holocaust victim testimony is taken into account. Indeed, the scale of the disaster itself both at the time and subsequently acted as a stimulus for Jews to '[w]rite and record!', as the great historian Simon Dubnow is reported as imploring, in his last words before he was murdered in the Riga ghetto in December 1941.[16]

Admiration for the tenacity and bravery of those who followed Dubnow's command during the war has become widespread in the last decades of the twentieth century and the early years of the twenty-first. It has developed, in contrast to initial disinterest and even antipathy, into something akin to a state of awe. Such respect, often verging on sanctification, has sometimes obscured the importance of the writing process in constructing contemporary testimony.[17] As the Nazis moved towards a policy of extermination, the voluminous writing in the ghettos, as well as the fragments that survive which were produced inside and in transit to and from the concentration camps, including the diaries of the Sonderkommandos in Auschwitz (the Jewish inmates of the camp responsible for the disposal of the victims' bodies), often had a public quality.[18] The public purpose incorporated either one or both of two time-frames. First, accounts were written to inform contemporaries of what was happening so action could be taken by the Jews themselves or the Allies to avoid/stop the killing. Second, they were designed for posterity, so that the murder would never be forgotten. As Zalman Gradowski of the Sonderkommandos stated, resigned to death but still hopeful that the capsules in which they hid their diaries would survive and be

19

discovered: 'Let the world regard [their writings] at least as a very incomplete testimony from the tragic world in which we have lived'.[19] The historian Emanuel Ringelblum established the Oneg Shabbath archives in October 1939 with the aim of presenting 'a photographically true and detailed picture of what the Jewish population had to experience, to think and to suffer'. Those working for the archive, he wrote, 'understood how important it was for future generations that evidence remain of the tragedy of Polish Jewry. Some also understood that the collected material served the present as well, informing the world of the horrors perpetrated against the Jews.'[20]

Such writings, however, also had a private purpose: they helped the individual retain a semblance of personal identity at the point when the Nazis and their allies were attempting to destroy not only the physical but also the spiritual and moral well-being of their perceived enemies. As the novelist Aharon Appelfeld perceptively comments, Jewish journals written during the war 'are the final effort to preserve a shred of one's self before it is rubbed out. Naked anonymity was the gateway to death.'[21] The last entry of Chaim Kaplan's Warsaw ghetto diary, written on 4 August 1942 before his deportation to Treblinka ('If my life ends – what will become of my diary?'), is worth exploring further in relation to Appelfeld's analysis.[22]

These words of Kaplan are often reproduced as evidence of such diarists' greater 'concern for preserving a record of the incredible events they were witnessing than for their own survival'.[23] On the one hand, such writings were undoubtedly a form of resistance in the light of the Nazis' determination to destroy not only the Jewish world but also all evidence of the destruction process. On the other, they were deeply personal and individualised. Reflecting on the achievements of Oneg Shabbath some three years after its founding, Ringelblum wrote: 'Comprehensiveness was the main principle of our work. Objectivity was the second. We endeavoured to convey the whole truth, no matter how bitter, and we presented faithful unadorned pictures.'[24] One of the milk cans in which the Oneg Shabbath archives were hidden has been transferred to the United States Holocaust Memorial Museum in Washington. Its founding director, Jeshajahu Weinberg, described it as 'perhaps the Museum's most important historic artifact'. Indeed, great efforts have been made to make sure that the mud that attached to it underground will be pre-served – a past that was in hiding designed for posterity is thus exposed for all future generations. The sanctification of this object and the writings it represents is clearly central to the purpose of the Washington museum – it is designed to show, following the 'objective' tradition set by Ringelblum, the factuality of the Holo-caust.[25]

The editor of Kaplan's diary, Abraham Katsh, suggests that his subject's mission at the beginning of the Second World War was 'to devote all his efforts to preserving a record for posterity'. Kaplan's 'intention of objectivity', argues Katsh, was 'carried out with remarkable tenacity'.[26] Yet as early as October 1939 and the Nazi assault on Warsaw, Kaplan describes, in deeply personal, subjective terms, how 'I find it hard even to hold a pen. My hands tremble; I have lived through a catastrophe that has left me crushed and physically broken. And what is worse, even as I sit writing these lines, I am still not certain that the catastrophe is over; I only comfort myself with the hope that I will come out of this alive.'[27] Kaplan called his diary 'my scroll of agony'. Although there are many detailed accounts of the impact of persecution on Warsaw Jewry within it, it is the diary's literary quality and his wide-ranging references to Jewish religious and secular sources, as well as its very personal elusiveness, that gives the 'scroll of agony' its power: 'a living, active truth', in Kaplan's words.[28] In November 1940 Kaplan records that he had not written in his diary for six days. Kaplan's sense of duty to record, his 'responsi-bility to Jewish historiography', battles against his feeling of being 'completely broken. Jewish Warsaw has turned into a madhouse. A community of half a million people is doomed to die, and awaits execution of their sentence.'[29] Some twenty months later as the great deportations of Warsaw Jewry to Treblinka got under way and the terrible end seemed in sight, Kaplan reflected again on keeping his diary: 'Some of my friends and acquaintances who know the secret of my diary urge me, in despair, to stop writing. "Why?" For what purpose? Will you live to see it published? Will these words of yours reach the ears of future generations?' But Kaplan is unmoved and refuses to listen to them. The continua-tion of the diary 'to the very end of my physical and spiritual strength is a historical mission which must not be abandoned … Therefore I will not silence my diary!'[30]

In his last weeks Kaplan became obsessed with 'hiding my diary so that it will be preserved for future generations. As long as my pulse beats I shall continue my sacred task.'[31] Yet the emphasis placed by Kaplan himself and later commentators on his historical mission to record should not disguise the importance of the writing process not only as a form of resistance but also as a form of personal survival: 'Were it not for my pen, my delight, I would be lost'.[32] With obvious resonance of Anne Frank, he described his diary as 'my life, my friend and ally'.[33] Katsh points out that Chaim Kaplan began a personal diary 'as early as 1933', which then 'trained him' for his wartime writing.[34] It would be less anachronistic to suggest that to Kaplan, diary writing, often self-consciously, was his way of coming to terms with the complexities and difficulties of the world around him. His wartime diary is particularly significant as a piece of Holocaust literature and testimony because he constantly questioned the genre within which he was trying to express his own experiences and those around him. Chronology and especially the daily entry – that is, the very essence of a diary – cumulatively break down under the Nazi assault. Kaplan writes in June 1942: 'I do not exaggerate when I say that we have reached a state of lack of breath. There is simply no air. Every minute is like a thousand years. Every day is a never-ending eternity.'[35] Similarly, the school teacher Abraham Lewin wrote a few months later after the majority of Warsaw Jews had already been deported that whilst the 'days themselves are full of radiance and light, glorious sun-filled days at the close of autumn', for the Jews 'here in our cramped and gloomy little world, the days are black, desolate, with a tedium which is in itself almost deadly'.[36]

Historians, literary scholars and others have been anxious to point out the difference between contemporary accounts such as diaries and post-war survivor accounts, generally favouring the former over the latter in terms of their usefulness and validity. They have failed, generally, to focus on the *genre* of writing and to explore how the form of the diary, for example, has influenced the mode of expression as well as its significance to the individual who created it. Anxious to treat the diaries as either sacred objects to be honoured or as sources of information to be mined scientifically, their importance as 'works of art' or as part of a longer intellectual and cultural tradition have often been ignored or relegated in importance.

David Roskies is one of the most sophisticated scholars of Jewish literary responses to extreme physical persecution in the first half of the twentieth century.[37] He has, however, effectively written the Oneg Shabbath archives out of the realm of comparison by suggesting that they, alongside what he calls 'the vast Library of Jewish Catastrophe written during the Nazi occupation', show that 'a new archetype of catastrophe emerged even as the events were unfolding ... [a] new consciousness in the midst of the Nazi terror'. They 'constitute a closed canon' and 'require a separate hermeneutics'. Ultimately, argues Roskies, 'they are sacred' but their sanction 'does not come from God. They derive their authority from the dead whose deeds they chronicle.'[38]

Similarly Sara Horowitz has written of ghetto narratives from Warsaw and how they 'place special interpretive responsibilities on us':

> Shimon Huberband's [from Oneg Shabbath] difficult handwriting, his idiosyncratic Yiddish, and the physical erosion of his manuscripts make it impossible for us to read him clearly. The series of slim notebooks which form Adam Czerniakow's diary are often so cryptic and spare that we cannot assuredly recognize the events to which he refers. Jan Korczak's writing is even more impressionistic, personal, enigmatic. That we cannot ask Hubberband to clarify, Czerniakow to elaborate, or Korczak to explain is a measure of our loss. Yet, however fragmented, these works must stand in for their authors.[39]

We need to ask: are the responsibilities and difficulties located by Horowitz different from those placed on any examination of a diary or memoir? There will always be elements to a diary that are unknowable, even to those who are writing them: the diarist is often exploring questions of identity and experience, and not, through the written word, producing a definitive account of them.

In the case of diaries written in the ghetto the need is to contextualise them through time and place and the individuality of the author. It is also crucial in the case of a collective body such as Oneg Shabbath to place them in the context of its intellectual forebear, YIVO, the Jewish Scientific Institute, formed in Vilna in 1925. YIVO encouraged and trained ordinary Jewish people to collect material concerning their everyday lives and encouraged autobiographical writing.[40] Moreover, as Samuel David Kassow has pointed out, 'YIVO, of course, was a diverse institution, and one need only point to the diary of Zelig Kalmanovitch [in Vilna] to realize that YIVO veterans could see the ghetto experience in radically different ways' – unlike Ringelblum, Kalmanovitch was a supporter of the Judenrat.[41] Moreover, it would be wrong to place YIVO in an exclusively Jewish context. It owed, for example, much to the interdisciplinary work and the development of the life story approach developed first at the University of Chicago, especially by W. I. Thomas and Florian Znaniecki in their *Polish Peasant in Europe and America* (1918–20).[42] Holocaust testimony, like all testimony, needs to be treated with care and subtlety. If it is regarded as unique and incomparable, however, its dynamic quality, indeed its very richness, is in danger of being lost.

The horror of the Holocaust and the contemporary impulse it created to record have clouded consideration of the point that '[t]he motives for diary writing are perhaps as many and varied as are the diaries themselves'.[43] Diaries, including those which are less articulate, have still to be analysed for their literary qualities.[44] As James Young has highlighted in his *Writing and Rewriting the Holocaust*, '[i]f the diarists' and memoirists' literary testimony is evidence of anything else, it is of the writing act itself. That is, even if narrative cannot document events, or constitute perfect factuality, it can document the *actuality* of writer and text.'[45] It is necessary to go further than Young, however, and differentiate as acts of writing the diary from the memoir (and, as will be shown shortly, the genres within the latter category).

The diary is a particular form of autobiographical writing with its own traditions and possibilities. Diaries are often presented as an early form of or the notes towards an autobiography. Instead they should be seen, as Felicity Nussbaum argues, as 'the thing itself, not a failed version of autobiography'. In many ways, diaries are more complex than other forms of autobiography: 'Diary serves the social/historical function of articulating a multiplicity of contestatory selves, of unstable and incoherent selves at an historical moment when that concept is itself the object of contest'.[46] Such comments need to be kept constantly in mind when dealing with Holocaust diaries. The author, paediatrician, educator and broadcaster Janusz Korczak was the head of a Jewish orphanage in Warsaw during the war, his life a constant battle to provide physically and spiritually for the two hundred children under his charge. Food and medicine had to be begged for and yet in spite of his efforts, and those of his equally remarkable staff, sickness was all around him. Yiddish poet Aaron Zeitlin highlights the vital role diary writing played for Korczak: 'In such surroundings, in that state of health, after such a day, he no longer has the strength or will to write for publication: he can only talk to himself on paper, making notes in haphazard abbreviations, almost a cipher; something of his chance thoughts, some memories, a fleeting impression ... The *Diary* has become no more than a register of psychological moments.' Zeitlin also lyrically stresses its complexity as an autobiographical act, confirming Nussbaum's analysis: 'This is neither the legendary Korczak nor the real Korczak. This is a man fragmented into moments, impulses, fibers – a third being, uncoordinated; the writing is more mysterious in its trembling close-up, in its burning sincerity.'[47]

Even Anne Frank's diary, written and rewritten by its author in contrast to Korczak's to achieve cohesion and narrative progression, reveals what she herself describes as a 'bundle of contradictions'. Her last entry, dated 1 August 1944, ends, having describing herself as 'split in two', by outlining her desire 'to find a way to become what I'd like to be and what I could be if ... if only there were no other people in the world'.[48] Veteran or novice writers, those who kept diaries in the Holocaust show that the relationship between writing and self, events and their descriptions, is never straightforward.

In 2002, two remarkable books of contemporary testimony relating to the ghettos in Vilna and Warsaw were translated into English. Their publication in the early twenty-first century reflects the progress that has been made in accepting the importance of ordinary people's writing in the Holocaust. A close examination of the presentation of these diaries and accounts shows the way forward with a more sophisticated response to such writings, but also some of the earlier lingering limitations of dealing with various genres of Holocaust testimony.

The first was published under the title *Words To Outlive Us: Eyewitness Accounts from the Warsaw Ghetto*. Edited by Michal Grynberg of the Jewish Historical Institute of Warsaw and published in Polish in 1993, it consists of the written testimony of twenty-nine individuals and is organised into six sections – 'Life

Within the Walls', 'Ghetto Institutions', 'Roundups, Selections, and Deportations', 'Passive and Active Resistance inside the Ghetto', 'On the Other Side of the Walls', and 'Liberation'. As the English translator of these documents, Philip Boehm, highlights, the twenty-nine were of different age, background and experience. Moreover, these previously unpublished testimonies varied in form from diary to report. Boehm, a playwright and author himself, acknowledges that their 'styles range from exceedingly simple to overtly literary; one account is written as a dialogue, and one was transcribed from dictation immediately after the war'.[49] Further acknowledging the individuality of the authors and the nature of their texts, biographical details and information about their writings are provided in the volume. Recognising that what is provided in this respect is often fragmentary and incomplete, Boehm encourages readers able to provide additional information to contact the publisher.

None of those whose work is reproduced in *Words To Outlive Us* were particularly prominent in the Warsaw ghetto. That care and attention has been paid to ensure that the reader is not simply left with their words alone shows that it is now possible to take seriously the testimony of ordinary people who suffered in the Holocaust. Yet Boehm's brief comments on the style of the writings are not pursued further in the collection. Instead, the reader is given small chunks of writing, edited so that they fit more or less neatly into the six categories chosen. As Boehm concedes, '[o]ut of these various points of view, a collective story unfolds'.[50] With care, readers can piece together the individual elements of testimony which weave in and out of the six categories. Furthermore, they can compare and contrast the various genres of writing from individuals with very different backgrounds and explore how the variations in literacy practice impact on specific subject matter such as resistance and leadership. Nevertheless, such neat 'packaging' of this testimony into categories inevitably undermines the integrity of each individual writing and the complexity of even apparently 'simple narrations' can be obscured. The publication of *Words to Outlive Us* thus recognises the importance of ordinary people's testimony for its own sake even if the presentation of the writing is uneven and at times unhelpful. At its best, the collection encourages the reader to get to grips with the full potential of the material as both literature *and* history. One excellent example is provided by the diary of Helena Midler, in hiding in the 'Aryan' side of Warsaw. Nothing is known about the author, but her diary, written in Polish, for November–December 1944 survived the war. Her entry for 16 November is typical of her self-reflexive approach to diary writing, which in spite of or even because of its scarcity of detail provides a remarkable insight into her situation:

> I long for the patter of autumn rain, long for the monotonous music of tiny droplets against the windowpane, for the sad, gray, overcast November sky, and I long for thoughts at twilight, which – sad though they may be – never begin with the words 'If I survive' and are never burdened with the heavy doubt that all thinking is pointless and empty, because in the end I won't survive anyway ...
>
> Like a miser I eagerly lock all my pain in the strongbox of my heart, from where, in occasional outbreaks of sincerity, I take out a coin to give to whomever I'm talking to; then I close the box and carefully turn the little key, since there is no one who can help me. The person in the crowd is always alone, always alone.[51]

The second example of translated testimony published in 2002 was the diary of Herman Kruk, covering the experiences of the Vilna ghetto and related concentration camps from 1939 to 1944. Kruk was, in many respects, a one-person version of Oneg Shabbath in Warsaw. He was, like Ringelblum, linked to YIVO. As the librarian in the Vilna ghetto, and a political activist (a member of the left-wing Bund), he was in a good position to gather material as well as write his detailed diary of life during the Second World War. His diary was first published in Yiddish in 1961. The English version is complex, including the footnotes provided in the earlier version, corrections, and material written by Kruk that had not come to light by 1961. Piecing the material together, related its later editor, Benjamin Harshav, was like putting together 'a half-lost mosaic'.[52]

The approach to publishing Kruk's testimony is the reverse of that adopted in *Words to Outlive Us*. Even though edited to exclude the related documentation gathered by Kruk, it amounts to several hundred thousand words. Moreover, Benjamin Harshav, Professor of Hebrew and Comparative Literature at Yale University, provides a detailed introduction to Herman Kruk, including not only the context of the diaries but also an analysis of what he calls the 'three concentric circles' of Kruk's writing. These were 'his private life and personal responses to events; the life of his party and extended family, the "Bund" and the Bundists; and the world of the ghetto as a whole'. Harshav also identifies four 'modes of discourse' in Kruk's diaries: Kruk's own notes on developments in the ghetto, his reactions to documentation, recording witness accounts, and an attempt at an overview chronicle of the whole situation. As Harshav adds, 'Kruk did not decide between these genres and their rather diverse tones of discourse. He wrote them simultaneously, as complementary kinds of documentation.'[53] It is disappointing, given this subtle and multi-layered analysis of Kruk's writing, that Harshav does not pursue this literary approach further. Indeed, Harshav ultimately dismisses the diarist for the quality of his language, which was 'rather poor'. Such an elitist approach to ordinary testimony is bound to lead to its importance being limited to the historical information contained, which in the case of Kruk happens to be of major significance. Harshav therefore concludes that he 'shall let the diaries speak for themselves'.[54] But this is hardly to do them justice as pieces of the remarkable literacy practice of an ordinary man: diaries, like any genre of writing, never simply 'speak for themselves'. Kruk's diaries were, as he stated in his last writings, to provide a 'trace' for future generations. His motive, however, was not simply to be a contemporary historian, or a provider of material for the future historian: 'I write because I must write – a consolation in my time of horror'.[55]

The publication of these two books in 2002 is thus hopeful as a way forward in confronting victim testimony – even if the tendencies towards expecting a 'collective' voice to emerge to honour the memory of those murdered, and a degree of patronisation, still persist. Understanding the richness and complexity of testimony such as that of Herman Kruk or Helena Midler requires an approach that draws from many disciplines, one that recognises the intrinsic worth of ordinary people and one that takes seriously the literacy practices and individuality of their writing. The attempt by the doyen of Holocaust studies, Raul Hilberg, in his analysis of sources, to divide and prioritise diaries as 'documents' and post-war recollections as 'testimony' is therefore simplistic and misleading but unfortunately widely adhered to by many scholars of the subject.[56] Utilised to show the reality of the experience of the Holocaust, ghetto and other diaries, the literariness and complexity of these forms of testimony have been underval-

[margin handwritten note: ordinary people play very important role in the whole of the Holocaust.]

ued, including the most famous text connected to the Second World War, *The Diary of Anne Frank*.[57] The same is true as we will now see for post-war testimony, with the additional burden that its 'reliability' has been seen as fundamentally suspect.

Confronting post-war testimony

From the late twentieth century, the apparently obvious need and rectitude of collecting testimony almost as a form of rescue archaeology[58] as the survivors dwindle in numbers has subsumed almost all the energy of those involved, even to the extent of obscuring the dilemma of whether it has been appropriate to the needs of all those interviewed. The remaining sections of this chapter will outline how this mass of post-war material has been collected and has subsequently been used by historians, film and documentary makers, museums and others, how survivors have responded to it, and how it might be taken forward. Before then, however, it is necessary to summarise briefly the place of survivor/victim testimony in Holocaust representation in the years following the Second World War.

The testimony of Holocaust victims has not been static in relation to quantity, focus or purpose. Yad Vashem has estimated that from 1945 to 1949 some seventy-five Holocaust memoirs were published, and for the first half of the 1950s the numbers were even smaller. From the 1960s, however, with an initial impetus from the Eichmann trial, the numbers started to show a year-on-year increase, with only a few exceptions. In 1995 alone the number of memoirs had increased to 180. Analysing these figures, Robert Rozett, director of the Yad Vashem Library, has placed the emphasis on changes in the survivors themselves. The impulse in more recent years, he argues, has been to leave a record for children and grandchildren as the survivors reach the end of their lives.[59] The internal factors certainly must not be dismissed, but they cannot be taken in isolation in explaining why survivors have and have not provided their testimony since 1945.

Immediately after the war, many of the accounts were written in Yiddish and Hebrew, clearly for a Jewish audience in some ways as memorials to the loss. It has been suggested by his son that Władysław Szpilman in 1945 wrote his account of survival, published in Polish the following year as *Death of a City*, 'for himself rather than humanity in general'.[60] A powerful memoir of life in the Warsaw ghetto and then in hiding on the Aryan side, it slipped into obscurity, suppressed by the Stalinists within Poland.[61] It was then rediscovered and published in English in the late 1990s, before being made into an award-winning film, *The Pianist* (2002).[62] Szpilman was involved with the Jewish resistance, helping to smuggle arms into the ghetto, although he 'mentions this brave deed modestly and only in passing'. His is an anti-heroic account of the Warsaw ghetto and his experiences in general. After several months in hiding he related his mood of despair: 'it seemed to me quite likely that this state of affairs might never end. And then what would become of me? After years of pointless suffering I would be discovered one day and killed.' As Wolf Biermann suggests: 'Wladyslaw Szpilman describes it in such a way that we can get a deeper understanding of something we already suspected: prisons, ghettos and concentration camps ... are not designed to ennoble the character. Hunger does not bestow an inner radiance.'[63] The critical and commercial success of Szpilman's memoir over half a century after it was originally written suggests, perhaps, a greater maturity in the reception of Holocaust testimony. It highlights again Greenspan's comments about the importance of taking account of the expectations of the reader in understanding the dynamics of survivor accounts.

Those published in English immediately after the war were there to inform, to add to the proof of evidence. Primo Levi, according to his biographer, found that the hardest part of writing his account of the camps, published as *If This Is a Man* (1947), was containing his anger: he feared that if 'he gave way to grief or moral outrage it would tarnish his credibility as a witness'.[64] The difficulty faced by Primo Levi in getting his memoirs published is indicative of the struggle for recognition not of Nazi crimes, but of the impact they had on their victims – it was rejected by a major American publishing house and then seven Italian publishers and sold only half of its print run of 3,000 copies.[65] If Jewish victims were marginalised, this is even more so of the others persecuted under the Third Reich. In the post-war trials, for example, in the thousands upon thousands of pages of evidence and testimony there was little mention of the Romanies, perhaps half a million of whom were murdered in the war.[66] Over fifty years later, the

Gypsy Holocaust, or Porajmos, remains to be recognised, historicised and memorialised. In 2000, at the Fifth World Romani Congress in Prague, a 'Declaration of a Nation' was proclaimed. Its second sentence tellingly reads, with the style and spelling of the original preserved: 'We, a Nation of which over half a million persons were exterminated in a forgotten Holocaust, a Nation of individuals too often discriminated, marginalized, victim of intollerance and persecutions, we have a dream, and we are engaged in fulfilling it'.[67]

Moreover, there were projects to interview Jewish survivors or to encourage them to write down their testimony in the last months of the war and immediately after. In some cases their use was intended as a form of memorial to those who had been murdered, as in the creation of Yizkor Books for the destroyed Jewish communities in east European towns and villages. The material collected was largely confined to the personal domain or in small-scale publications in Yiddish. The Yizkor Books represented the printed version of what Deborah Dwork has referred to as the survivors' 'islands of speech' in a post-war world that was largely indifferent or hostile to their memories. Revealing the dynamic nature of such testimonies which have never been fixed in time or place, Rosemary Horowitz suggests that the Yizkor Books 'reflect an ongoing interpretation of the Holocaust by the survivors themselves'.[68]

Survivor testimonies were also used as both legal and historical evidence of atrocities in order to confirm the 'real' nature of Nazism.[69] With regards to the latter, underfunded bodies created before, during or immediately after the war, such as the Wiener Library in London, the Centre de Documentation Juive Contemporaine in Paris and the Jewish Historical Institute in Warsaw, carried out early and often uneven interviews with Jewish survivors about their war experiences.[70] The only major independent academic study of survivors that was more concerned to gather information on the impact on the individual, rather than to act as qualitative proof of the evils of Nazi-Fascism, was carried out by the psychologist David Boder. In 1946 Boder interviewed 109 people, largely but not exclusively Jewish, in displaced persons camps across the continent. Significantly, funding of the project and publication of its results proved difficult.[71]

With regards to the legal sphere, post-1945 war crimes trials tended to marginalise or discount survivor evidence in favour of documentary evidence – an eclipsing which reflected legal tradition, especially in the USA, as well as the lack of status and respect given to the victims of Nazism.[72] Moreover, the early historians of the Holocaust from Leon Poliakov to Raul Hilberg not only based their work on the material collected at the trials, but shared the prejudices of those responsible for them against using the testimony of the survivors. Poliakov, for example, in his *Harvest of Hate*, first published in French in 1951, stated that 'wherever possible, to forestall objections, we have quoted the executioners rather than the victims'.[73] The tiny number of scholars who were engaged in the early stages of creating a history of the Holocaust were thus part of a world that at best told survivors to forget and get on with re-building their lives and at worst dumped them in displaced persons camps, an integral part of the mass of 'unwanted' refugees across Europe.[74]

In the sphere of historiography, the social history revolution in which the collection of oral testimony was central did not gather serious momentum until the 1960s. Thus in 1952 Gerald Reitlinger, the British Jewish historian and author of *The Final Solution* (after Poliakov's account the first overview of the Nazi policy of extermination), could write that he did not consider using the testimony of the 'hardy survivors', because they 'were seldom educated men'.[75] Reitlinger, typical of the history profession, was a product of an education at an exclusive private school and Oxford University.[76] Equally, in sociology, the dabbling in life history analysis coming out of the Chicago school in the inter-war period suffered from 'utter rejection' by the 1950s in favour of mass quantitative social survey work in which the individual was totally subsumed.[77] It was significant that when Yad Vashem in Jerusalem did begin to actively collect written and oral testimony in the mid-1950s it was part of what its director called 'scientific research', following in many ways the approach of pre-war Jewish research bodies such as YIVO and Oneg Shabbath during the war itself.[78] The questionnaire it developed to interview survivors included nearly five hundred questions, enabling standardisation (and presumably quantification) of responses.[79] In terms of general intellectual currents, it has taken the 'history from below movement' (alongside the more recent return to favour of qualitative, interdisciplinary approaches to the study of society, partly prompted by the pluralistic impulses of postmodernism) to enable fresh responses to Holocaust testimony. If we move from a theoretical level to one of implementation, however, it is apparent that we have reached a stage where few would seriously replicate the view of a Poliakov or a Reitlinger in terms of using Holocaust testimony, but that problematising its use and collection is a different matter again.

In 1986 Martin Gilbert published his *The Holocaust: The Jewish Tragedy*.[80] Until this book, the author was very much an elite political-diplomatic historian, associated particularly with his multi-volume life of Winston Churchill.[81] In apparent contrast, Gilbert's *The Holocaust* attempts a moving social history of the event. It is, in his words, 'an attempt to draw on the nearest of the witnesses, those closest to the destruction, and through their testimony to tell something of the suffering of those who perished, and are forever silent'.[82] In fact, with his insistence on chronology, and the use of extensive contemporary sources, including diaries and reports, as well as later oral and written testimony, Gilbert's *The Holocaust* is more at one with the rest of his prolific writings than first appears. Just as his account of Churchill progresses day by day, so the Holocaust material is brought together 'into a single chronological narrative', which Gilbert himself suggests is 'set out rather like a diary'.[83]

The centrality of victim testimony in its various forms marks out this book as pathbreaking. Its popular reception was and continues to be very positive, reflecting a greater concern not only with the subject matter but also the respect shown to Holocaust survivors, almost all of whom have been very favourable towards Gilbert's work.[84] Indeed, *The Holocaust: The Jewish Tragedy* has gained status as an almost semi-sacred text, its use recommended for commemoration of Yom Hashoah. As George Steiner put it, '[t]his tome is an archivist's Kaddish, the never-to-be-silenced act of remembrance and prayer for the dead'.[85] Its reverential approach to victim testimony has clearly met the emotional need of a wide readership, Jewish and non-Jewish. Many reviewers, perhaps inspired by misplaced guilt, have written how they felt duty-bound to read to the end its harrowing descriptions of the terror inflicted on the Jews of Europe.[86]

In some respects Gilbert's book remains exceptional. No one subsequently has attempted a detailed chronology of the Holocaust based on the testimony of the persecuted.[87] Nevertheless, the approach of reproducing testimony as an *illustrative device*, 'used only in a complementary way' to show the development of the Nazis' campaign of extermination, has become almost standard.[88] Many recent documentary series, including the BBC's award-winning *The Nazis: A Warning from History* (1997), use the words of ordinary people to reveal the extraordinary everyday detail of mass murder and its origins, replicating Claude Lanzmann's *Shoah*, including the antagonistic approach to the interviewing of perpetrators and bystanders. But this new, superficially more inclusive social history has its limitations. Sometimes, the information imparted is banal, sometimes it is breathtaking. It is rarely included, however, in a way that would disrupt the general narrative structure of the documentary. The words of the eyewitnesses are used to bring home the reality of what racism or mass murder meant in practice. Yet the testimony itself, if not always in the form of soundbites, is rarely allowed to have space to reveal its own internal dynamics, especially in relation to the rest of the person's life story.[89]

Returning to Gilbert, a similar approach to testimony has been used in his later *Holocaust Journey: Travelling in Search of the Past* (1997), a diary of a two-week field trip across the continent of Europe. Precise dates from the extermination process are never far from the surface of this moving if somewhat Pooteresque account. Nevertheless, the format forces Gilbert to move beyond the reliance on chronology alone and embrace the importance of geography in confronting the Holocaust. At its best, the interplay between history, memory and landscape in *Holocaust Journey* enables a more interesting and revealing approach to the use of testimony, allowing it to be contextualised by time, place and interpretation.

A similar stage of incorporation of Holocaust testimony has been reached, it must be suggested, in historiography, typified perhaps in Saul Friedländer's synthetic overview *Nazi Germany and the Jews: The Years of Persecution 1933–39* published in 1997.[90] Friedländer has not only been an outstanding historian of the Holocaust but is a pioneer of the study of the memory of the event.[91] As Michael Burleigh has written: 'Friedländer is the most astute, sophisticated and stylish historian of the Holocaust working in any language today'.[92] The book is a remarkable achievement, but it is, given Friedländer's general subtlety of approach and his awareness of the potential conflict between history and memory, disappointing in its use of testimony.

Friedländer, as a historiographer, is well aware of the tendency to remove the victim when dealing with Nazi antisemitism. He thus states in his introduction that his 'study will attempt to convey an account in which Nazi policies are indeed the central element, but in which the surrounding world and the victims' attitudes, reactions and fate are no less an integral part of this unfolding history'.[93] His justification of this approach will be quoted at length:

> In many works the implicit assumptions regarding the victims' generalized hopelessness and passivity, or their inability to change the course of events leading to their extermination, have turned them into a static and abstract element of the historical background. It is too often forgotten that Nazi attitudes and policies cannot be fully assessed without knowledge of themselves. Here, therefore, at each stage in the description of the evolving Nazi policies and the attitudes of German and European societies as they impinge on the evolution of those policies, the fate, the attitudes, and sometimes the initiatives of the victims are given major importance. Indeed, their voices are essential if we are to attain an understanding of this past. For it is their voices that reveal what was known and what *could* be known; theirs were the only voices that conveyed both the clarity of insight and the total blindness of human beings confronted with an entirely new and utterly horrifying reality. The constant presence of the victims in this book, while historically essential in itself, is also meant to put the Nazis' actions into full perspective.[94]

Friedländer certainly honours his word in including the perspective of Jews throughout this book. And yet ultimately there is a sense that these are tacked on to what is the essence of the narrative structure – one created and driven by the Nazis. The presence of the Jews humanises the text and shows what happens when discriminatory legislation is put in place and violence inflicted upon a minority. But Friedländer's critical approach to sources relating to high-level Nazi documentation is largely absent in relation to the diaries, written and other testimony of the Jews. They are there ultimately to illustrate the nature of Nazism, as is the case with the majority of documentary and museum presentations of the Holocaust today, such as the United States Holocaust Memorial Museum and the Imperial War Museum's Holocaust exhibition and Steven Spielberg's award-winning film *The Last Days* (1999). (In the process, by including *Jewish* evidence, the particularity of Nazi racism is illustrated, and in skilled hands, such as Friedländer's, the dilemmas facing the Jews are highlighted.[95])

In more polemical works, such as Daniel Goldhagen's *Hitler's Willing Executioners*, Jewish voices, either from sources or more often as imagined by the author, are there *purely* to show the full horror of German mass murder. In the process, integrity is lost and Goldhagen's work verges on the pornographic in its description of violence.[96] (In contrast, see the understated and unvoyeuristic account of the same action in Christopher Browning's *Ordinary Men: Police Battalion 101 and the Final Solution in Poland*, 1992.) But even with the exceptionally good, self-aware work of Saul Friedländer, there is no way that victim testimony is allowed to disrupt the harmony of the narrative flow. The testimony is tidy and coherent. It is rarely problematised.[97] Here, it must be argued that we have reached a real stumbling block, and its implications will be teased out in the remainder section of this chapter.

Approaches to the evidence collected through oral testimony have gone through several clear stages. In its first major wave in the 1960s there was an excitement that here was the way to reach parts of history, especially of the oppressed and marginalised, that other, 'traditional' sources could not reach. All that was needed was a sufficient number of testimonies to ensure a reliable sample to recover the experiences of the working classes, women, immigrants and so on.[98] In fact, this approach, privileging numbers over quality, typified many of those involved in the early stages of Holocaust survivor interviewing. Ball-Kaduri, working at Yad Vashem in the 1950s, reported a conversation between Dr Reichmann of the Wiener Library and Professor Koebner of the Hebrew University about witness testimony: 'If I find only one piece of evidence, it does not mean anything to me; if I have ten records that is good; but if I have a hundred, then the evidence is conclusive'. Ball-Kaduri queried whether one piece of evidence on its own was valueless, 'especially in the field of active Jewish life there are cases where only one witness has survived'. Such an account, however, was again only important as an illustration and not because the individual was of significance in his/her own right. With the situation of the Jews in Germany in the years from 1933 to 1938, what happened was already 'known'. Writing in 1959, Ball-Kaduri argued that in this case '[w]hoever experienced the suffering there and escaped in time, can hardly add anything of importance, after the passing of so many years'.[99]

In the early years of oral history it was assumed that there was no need for an 'anthropological gap' – the self-doubt and awareness of what could not be grasped by a participant-observer which has typified the discipline of anthropology since 1945, in which the approach of life history has the longest pedigree.[100] Interviewers and interviewees spoke the same language and met as equals. Indeed, marginalised groups would be empowered by knowing their own history and could even undertake it themselves. Next came the easy critique, especially from those within academia who were always unhappy about the populist nature of the oral history bandwagon. Opponents argued that the testimonies gathered could not be relied upon for accuracy and were subject to biased questioning. More recently, however, and certainly in the last decade, the mythologies created within individual life stories, rather than being seen as an inherent weakness, have been celebrated as one of their great strengths. Using insights gained from psychology and literary and cultural studies, the construction of life story has become increasingly sophisticated.[101] How individuals put together their lives in a coherent way tells us as much about their lives *now* as it does about their past experiences. All are bound together in creating the individual's identity. With this development in the approach to oral testimony, however, there is a potential tension between the users and the interviewed, an anthropological gap that would not necessarily have been recognised say in the 1960s had such work been carried out. In contrast, it is largely absent in survivors' responses to the work of Martin Gilbert, who, whilst selecting testimony to fit into a generally chronological framework, never intervenes in the text itself.

It is crucial for scholars and others to be sensitive in their use, or absence of use, of Holocaust testimony. They have to take it seriously, revealing its own internal dynamics, which might mean revealing its strong mythologies and contradictions – the real nature of any life story as has been shown even with the chronologically more specific ghetto diaries in the earlier part of this chapter. For scholars and others to lose that critical perspective is ultimately not to honour the survivors, but to do them damage, as has become so apparent with the Wilkomirski *Fragments* affair.

In 1995 Binjamin Wilkomirski, a Swiss classical musician, published an account of a Polish Jewish childhood in the war. Translated into English the following year, it won literary prizes across the world and was praised for its bravery and authenticity in relating the child's experience of the Holocaust.[102] It later emerged that Wilkomirski had in fact been adopted as a child and raised in a Swiss orphanage (becoming Bruno Dossekker from Bruce GrosJean).[103] Read critically, and obviously now with the advantage of hindsight, the account cannot be that of the author's own childhood, but it is surely significant that many people wanted it to be true, both the general public and even more so the very young survivors of the Holocaust. The latter have been largely marginalised in writing on the Holocaust, and to many child survivors the stark beauty of Wilkomirski's prose managed to give much-needed status to their memories.[104] It is also important not to dismiss, simply out of the fear of providing ammunition to Holocaust deniers, other accounts which in part are deliberately distorted by their authors, such as the case in the early 1970s of Martin Gray's *For Those I Loved*.[105] Gray took his story from the Warsaw Ghetto to Treblinka, which he had not experienced, with the death camp added to his narrative so that he (or his ghost-writer, Max Gallo, 'a writer of some notoriety'[106]) could tell the 'whole' story of the Holocaust. Gallo argued that the chapter on Treblinka was necessary 'because the book required something strong for pulling in readers'. Of much greater significance was Gray's response when confronted by the investigative journalist Gitta Sereny with the fact that 'he had manifestly never been to, nor escaped from Treblinka': 'But does it matter? Wasn't the only thing that Treblinka *did* happen, that it *should* be written about, and that some Jews should be shown to have been heroic?'[107] To Sereny, writing in 1979, it *did* matter: 'Every falsification, every error, every slick re-write job is an advantage to the neo-Nazis'. Gray, unwittingly, was assisting the so-called revisionists.[108]

Since then, Holocaust denial has become more organised, utilising the potential of the electronic media, but is still no less marginal both in terms of academic respectability and in popular acceptance of its message. To allow deniers, most of whom belong to organised racist groupuscules, to determine the representation of the Holocaust is surely absurd, ultimately giving them power by default. In the case of Gray, the inclusion of the chapter on Treblinka does not invalidate the text as a whole but helps to problematise it. It reveals much about the author's identity *and* the context in which he and (unusually in this example) his ghost-writer were working – a time in which memoirs about the Holocaust and interest in the subject were at a low ebb. Whilst it is true that deniers continue to refer to the book on their websites, it is misleading and unnecessary to argue as Gary Mokotoff, a member of the Jewish Book Council in the United States, has done that it has been 'exposed as fiction'. Mokotoff, by linking *For Those I Loved* with *Fragments*, argues that '[t]hese kinds of pseudo-memoirs may do real damage to survivors, by rendering each Holocaust memoir suspect'. Alternatively, it must be suggested, they act as reminders to read and listen to such accounts critically, on one level for their veracity but more importantly to understand their internal dynamics.[109]

More recently, Deli Strummer, a young Austrian Jew who survived Theresienstadt, Auschwitz and Mauthausen, was 'exposed' when it was found that in her memoir, published in 1988, and in a later educational video she falsely killed off her survivor husband whom she claimed had died in Dachau concentration camp. Strummer had also given her testimony to the Fortunoff Video Archive for Holocaust Testimonies at Yale University. Reading the published account, and listening again to the Yale tape, Lawrence Langer, who has produced a monograph on the Fortunoff Video Archive, and Raul Hilberg, one of the great historians of the destruction process, pointed out other aspects of her war experiences that were factually inaccurate, such as gassings at Mauthausen in early May, a week after these had ceased to occur. In relation to invented reality within a testimony, Langer claimed that he had 'never encountered anything like this before'. In fact, according to Libby Copeland of the *Washington Post*, 'Deli Strummer is a Holocaust survivor who wittingly or not altered numerous elements of her story. Her account is clearly longer, more harrowing and more miraculous than what actually happened.'[110]

In such examples, the very desire of the authors to please their intended audiences, and to elicit their full respect and possibly sympathy, with narrative cohesion and Holocaust clichés, suggests the essential need to contextualise such testimonies in time and place and not to regard them as *sui generis*, that is of their own kind and therefore beyond comparison. Mary Chamberlain and Paul Thompson have argued that '[a]ny life story, whether a written autobiography or an oral testimony, is shaped not only by the reworkings of experience through memory and re-evaluation but also always at least to some extent by art'. Although historians and literary critics, because of their elitist assumptions, have been slow to take them on board, there are genres within the autobiographies and testimonies of ordinary people which inevitably bring expectations: 'common assumptions between writer, speaker and audience of conventions, manner and tone, forms of delivery, timings, settings, shapes, motifs and characters'.[111]

It has been argued by those working on the Yale Fortunoff Video Archive that there are 'simplifications which can be described as metonymies'. Geoffrey Hartman observes how 'every Auschwitz survivor seems to have gone through a selection by Mengele, as if he manned his post 24 hours a day'. Yet Hartman argues that 'a remarkable degree of precision remains, because the memory of evil is first and last the memory of an offence, independent of the injustice suffered'.[112] Problematising the same material even less, Lawrence Langer dismisses the question of '[h]ow credible can a reawakened memory be that tries to revive events so many decades after they occurred'. He answers that '[t]here is no need to revive what has never died. Moreover, though slumbering memories may crave reawakening, nothing is clearer in these narratives than that Holocaust memory is an insomniac faculty, whose mental eyes have never slept.' Langer then proceeds to create the category of 'deep memory' to analyse the video testimonies he has examined.[113]

Similarly, Shoshana Felman and Dori Laub's literary and psychoanalytic analysis of the Yale testimonies argues that factual inaccuracies in the tapes are insignificant.[114] Langer, Felman and Laub provide a naive and ultimately patronising attitude to the survivor testimonies, failing to acknowledge how the interviewees often strive to fit into the genre expected of them. It is therefore not surprising that Langer was so astonished by the Deli Strummer controversy that he had to regard it as almost unique, refusing to recognise its wider significance,[115] or that Felman and Laub could write of the significance of Martin Gray being 'forced to witness the destruction of his entire family in the flames of Warsaw and Treblinka' oblivious to the fact that he saw no such thing.[116]

Academics have been slow to recognise the importance of ordinary survivors' testimony. In the historical profession, the dismissive approach has still to go away. In 1992 David Bankier suggested in his study of German popular opinion during the Nazi era that such sources 'hardly constituted firm historical evidence' and could at best only 'be used simply to illustrate or add colour to an account based on less subjective sources', a statement that replicates almost exactly comments made by prosecutors at the Nuremberg trials.[117] More recently, the intellectual historian Peter Novick has suggested that survivors' memories 'are not a very useful historical source'. Further revealing Novick's inability to understand the nature of survivor testimony, he qualifies himself by suggesting 'some may be, but we don't know which ones'.[118] An elitist response has also typified literary studies in which the 'study of authentic first-hand accounts has by no means kept pace with the generally increased attention of historians to the Nazi period'. Andrea Reiter is one of the very few within that discipline who has examined the 'quite distinctive quality' of 'ordinary' concentration camp reports, asking questions such as 'which linguistic devices, which genres, do the survivors rely upon to communicate their experiences? How does literature in the broadest sense, and language and genre more narrowly, become a means of coming to terms with life?'[119] If it is true that 'Holocaust testimony is not usually published because it possesses artistic merit', we still need to return to it bearing in mind Chamberlain and Thompson's maxim that any life story is to some extent always shaped by art.[120] In psychology, which has dominated the study of the survivor,[121] only Henry Greenspan, who has interviewed survivors in a much more informal way than the Yale project over a period of decades, has paid full justice to the process by which an individual's story is made and remade. For Greenspan, the stories of survivors are part of a dynamic process, they evolve and are ultimately influenced by their lives before and after the Holocaust as well as by the expectations of their listeners. In short, we are close here in such nuanced work to the concept of genre(s) in the testimony of ordinary survivors. Greenspan justifies his study by reversing the usual approach: 'In the midst of contemporary claims about all we are supposed to "get *out* of" survivors' testimony – its uses and benefits – I have emphasised that it has not become less urgent to think about how we "get *into*" all that survivors have to retell'. He concludes that 'to listen to survivors is to listen to survivors. No other purpose is required.'[122]

Historians, mirroring exactly those in the legal sphere, have a tendency to require survivor testimony to meet a factual accuracy in terms of dates and detail which they rarely if ever provide. Literary scholars have now begun to incorporate works such as those by Primo Levi and Elie Wiesel into the 'canon' but have done so at the expense of the accounts of ordinary survivors. Psychologists have tended to view survivors only with regard to the trauma of their memory, sometimes dismissing those who were very young and were deemed not to have any recall of their Holocaust childhoods. In terms of audience, it is therefore not surprising that very young survivors, largely written out of the history and memory of the Holocaust, should be so resistant even now to reject *Fragments*, the narrative cohesion of which gives their lives meaning and recognition.[123] Such deception is, of course, relatively rare, but it forces us to read and listen to testimonies with greater care, relishing their very messiness, and to take seriously why, in the less common cases of Gray and Strummer, the authors *deliberately* changed their endings – heroism in one case and pathos in the other.

More generally, it is often what is *not* said as well as what is included and emphasised that is significant. Indeed, it has been argued that silence in testimony and autobiography forms a genre in itself.[124] This is illustrated by the remarkable investigative work carried out by the historian Mark Roseman in relation to German Jewish survivor Marianne Ellenbogen, in which oral and written testimony have been placed alongside a range of contemporary and legal sources (diaries, letters, memoirs, records from the resistance and the Nazis, and post-war restitution documents) to reveal the complex layers of memories in the construction of her life story for the Nazi era. What is revealing, argues Roseman,

is often not the contrast between the *written* and the *spoken* but rather that between perceptions and memories 'fixed' or recorded at different points of distance from the events which they describe, that is, in reports and letters *then*, in interviews and conversations *now*. In any case, when the content of Marianne's interviews was compared with sources from the Nazi and post-war periods, a number of important differences and discrepancies emerged. So much so, that the process by which Marianne's past life regained shape in the present sometimes felt like a detective story (albeit a harrowing and tragic one) as a chain of clues and witnesses forced consecutive reappraisals of the events of more than fifty years ago.[125]

Used freely and fully, oral and other forms of Holocaust testimony are likely to be disruptive and difficult. Donald Niewyk has said that 'close attention to survivors' accounts [might buy] texture and historicity at the expense of coherence' but he adds that 'it is a risk we need to take if we are to grasp the complexity of the process and approach an understanding of what happened to the victims'.[126] At present the dominant usage of survivor accounts is distorted – they are ironed out and re-arranged so as to provide narrative cohesion. For example, tens of thousands of video interviews have been carried out by the Spielberg Foundation, producing hundreds of thousands of hours of testimony. By a massive indexing operation it is possible that this archive could be used highly effectively to trace the Holocaust at particular places if not at exact times. But how these video tapes are to be used beyond the merely illustrative seems to have been a question left unexplored.[127]

If such representation of testimony is to do justice to the depth and wealth of material, the answer is not in the Spielberg film directed by James Moll, *The Last Days* (1999).[128] This achieves cohesion by focusing on one place in what was (even given the warning implicit in the next chapter about seeing any part of the 'final solution' as its essence) a rather unrepresentative part of the Holocaust – namely the sudden and intensive murder of Hungarian Jews in the summer of 1944 – and further by reinterviewing the survivors or rearranging their testimony to produce an account made up of soundbites where both survivor and liberator are part of a clear storyline. Indeed, on only one occasion in the film did the testimony of a survivor last for more than forty-five seconds. Significantly it came from Dario Gabbai, a Greek member of the Sonderkommando. It was included within the film to illustrate the functioning of the gas chambers working at their full capacity in Auschwitz rather than to explain how Gabbai came to be in the camp in the first place. Likewise, the only other slightly extended testimony came from a former Nazi doctor to show how the final solution was implemented in its most systematic form.[129]

It is not surprising that film-makers, museum curators and publishers like neat, packageable narrative structures. The Imperial War Museum's Holocaust Gallery, following Washington, follows a strict chronology led by the Nazi rise to power. At the United States Holocaust Memorial Museum its first director, Jeshajahu Weinberg, stated that '[p]ersonal narrative is woven into the text so history is made incarnate through the experience of men, women, and children who went through the event'. At the Imperial War Museum, the victims are certainly not silenced – oral testimony is more prominent than in Washington – and visitors hear briefly about their lives before and after as well as during the years of persecution. Yet the use of this testimony is not central to the display as a whole: just as documentary evidence was deemed as 'proof positive' in the post-war trials, so artefacts, most relating to the process of extermination, are central to the huge national museum displays in the capitals of the two leading former Allied nations. Survivor testimony is yet again marginalised and used to illustrate the impact of what the Nazis did rather than being part of an intensive study of survivors' lives as a whole. As the director of the Imperial War Museum, Robert Crawford, puts it: the survivor-witnesses 'provide a poignant, intimate enhancement to the main historical narrative'. In both museums, enormous attention has been paid to making sure that all exhibits have, in Weinberg's words, 'proven provenance' in order '[t]o preclude definitively revisionist declarations'.[130]

Ironically, such attitudes have led to the exclusion of Holocaust-related memoirs as when in September 2000 the Washington Museum refused to host a book-signing because the author had referred to the unproven manufacture of soap from human remains at Auschwitz. A spokeswoman for the museum defended the action, arguing that '[s]ingling out a memoir for a book-signing implies a level of endorsement of its contents' and in this particular case would risk providing fodder to the revisionists.[131] David Cesarani has written that at a time of Holocaust denial, we '*want* the survivors to remember it all and be able to articulate it, to *prove* by virtue of their very existence that it happened'. But, as he adds, 'these expectations place too great a burden on the survivor-writer'. It does not follow, however, that when testimony is published with 'inaccuracies' in detail, it 'is a hostage to fortune, a gift to Holocaust deniers'.[132] As two publishers of such accounts wrote in response: 'we are not concerned to joust with Holocaust deniers and revisionists. They will always find some little detail to damn a book.'[133]

Survivor testimony, whether in written, oral or video form, has to be taken seriously on its own terms as life history of ordinary people before, during and after persecution. It becomes distorted or manipulated if used crudely as a weapon against denial or as simply a provider of 'colour' or texture to educational, museum or artistic representations of the Holocaust. If slowly we have started to listen to survivors, we should also respect the desire of some to keep their silence. As Novick suggests, 'it's clear that for many survivors all the attention paid to the Holocaust has been gratifying, and helped scars to heal; for others it has reopened old wounds and given rise to nightmares once quiescent'.[134] Claude Lanzmann's bullying of Treblinka survivor Abraham Bomba in his film *Shoah* (1985) – 'You have to do it', when asking him to describe preparing friends for the gas chamber – can have no ethical justification, historical or artistic.[135] Lanzmann's *Shoah* was subtitled 'An Oral History', but in the process of providing a counter-myth to attempts at earlier representations of the Holocaust through history and chronology, he is interested in showing only the violence of the destruction process, in which there is absolutely no place for the life story of the survivors, whom he largely represents as having died in all but body.[136] Forcing survivors to give testimony, or ignoring their lives before and after, is to add another form of abuse that began with their persecution, continued after the war in neglect and marginalisation, and now expects too much from them at the same time as ignoring the very complexity of their accounts.[137]

The Holocaust testimony collected in the 1940s through to the 1970s by David Boder and institutions such as Yad Vashem focused almost solely on the years of destruction. For example, the questionnaire designed by Yad Vashem had less than 1 per cent of its questions relating to the pre-war period.[138] In the 1980s projects such as those at Yale University and the National Sound Archive in London moved towards a life story approach, mirroring the dominant trend in oral history as a whole.[139] Nevertheless, as we have seen, it is extremely rare in almost all manifestations of Holocaust representation, whether academic or artistic, for this life story material to be used other than in brief, fragmented form. As a result, the totality of the individual concerned is at best obscured and at worst utterly subsumed. But is an alternative approach to Holocaust testimony a realistic possibility, given commercial and other practical realities?

For survivor oral testimony to be interpreted according to its strengths would require a shift towards a life story approach and for the strands of history and memory to be woven together to show the full complexity of survivor identity. For the curator, the film-maker and the historian, focusing on the victims creates immense practical problems, not least where and when to start and finish. As Lawrence Langer puts it, trying to make sense of the Yale Holocaust video collection, 'the Holocaust has a different beginning for each witness'. Returning to Martin Gilbert's *The Holocaust*, a lead is given in providing a victim-centred account. It is, however, a misleadingly deceptive one through the use of a strict and straightforward chronology that ultimately makes a nonsense of the life story of each individual introduced. If Gilbert attempts to provide a diary of the Holocaust, it is never that of any one person. In this respect his attempt to humanise the Holocaust is to an extent counter-productive.[140] The chaos and the rupture in the lives of the victims are obscured in the desire to achieve smoothness. But can popular representations, including within the writing of history, deal with the full complexity of the ordinary life as well as letting the visitor or reader tease out the mythologies entangled in such stories?

If the answer is to be yes, it will require an acknowledgement from all concerned that it will not be easy – but then should any representation or commemoration of the Holocaust accept a simplistic idea of closure, a story with a neat beginning, middle and happy ending (whether in the form of concentration camp liberation or the creation of the state of Israel)? The museum/memorial work of Daniel Libeskind in Berlin shows that Jewish history incorporating the Holocaust, and confronting individual testimony in its entirety, can be represented in a complex way, allowing for disjunction and confusion, but still able to make itself accessible to the public.[141] There is an equal danger, as with such famous writers as Elie Wiesel or Anne Frank, of 'privileging a particular story or in assuming that there is a single story to be told'. Mary Lagerwey, in particular, has queried the notion of a representative Holocaust story: 'Perhaps Auschwitz engulfed individual differences, whether of gender, nationality, or intellect. Perhaps ...'.[142] Terrence des Pres, in his *The Survivor: An Anatomy of Life in the Death Camps* (1976), suggests that a 'vast body of literature has ... come into being – diaries, novels, documentary reports, simple lists and fragments ... which all tell one story'. Yet even his simplistic analysis and attempt to provide 'a medium through which these scattered voices might issue one statement' breaks down within the text as the authors chosen by des Pres stamp their own individuality on the experiences they describe.[143]

Testimony forces us to think qualitatively and we have to face the fact that to do it justice may require working with smaller rather than larger numbers of individuals; this allows, however, through the greater self-reflectivity of those collecting and utilising the material, for the richness of testimony to come to the fore, including its contradictions and mythologies.[144] It is a radical vision, but in the end choosing confusion over smoothness in the representation of life story testimony, whether contemporary or post-war, is to do greater justice to the way the Holocaust was actually experienced on an everyday level. Primo Levi wrote and re-wrote his Holocaust testimony with obsessive care. Indeed, it has been suggested that no other survivor 'has written down and reflected on his memories of the camps over such a long period of time – from 1944/5, when he wrote scraps of notes in the Buna lab at Monowitz, until his death in 1987'.[145] *The Drowned and the Saved* (1986), his last attempt to confront the past and its relationship to the present, was, in Levi's words, 'drenched in memory ... it draws from a suspect source, and must be protected against itself ... it contains more considerations than memories, lingers more willingly on the state of affairs such as it is now than on the retroactive chronicle'.[146] Levi, as Robert Gordon suggests, had wrestled 'with the processes and representation of memory' from his first published account of his experiences in Auschwitz, *If This Is a Man* (1947). This book itself became 'an object of memory for Levi over the course of decades to come, blocking at times his access to the direct memories of his experiences themselves'.[147]

Levi's concerns about the memory process parallel those of

Janusz Korczak in his contemporary Warsaw diary. Korczak, however, was far less concerned about any distortion caused in constructing his testimony. He wrote in May 1942 that he did not

> know how much of this autobiographical stuff I've already scribbled down. I cannot bring myself to read it and examine the overload. And I'm increasingly in danger of repeating myself. What's even worse, the facts and experiences may be, must be and will be told differently each time as regards the details. But never mind. It only proves that the moments to which I constantly return were experienced deeply.[148]

If the complex and often contradictory nature of Holocaust testimony, including its intricate relationship with memory, is not accepted, we are in danger of fast settling, especially in the commercial world in which an increasing amount of Holocaust commemoration is located, for representation that reduces the subject matter to a simplistic morality tale – one shorn of its specific historic context in which is explored when, where and *who* was affected. In this respect, the failure to realise the Shoah Centre in Manchester, designed by Libeskind (see frontispiece), does not bode well for the future.[149] The project, finally abandoned in the early 2000s, was to have focused on the life story testimony of survivors as its major form of Holocaust representation.

The Manchester Shoah Centre faltered partly through a lack of financial will and partly through its radical vision. Nevertheless, its apparent non-success can be reinterpreted if it is regarded as a form of what in Germany has developed as Holocaust counter-monuments. They include the work of Jochen Gerz and Esther Shalev-Gerz in Hamburg, a 12m pillar that literally disappeared into the landscape. As James Young states: 'How better to remember forever a vanished people than by the perpetually unfinished, ever-vanishing monument?'.[150] In these works the very absence of presence reflects the vacuum created by the destruction process, removing the clear categories of 'then' and 'now' and thereby recognising the necessity of ongoing Holocaust memory work.

The Shoah Centre was to have been located opposite the Imperial War Museum North (IWMN) in reclaimed land around the Manchester Ship Canal. The IWMN, also designed by Libeskind, *was* built, and opened in 2002. Its narrative of the Second World War, whilst containing a local slant, is generally universal, and the story of the Holocaust fits within and does not disrupt its overall approach. The Shoah Centre would have complemented the ideological framework adopted by Libeskind for the IWMN with its desire to show the fundamental dislocation caused by twentieth-century world conflict: 'I have imagined the globe broken into fragments and taken the pieces to form the building – three shards – together they represent conflict on land, in the air and on water'.[151] At the same time, the Shoah Centre would have challenged the IWMN through its more particularistic slant – focusing largely on Jewish victims. The testimony would have come largely from survivors who settled in the Manchester region after the war.

The Shoah Centre intended to connect the city of Manchester to the destruction process on the continent at various levels: first, and most straightforwardly, through local responses and reactions, positive and otherwise, to the persecution of Jews and others from the rise of Nazism to its defeat in 1945; second, and with more complexity, to show the impossibility of separating out the local from the national and global through the testimony of the survivors. By taking their life stories seriously, the proposed museum would have highlighted the importance of place identity to these individuals – before, during and after the Holocaust. Manchester would then have been linked to the villages, towns and cities of the continent in which these people grew up, as well as to the everyday sites of destruction. Concentrating on a small number of testimonies would have enabled those visiting the Shoah Centre not just to humanise the victims but to begin to understand the complexity as well as the ordinariness of the worlds that were destroyed and the ordinary places that became killing fields. The process of 'bringing home' the Holocaust would have been extended to make connections, though far from simplistic comparisons, with the forms of racism and intolerance that are part of the everyday life of England's second city, no matter how strong its liberal reputation.

Although questions of representativeness would not have been totally avoided, such as the sex and forms of Jewish identities of those whose life stories were chosen, the Shoah Centre would have acknowledged the impossibility of telling *all* the stories of the Holocaust. Indeed, it would have seen the qualitative aspects of its representation as a virtue rather than an inherent weakness. The Holocaust Exhibition at the Imperial War Museum in London, which arguably has the most extensive use of testimony in any equivalent display, is still driven by the (relatively) clear chronology provided by the Nazi destruction process. In contrast, the Shoah Centre in Manchester would have relished the messiness created by embracing the life stories of ordinary people to whom something extraordinary happened. Most importantly, the visitor would have been forced to confront the actual process of providing testimony: what it means to those giving *and* receiving it. Its exhibition would have lacked a simplistic form of story telling, but it would have forced the visitor to confront the fact that the Holocaust was not experienced by its victims as the coherent narrative in which it is now increasingly packaged.

The Shoah Centre is thus absent from the memorial landscape of post-industrial Manchester, birthplace of an industrial modernity that in its most destructive form manifested itself through the Holocaust. It can, however, like the countermonuments of Germany, still play a vital role in Holocaust memory work. To quote James Young again: '[The] countermonument recognizes and affirms that the life of memory exists primarily in historical time: in the activity that brings monuments into being, into the ongoing exchange between people and their historical markers, and finally, in the concrete actions we take in light of a memorialized past'.[152] At present, victim testimony is almost exclusively, if well-meaningly, used to provide supplementary forms of Holocaust representation that serve the purpose of either giving a human face to the millions murdered or to show the vileness of what was done to them. The challenge now is to confront the testimony of the victims both qualitatively (dealing with less in terms of the life stories represented can, in this case, mean much more in relation to the engagement with the material) and reflectively (acknowledging context and genre, even in the most apparently simple accounts). Ultimately, it is important to accept that how we remember the Holocaust, including through the various genres of victim testimony, 'is not against history but part of a process of inserting memory into history'.[153] There would be a tragic irony if Holocaust testimony, with all its potential nuances, became integral to the telling of a story so polished that we actually lost sight of the individual in any meaningful sense.

Holocaust testimony should be studied seriously through critical engagement because the lives of ordinary people, and their ways of telling their life stories, matter. That said, we should not expect the impossible from Holocaust testimony. It will rarely, for example, contribute knowledge to our understanding of the politics of implementation, which is located, as will become clear in the following two chapters, in an obviously related but nevertheless discrete (if complex and fast evolving) historiography.

Notes

1   By 1999, the Survivors of the Shoah Visual History Foundation, founded by Steven Spielberg in 1994, had gathered some 50,000 testimonies. See Michael Berenbaum, 'Prologue', in *The Last Days* (London, Weidenfeld & Nicolson, 1999), p. 9. Yad Vashem in Jerusalem has tens of thousands of written testimonies.

2   Primo Levi, *The Drowned and the Saved* (London, Michael Joseph, 1988), pp. 1–2.

3   Tony Kushner, *The Holocaust and the Liberal Imagination: A Social and Cultural History* (Oxford, Blackwell, 1994), ch. 7.

4   Henry Greenspan, *On Listening to Holocaust Survivors: Recounting and Life History* (Westport, Ct., Praeger, 1998), pp. 169–70.

5   Raul Hilberg, *Sources of Holocaust Research: An Analysis* (Chicago, Ivan R. Dee, 2001), p. 49.

6   Raul Hilberg, *The Politics of Memory: The Journey of a Holocaust Historian* (Chicago, Ivan R. Dee, 1996), p. 133.

7   Raul Hilberg and Stanislaw Staron, 'Introduction', in Raul Hilberg, Stanislaw Staron and Josef Kermisz (eds), *The Warsaw Diary of Adam Czerniakow* (New York, Stein and Day, 1979), p. 25.

8   Raul Hilberg, *Perpetrators, Victims, Bystanders: The Jewish Catastrophe 1933–1945* (New York, HarperCollins, 1992).

9   Raul Hilberg, *The Destruction of the European Jews* (Chicago, Quadrangle Books, 1961), p. v.

10   Levi, *The Drowned and the Saved*, orig. in Italian, 1986, pp. 63–4.

11   Elie Wiesel, 'Trivializing Memory', in idem, *From the Kingdom of Memory: Reminiscences* (New York, Schocken, 1990), pp. 165–6.

12   Yehuda Bauer, 'Against Mystification', in idem, *The Holocaust in Historical Perspective* (London, Sheldon Press, 1978), p. 44.

13   Gayatri Chakravorty Spivak, 'Can the Subaltan Speak?', in G. Nelson (ed.), *Marxism and the Interpretation of Culture* (Basingstoke, Macmillan, 1988), pp. 271–313, esp. pp. 294, 308.

14   John Blassingame, *The Slave Community: Plantation Life in the Antebellum South* (New York, Oxford University Press, 1972), p. 325 covers twenty accounts written by slaves manumitted by their masters and a further twenty-six written by fugitive slaves. In the 1930s interviews

with former slaves were carried out. The overall number is still tiny.

15   Posen speech, 4 October 1943, reproduced in Lucy Davidowicz (ed.), *A Holocaust Reader* (New York, Behrman House, 1976), pp. 132–4.

16   Martin Gilbert, *The Holocaust: The Jewish Tragedy* (Glasgow, Collins, 1986), pp. 229–30.

17   See, for example, the comments made by Ruth Wisse in Robert Moses Shapiro (ed.), *Holocaust Chronicles: Individualizing the Holocaust Through Diaries and Other Contemporaneous Personal Accounts* (Hoboken, N.J., KTAV, 1999), pp. xvii–iii on the need for special treatment of ghetto diaries 'perhaps as moral compensation for the indignity visited on these people when they lived'.

18   Nathan Cohen, 'Diaries of the *Sonderkommandos* in Auschwitz: Coping with Fate and Reality', *Yad Vashem Studies*, vol. 20 (1990), pp. 273–312.

19   Ibid., p. 287.

20   Emanuel Ringelblum, 'O.S.', written late December 1942 and reproduced in Joseph Kermish (ed.), *To Live With Honor and Die With Honor* (Jerusalem, Yad Vashem, 1986), pp. 7–8.

21   Aharon Appelfeld, 'Individualization of the Holocaust', in Shapiro (ed.), *Holocaust Chronicles*, p. 5.

22   Abraham Katsh (ed.), *Scroll of Agony: The Warsaw Diary of Chaim A. Kaplan* (London, Hamish Hamilton, 1966), p. 318.

23   Ruth Wisse, 'Introduction', in Shapiro (ed.), *Holocaust Chronicles*, p. xv.

24   Ringelblum, 'O.S.', p. 9.

25   Jeshajahu Weinberg and Rina Elieli, *The Holocaust Museum in Washington* (New York, Rizzoli, 1995), pp. 17, 106–7; Edward Linenthal, *Preserving Memory: The Struggle to Create America's Holocaust Museum* (New York, Viking, 1995), pp. 108, 158; Michael Berenbaum, *The World Must Know: The History of the Holocaust as Told in the United States Holocaust Memorial Museum* (Boston, Little, Brown & Co., 1993), pp. 92–4.

26   Katsh, 'Introduction', *Scroll of Agony*, p. xiii.

27   *Scroll of Agony*, pp. 22–3, diary entry for 1 October 1939.

28   Ibid., p. 103, entry for 20 February 1940.

29   Ibid., p. 206, entry for 26 November 1940.

30   Ibid., pp. 302–3, entry for 26 July 1942.

31   Ibid., p. 313, entry for 31 July 1942.

32   Ibid., p. 213, entry for 16 December 1940.

33   Ibid., p. 278 entry for 13 November 1941.

34   Katsh, 'Introduction', *Scroll of Agony*, p. xiii.

35   *Scroll of Agony*, pp. 281–2, entry for 27 June 1942.

36   Antony Polonsky (ed.), *A Cup of Tears: A Diary of the Warsaw Ghetto* (Oxford, Blackwell, 1988), p. 193, entry for 30 October 1942.

37   See, for example, his *The Literature of Destruction: Jewish Responses to Catastrophe* (Cambridge, Mass., Harvard University Press, 1984).

38   David Roskies, 'The Library of Jewish Catastrophe', in Geoffrey Hartman (ed.), *Holocaust Remembrance: The Shapes of Memory* (Oxford, Blackwell, 1994), p. 41.

39   Sara Horowitz, 'Voices from the Killing Ground', in Hartman (ed.), *Holocaust Remembrance*, p. 44.

40   Lucjan Dobroszycki, 'YIVO in Interwar Poland: Work in the Historical Sciences', in Yisrael Gutman et al. (eds), *The Jews of Poland Between Two World Wars* (Hanover, University Press of New England, 1989), pp. 494–518; Samuel David Kassow, 'Vilna and Warsaw, Two Ghetto Diaries: Herman Kruk and Emanuel Ringelblum', in Shapiro (ed.), *Holocaust Chronicles*, pp. 176–8.

41   Kassow, 'Vilna and Warsaw', p. 176; Zelig Kalmanowitsch [Kalmanovitch], 'A Diary of the Nazi Ghetto in Vilna', *YIVO Annual*, vol. 8 (1953), pp. 9–81.

42   Barbara Kirshenblatt-Gimblett, 'Coming of Age in the Thirties: Max Weinreich, Edward Sapir and Jewish Social Science', *YIVO Annual*, vol. 23 (1996), pp. 1–103; Martin Bulmer, *The Chicago School of Sociology* (Chicago, University of Chicago Press, 1984), ch. 4.

43   Liz Bloom, 'The Diary as Popular History', *Journal of Popular Culture*, vol. 9 (Spring 1976), pp. 794–5.

44   Steven Kagle, 'The Diary as Art: A New Assessment', *Genre*, vol. 6 (1973), pp. 416–27, esp. p. 425.

45   James Young, *Writing and Rewriting the Holocaust: Narrative and the Consequences of Interpretation* (Bloomington, Indiana University Press, 1988), p. 37.

46   Felicity Nussbaum, 'Toward Conceptualizing Diary', in James Olney (ed.), *Studies in Autobiography* (New York, Oxford University Press, 1988), pp. 132, 137.

47   Aaron Zeitlin, 'The Last Walk of Janusz Korczak', in Janusz Korczak, *Ghetto Diary* (New York, Holocaust Library, 1978), p. 72.

48   Anne Frank, *The Diary of a Young Girl* (London, Penguin Books, 2000), pp. 332–4.

49   Philip Boehm, 'Introduction', in Michal Grynberg (ed.), *Words to Outlive Us: Eyewitness Accounts from the Warsaw Ghetto* (London, Granta Books, 2003), p. 3.

50   Ibid.

51   Ibid., pp. 374, 376.

52   Benjamin Harshav (ed.), *Herman Kruk: The Last Days of the Jerusalem of Lithuania: Chronicles from the Vilna Ghetto and the Camps, 1939–1944* (New Haven, Yale University Press, 2002), p. xviii.

53   Harshav, 'Introduction', in ibid., pp. xxvi–xxviii.

54 Ibid., p. xxix.

55 Ibid., pp. v–vi.

56 Raul Hilberg, *Sources of Holocaust Research* (Chicago, Ivan R. Dee, 2001), p. 20; see also Lawrence Langer, *Admitting the Holocaust* (New York, Oxford University Press, 1995), pp. 41–2.

57 See Hyman Enzer and Sandra Solotaroff-Enzer (eds), *Anne Frank: Reflections on Her Life and Legacy* (Urbana and Chicago, University of Illinois Press, 2000), part 2: 'Writer and Rewriter'.

58 This is the approach, for example, of the National Life Story Collection at the British Library, London, in response to an industry closing down – workers and those associated with the industry are located to provide an archive of lives in danger of oblivion. See, for example, Alan Dein and Rob Perks, *Lives in Steel* (CD Rom, National Sound Archives, London, 1993), carried out when the steel industry in Britain was being decimated – the background to the film *The Full Monty*, set in Sheffield, 'steel city'.

59 Robert Rozett, 'The Scribes of Memory', *Yad Vashem Magazine*, vol. 10 (Summer 1998), pp. 6–7.

60 Andrzej Szpilman, 'Foreword', in Wladyslaw Szpilman, *The Pianist* (London, Phoenix, 2002), p. 8.

61 Wolf Biermann, 'Epilogue', in Szpilman, *The Pianist*, p. 211.

62 It was published by Victor Gollancz in 1999. Roman Polanski directed the film which won the Palme D'Or at the 2002 Cannes Film Festival.

63 Szpilman, *The Pianist*, pp. 126, 137; Bierman, 'Epilogue', pp. 213–14.

64 Ian Thomson, *Primo Levi* (London, Hutchinson, 2002), p. 240.

65 Robert Gordon, *Primo Levi's Ordinary Virtues: From Testimony to Ethics* (Oxford, Oxford University Press, 2001), p. 56; Thomson, *Primo Levi*, pp. 242–4, 253.

66 Donald Kenrick and Grattan Puxon, *The Destiny of Europe's Gypsies* (London, Heinemann, 1972); Guenter Lewy, *The Nazi Persecution of the Gypsies* (Oxford, Oxford University Press, 2000).

67 Reproduced in Thomas Acton and Ilona Klimova, 'The International Romani Union', in Will Guy (ed.), *Between Past and Present: The Roma of Central and Eastern Europe* (Hatfield, University of Hertfordshire Press, 2001), p. 216.

68 David Roskies, 'The Library of Jewish Catastrophe', in Hartman (ed.), *Holocaust Remembrance*, pp. 33–41; Annette Wieviorka and Ithok Niborski, *Les Livres du Souvenir Memoriaux juifs de Pologne* (Paris, Editions Gallimard, 1983); Deborah Dwork, paper at 'Lessons and Legacies VI: The Presence of the Holocaust' International Conference, Northwestern University, November 2000; Rosemary Horowitz, 'Reading and Writing

During the Holocaust as Described in Yisker Books', in Jonathan Rose (ed.), *The Holocaust and the Book: Destruction and Preservation* (Amherst, University of Massachusetts Press, 2001), p. 129.

69   For example, *The Black Book* was material collected by the Soviet Jews Ilya Ehrenburg and Vasily Grossman from 1943 onwards to gather material for war crimes trials and to document the fate of the Jews through all forms of autobiographical material. Its publication after the war was suppressed by the Soviet Union. See Joseph Kermish, 'The History of the Manuscript', in *The Black Book* (New York, Holocaust Library, 1980), pp. xix–xxvi.

70   Some of the Wiener Library interviews have recently been reproduced in microfilm form: *Archives of the Wiener Library – Testaments to the Holocaust* Section 2 *Eyewitness Accounts* (Woodbridge, Primary Source Media, 1998). On the problems facing those involved in the early stage of testimony collection, see K. Ball-Kaduri, 'Evidence of Witnesses, its Value and Limitations', *Yad Washem Studies*, vol. 3 (1959), p. 88.

71   Some of the results were published by Boder under the title *I Did Not Interview the Dead* (Urbana, University of Illinois Press, 1949). Thirty-four of the interviews are reproduced in Donald Niewyk (ed.), *Fresh Wounds: Early Narratives of Holocaust Survival* (Chapel Hill and London, University of North Carolina Press, 1998). See Niewyk's introduction, pp. 1–6, for the background to Boder's work.

72   See especially Donald Bloxham, *The Holocaust on Trial: The War Crimes Trials in the Formation of History and Memory* (Oxford, Oxford University Press, 2001).

73   Leon Poliakov, *Harvest of Hate* (London, Elek Books, 1956), p. xiv.

74   Kushner, *The Holocaust and the Liberal Imagination*, ch. 7.

75   Gerald Reitlinger, *The Final Solution: The Attempt to Exterminate the Jews of Europe 1939–1945* (London, Vallentine, Mitchell, 1953), p. 531.

76   See *The Times*, 21 March 1978.

77   Daniel Bertaux, 'Preface', in idem (ed.), *Biography and Society: The Life Story Approach in the Social Sciences* (Beverly Hills, Calif., Sage, 1981), p. 1.

78   Benzion Dinur, 'Problems Confronting "Yad Washem" in its Work of Research', *Yad Washem Studies*, vol. 1 (1957), p. 21.

79   Zvi Bar-On and Dov Levin, 'Problems Relating to a Questionnaire on the Holocaust', *Yad Washem Studies*, vol. 3 (1959), pp. 91–117.

80   Gilbert, *The Holocaust*.

81   Martin Gilbert, *Churchill: A Life* (London, Heinemann, 1991), which synthesises the multi-volume biography which Gilbert produced from 1971 through to 1988.

82   Gilbert, *The Holocaust*, p. 18.

83   Gilbert has stated that 'chronology is the key to understanding

everything' in the *Observer*, 28 December 1986; Martin Gilbert, 'The Witnesses of the Holocaust', *Sunday Times*, 12 January 1986.

84   For survivor responses, see Hugo Gryn's review in *Jewish Chronicle*, 7 February 1986. It was at the prompting of survivors in Britain that Gilbert began work on the project, which took ten years to complete.

85   George Steiner reviewing *The Holocaust* in the *Sunday Times*, 9 February 1986.

86   See, for example, quotes from reviewers reproduced in the paperback edition.

87   But see Gustavo Corni, *Hitler's Ghettos: Voices from a Beleaguered Society 1939–1944* (London, Arnold, 2002), who does so for a specific aspect of the Holocaust. On pp. 3–4 Corni rejects the use of oral testimony, however, as lacking any sense of narrative. Such a dismissal runs against the life history approach to oral history which has become dominant since the 1980s.

88   Ibid., p. 2.

89   Martin Gilbert, *Holocaust Journey: Travelling in Search of the Past* (London, Weidenfeld & Nicolson, 1997). Laurence Rees, *The Nazis: A Warning from History*, BBC2, screened in six parts from 10 September to 15 October 1997. Amongst other awards it won a BAFTA Best Factual Film and a George Foster Peabody Award in 1997. The fifth programme, 'The Road to Treblinka', was broadcast on 8 October. The lack of depth in the testimony is exposed more blatantly when it is reproduced in the printed version of the series with the same title and also written by Laurence Rees, published by BBC Worldwide, London, 1997. It should be added that this quality series is in a category of its own, having benefited from the input of its historical advisor, Ian Kershaw. Its pale imitators on both sides of the Atlantic, most recently in the German television series *Holokaust* (2000), become merely sensationalist.

90   Saul Friedländer, *Nazi Germany and The Jews: The Years of Persecution 1933–39* (London, Weidenfeld & Nicolson, 1997).

91   See, for example, his collected essays, *Memory, History and the Extermination of the Jews of Europe* (Bloomington and Indianapolis, Indiana University Press, 1993).

92   Burleigh quoted on the cover *Nazi Germany and the Jews*.

93   Friedländer, *Nazi Germany and the Jews*, p. 2.

94   Ibid.

95   The relatively marginal status of Jewish testimony is revealed in chapters 9 and 10 relating to Kristallnacht and its aftermath.

96   Daniel Goldhagen, *Hitler's Willing Executioners: Ordinary Germans and the Holocaust* (Boston, Little, Brown & Co., 1996). See, for example, Goldhagen's approach to the initial killing operation of police battalion 101 in Jozefow: 'they chose to walk into a hospital, a house of healing, and to shoot the sick, who must have been cowering, begging and screaming for mercy. They killed babies ... In all probability, a killer either shot a baby in its mother's arms [or] held it at arm's length by the leg ... Perhaps the mother looked on in horror. The tiny corpse was then dropped like so much trash and left to rot' (pp. 215–16).

97 This is true of Friedländer's use of the exceptionally rich and powerful testimony of Victor Klemperer. See *Nazi Germany and the Jews*, pp. 58–9, 126, 324. These diaries were published in Germany in extensive form in 1995.

98 The approach is best summarised in the first edition of Paul Thompson, *The Voice of the Past: Oral History* (Oxford, Oxford University Press, 1978), ch. 4 'Evidence'.

99 Ball-Kaduri, 'Evidence of Witnesses', p. 89.

100 Judith Okely and Helen Calloway (eds), *Anthropology and Autobiography* (London, Routledge, 1992), and for one of the leading post-war practitioners and its implementation see Clifford Geerz, *Local Knowledge* (London, Fontana, 1993).

101 For a summary of approaches, see Raphael Samuel and Paul Thompson, 'Introduction', in idem (eds), *The Myths We Live By* (London, Routledge, 1990), pp. 1–22. See also the second edition of Thompson's *The Voice of the Past* (Oxford, Oxford University Press, 1988). In the preface Thompson wrote that '[i]n the ten years since I first wrote this book much has happened'. In chapter 4, on 'Evidence', he introduced a new section on subjectivity, and he added a totally new chapter on 'memory and the self'.

102 Binjamin Wilkomirski, *Fragments* (Basingstoke, Picador, 1996). For a sensitive account of the 'affair', see Elena Lappin, 'The Man With Two Heads', *Granta*, no. 66 (Summer 1999), pp. 9–65.

103 Blake Eskin, *A Life in Pieces* (London, Aurum Press, 2002) for an insightful overview.

104 Christopher Oligiati's documentary on the affair, *Child of the Death Camps: Truth and Lies* (BBC1, 3 November 1999), included child survivor groups supporting Wilkomirski. See also Eskin, *A Life in Pieces*, passim.

105 Originally published in France in 1971, it had a wide circulation in English in its translation by Anthony White, published in the United States by Little, Brown & Co. and in Britain by Book Club Associates.

106 The description is by Philippe Lejeune, *On Autobiography* (Minneapolis, University of Minnesota Press, 1989), p. 195.

107 Gitta Sereny, 'The Men who Whitewash Hitler', *New Statesman*, 2 November 1979.

108 Ibid.

109 According to the figures produced by Yad Vashem, 1971 saw a particularly low number of survivor accounts published across the world – just twenty. See Robert Rozett, 'The Scribes of Memory', *Yad Vashem Magazine*, vol. 10 (Summer 1998), pp. 6–7. For Mokotoff, see Lappin, 'The Man with Two Heads', p. 49.

110 Libby Copeland, 'Survivor', *Washington Post*, 24 September 2000.

111 Mary Chamberlain and Paul Thompson, 'Introduction: Genre and Narrative in Life Stories', in idem (eds), *Narrative and Genre* (Routledge, London, 1998), pp. 1, 4.

112 Geoffrey Hartman, 'Learning from Survivors: The Yale Testimony Project', in idem, *The Longest Shadow: In the Aftermath of the Holocaust* (Bloomington and Indianapolis, Indiana University Press, 1996), pp. 136, 141. The article was originally published in *Holocaust and Genocide Studies* in Autumn 1995.

113 Lawrence Langer, *Holocaust Testimonies: The Ruins of Memory* (New Haven, Yale University Press, 1991), p. xv and ch. 1.

114 Shoshana Felman and Dori Laub, *Testimony: Crises of Witnessing in Literature, Psychoanalysis and History* (New York and London, Routledge, 1992), esp. ch. 2.

115 Langer, quoted in *Washington Post*, 24 September 2000.

116 Felman and Laub, *Testimony*, p. 65.

117 David Bankier, *The Germans and the Final Solution: Public Opinion under Nazism* (Oxford, Blackwell, 1992), pp. 118, 124.

118 Peter Novick, *The Holocaust and Collective Memory* (London, Bloomsbury, 2000), p. 275.

119 Andrea Reiter, *Narrating the Holocaust* (London, Continuum, 2000), pp. 1–2, 3.

120 David Cesarani, 'Shadows of Doubt', *Jewish Quarterly*, no. 164 (Winter 1996/97), p. 61; Chamberlain and Thompson (eds), *Narrative and Genre*, p. 1.

121 Thus in the entry in Israel Gutman and Geoffrey Wigoder (eds), *Encyclopedia of the Holocaust*, vol. 4 (New York, Macmillan, 1990), pp. 1426–8, survivors are dealt with under the sub-title 'Psychology of'.

122 Greenspan, *On Listening to Holocaust Survivors*, pp. 169–72.

123 Thus at the international Holocaust conference, 'Remembering for the Future 2000', held at Oxford in July 2000, well after the author had been 'exposed', many child survivors present were still deeply sympathetic towards Wikomorski and his book. For a brief but thoughtful discussion of accounts written by those who were children during the Holocaust see the epilogue to Reiter, *Narrating the Holocaust*, pp. 230–40, which includes discussion of Wilkomirski.

124 Diana Gittens, 'Silences', in Chamberlain and Thompson (eds), *Narrative and Genre*, pp. 46–62.

125 Mark Roseman, 'Surviving Memory: Truth and Inaccuracy in

Holocaust Testimony', *Journal of Holocaust Education*, vol. 8, no. 1 (Summer 1999), p. 2; idem, *The Past in Hiding* (London, Allen Lane, 2000).

126 Niewyk, *Fresh Wounds*, p. 1.

127 In 1999 the Foundation had gathered over 115,000 hours of testimony and had claimed to have developed 'an in-depth indexing system capable of cataloguing the wide range of historical, biographical and geographical data offered by each witness'.

128 *The Last Days* (James Moll, 1999, October Films).

129 The testimony of Gabbai is reproduced in *The Last Days*, pp. 157–9.

130 Berenbaum, *The World Must Know*, pp. xv, 3; *The Holocaust: The Holocaust Exhibition at the Imperial War Museum* (London, Imperial War Museum, 2000), p. 3. For critical overviews, see Linenthal, *Preserving Memory*, and for the Imperial War Museum see Donald Bloxham and Tony Kushner, 'Exhibiting Racism: Cultural Imperialism, Genocide and Representation', *Rethinking History*, vol. 2, no. 3 (1998), pp. 349–58 and Tony Kushner, 'Oral History at the Extremes of Human Experience: Holocaust Testimony in a Museum Setting', *Oral History*, vol. 29, no. 2 (Autumn 2001), pp. 83–94.

131 Details from *Jewish Chronicle*, 29 September 2000.

132 Cesarani, 'Shadows of Doubt', pp. 61–2.

133 Anthony Rudolf of Menard Books and Monika Bucheli of Chronos, letter to the *Jewish Quarterly*, no. 165 (Spring 1997), p. 4. See also Pierre Vidal-Naquet, *The Assassins of Memory: Essays on the Denial of the Holocaust* (New York, Columbia University Press, 1992).

134 Novick, *The Holocaust and Collective Memory*, p. 273. Felman and Laub, *Testimony*, passim, assume that giving testimony is automatically liberating for survivors, enabling them to become alive once again.

135 Claude Lanzmann, *Shoah* (1995) and as text *Shoah: An Oral History of the Holocaust* (New York, Pantheon Books, 1985), p. 117. Annette Wieviorka, 'On Testimony', in Hartman (ed.), *Holocaust Remembrance*, p. 23, comments that little of the testimony of the survivors is unfamiliar from trials and written accounts.

136 Claude Lanzmann, 'Shoah as Counter-myth', *Jewish Quarterly*, no. 121 (Spring 1986), pp. 11–12.

137 Vera Karoly, a Hungarian/Czech Jew who survived the Holocaust and came to live in Britain, was bullied into giving her testimony to the Spielberg Foundation. For an account of her experiences, given to the author, see *Kesher*, the magazine of the South Hampshire Jewish Community, September/October 1997 and her obituary in *Jewish Chronicle*, 13 June 2003. In terms of life history, whilst Roseman's *The Past in Hiding* is superb in confronting the various genres which he utilises in his account of Marianne, the account in essence deals only up to the end of the war and deals relatively briefly with her childhood.

138 Niewyk, *Fresh Wounds*, p. 4; Bar-On and Levin, 'Problems Relating to a Questionnaire', p. 103.

139 Paul Thompson, 'Sharing and Reshaping Life Stories', in Chamberlain and Thompson (eds), *Narrative and Genre*, pp. 167–81.

140 Gilbert in *Sunday Times*, 12 January 1986.

141 Helene Binet, *Jewish Museum Berlin: Architect Daniel Libeskind* (Berlin, G + B Arts International, 1999).

142 Mary Lagerwey, *Reading Auschwitz* (London, Sage, 1998), p. 63.

143 Terrence des Pres, *The Survivor: An Anatomy of Life in the Death Camps* (Oxford, Oxford University Press, 1976), pp. vi, 30. For a critique of his universalism see Lagerwey, *Reading Auschwitz*, p. 39.

144 In this respect Geoffrey Hartman's self-criticism of the Yale project is a useful way forward. See his 'Memory.com: Tele-Suffering and Testimony in the Dot Com Era', *Raritan*, vol. 29, no. 3 (Winter 2000), pp. 1–18.

145 Gordon, *Primo Levi's Ordinary Virtues*, p. 55.

146 Levi, *The Drowned and the Saved*, p. 21.

147 Gordon, *Primo Levi's Ordinary Virtues*, pp. 55–8.

148 Korczak, *Ghetto Diary*, pp. 113–14.

149 The project was led by Bill Williams, a pioneer of oral history in Britain and the major force behind the 'Living Memory of the Jewish People' project, part of the National Life Story Collection of the British Library.

150 James Young, *The Texture of Memory: Holocaust Memorials and Meaning* (New Haven, Yale University Press, 1993), ch. 1, esp. p. 31.

151 Imperial War Museum, *Imperial War Museum North* (London, Imperial War Museum, 2000), p. 45.

152 Young, *The Texture of Memory*, p. 48.

153 Gordon, *Primo Levi's Ordinary Virtues*, p. 58.

2

Perpetrators and perpetration part I: ideology and interpretation

One of the greatest challenges facing historians of the Holocaust is explaining how women and predominantly men were induced to murder or to contribute to murder. By one estimate, 100,000 Germans and tens of thousands of non-Germans were closely involved with the process that culminated in Jews being shot, gassed, starved, worked or beaten to death. 'Process' is the key word here, because the Holocaust was a culmination of pre-existing developments, if not an inevitable one. This chapter and the following one build towards the final point of addressing involvement, in all its different guises, in the act of murder. Given, however, that the situation was never a straightforward choice out of a clear blue sky, and in a neutral situation, as to whether or not to kill, or help to kill, and given also that perpetrators' motivations differed from case to case, we must first work towards understanding how various groups and individuals from Germany and beyond found themselves in the position of participant.

The most immediately evident contributory factor to the murder of the Jews is antisemitism. Whatever the precise course of development of the 'final solution of the Jewish question', Jews were slated to suffer because of anti-Jewishness. Despite the differences between earlier religious anti-Judaism and modern race-based antisemitism, the latter owed a debt to the former because it could feed into pre-existing stereotypes that were peculiar to Christian civilisation. Thus it was no accident that from the later decades of the nineteenth century onwards the popularisation of racial thought and 'social Darwinism' amongst the educated

European classes fostered a particularly malignant conception of 'the Jew' amongst all of the virulent pseudo-science propagated at the time. Indeed, it is inappropriate to distinguish too clearly between the rhetoric of 'Christian' and pseudo-scientific 'racial antisemitism', and it is simply wrong to believe of the images of Jews each conjured that one was somehow less negative than the other. In the modern age, anti-Judaism was dangerously *compounded* by a series of other ideological and cultural desiderata.

In medieval societies where religion was the key intercommunal cleavage, religious persecution was concomitantly important and severe. With the development of European nationalisms, particularly the ethno-nationalist models more generally adopted in eastern and central Europe from the second half of the nineteenth century, the principal cleavage of the age changed. Different forms of Christianity were co-opted as integral parts of national identity (Orthodoxy in the Ukraine, for instance, Catholicism in Croatia) and thus their counterparts (other Christian sects, Muslims, and, inevitably, Jews) became the subject of a different form of exclusion. In this new age of increasing loyalty to a state defined in terms of delineated geography and homogeneity of population, always more imagined than real, anti-Jewish stereotypes were reinforced by the fact that Jews might be identified as belonging to a higher, multinational collective.

This logic reached its zenith with the Jews cast as the emblematic group of apatrides[1] – the ubiquitous, stateless, trans-state minority, the modern counterpart to the anathematised early modern 'wandering Jew'. Unlike that other emblematic transstate minority in the European imagination, the despised Romanies, the Jews were even further stigmatised as somehow gaining power from this multinationalism, or better, 'non-nationalism'.[2] They were attributed as having a higher communal loyalty which, since it was not quantifiable in terms of a Jewish state or government, must be clandestine and therefore threatening. This was argued most influentially in the infamous document the 'protocols of the elders of Zion' with its depiction emanating from late Tsarist Russia of worldwide Jewish conspirators using any and every means of subversion against national systems.[3]

The power of these changing stereotypes and belief systems helps to explain why the generations-long processes of emancipation and assimilation of German Jews into the German national community unravelled so quickly in the 1930s. The very fact of emancipation could be blamed by antisemites for allowing Jews to infiltrate ever more deeply into their 'host' societies, while assimilation and even conversion seemed but a disguise for the playing-out of a communal agenda by 'hidden' Jews. Such suspicions gained considerably in strength from the time of the First World War onwards, and not just in Germany.

Even if 'ethnic'-based antipathy to Jews throughout Europe was not identical to Nazi discrimination on the spurious grounds of blood and genetics, other European countries independently adopted some comparable discriminatory legislation against Jews. Moreover, many German perpetrators of the 'final solution' acted according to motives that would have been entirely recognisable to ethnic-nationalists elsewhere: that is, they acted out of a general feeling that Jews and others were somehow 'different' from their own 'national group' without subscribing to the letter of extreme racist doctrines or Nazi policy. Indeed, the difference is often only slight between the out-and-out racist and the nationalist believing in the essence and destiny of peoples or the relationship between blood, soil and culture. The obsessively racist core of 'true believers' at the head of the Nazi state, and the flourishing profession of 'racial science' promoted therein, relied on more widely identifiable forms of German nationalism for support and frequently execution of their policies. Conversely, the 'ordinary' German actors became increasingly tightly bound to the Nazi project owing to the success of Nazi penetration into and mobilisation of mass society.

Genocide is almost by definition a state crime. The far-reaching power of the state has been in most cases of genocide essential to translate ideology into practice: its perceived legitimacy; its ability to draw upon the loyalty of its citizens, and to mobilise and unify their efforts; its control of the means of violence and coercion. The state is both *instrument* of genocide through its administrative and executive organs, and *instrumentaliser* of its citizens and other resources towards genocide. This is the real force behind Ian Kershaw's judgement that without Hitler the Holocaust would have been 'hardly conceivable', underlining the extremity of Hitler's personal antisemitism[4] but also the realisation that only by the historical happenstance of that particular individual being propelled into a position of supreme power could the German state have taken the road that it did, irrespective of the general colour and strength of German antisemitism at the time. At the most fundamental level, the peculiar extent and nature of the antisemitism of Hitler and his Nazi party milieu determined that Jews were singled out for particular attention.

Nevertheless, since, as is argued here, more everyday German ethnic-nationalism was a key legitimating factor in the state's crime, any attempt to contextualise the Holocaust must examine other state-led projects of radical exclusion on ethnic lines around the time of the Nazi period and within geographical proximity to Germany. With the break-up of major land empires during the First World War, the process of nation building in parts of eastern, central and southern Europe was characterised by a series of coercive state measures in pursuit of population homogeneity, and particularly assaults on minorities. This idea is the key to this chapter, which seeks to get away from the entirely Germano-centric approach that often dominates study of the perpetration of the Holocaust, and instead to place the Holocaust firmly in a temporal and spatial context that is essential to understanding why antisemitism and other German prejudices exploded into extreme persecution and murder when they did.

As to Germany itself, the exact relationship between state-sponsored Hitlerian racism and the implementation of mass murder is neither straightforward nor easily quantifiable. It is a central issue here, as it long has been. The old intentionalist position is not tenable as an explanation, for the simple reason that it illustrates little more than the self-evident: Hitler and his cohorts hated Jews. It does not account for developments in Nazi anti-Jewish policy in peace and in war. For this purpose 'functionalism' in its various forms was invented, though that, too, has been found wanting on vital counts of context and interpretation, particularly regarding the degree of ideological consensus across the Nazi power structure on the 'final solution'.

Above and beyond these debates, however, there is a growing gap between the fruits of detailed empirical research, often disseminated in German alone, and those of broadly philosophical reflections approaching the Holocaust as a unitary historical phenomenon and attempting to situate it within (or outside) our understanding of the rest of history at a metahistorical or even metaphysical level. Whatever their intellectual nuance, the latter approaches have tended to bolster simplistic popular comprehension of 'the Holocaust' as something entirely singular and morally separate, irrespective of the findings from the archives that show the messy development of the 'final solution' and its interlinkage with other Nazi genocidal campaigns. The present chapter deals with these macro-historical questions, leaving the detailed issues of individual and group participation and the internal dynamics of the Nazi system to chapter 3.

Across the European countries occupied by or allied to Germany the course of the persecution of the Jews was influenced by the type of governing regime, the length of occupation, local Jewish–gentile relations, geography, German economic policy and the state of the war. These conclusions are implicit in the recent wave of case studies of Nazi *Vernichtungspolitik* in eastern Europe, though they were also suggested in Helen Fein's pioneering sociological survey *Accounting for Genocide*.[5] Detailed regional examinations and studies of Nazi institutions and individuals have revolutionised our understanding of the complex nature of Nazi decision-making and implementation. The approach they adopt, however, only mirrors developments in the more advanced study of other 'epoch-making' events in history from the English civil war to the French revolution. To paraphrase René Descartes, the 'final solution' may only be rendered properly comprehensible – that is, in a way beyond imprecise reference to German anti-semitism or authoritarianism, or wartime radicalisation – by breaking it down into its contingent parts,[6] whether geographical, temporal or thematic.

The breadth and depth of knowledge we now possess is not on its own an unalloyed good, however. If the analytical process is to serve a genuinely explanatory purpose rather than just a deconstructive one – and such is arguably an unintended effect of the proliferating micro-studies of the 'final solution' – then the pieces will ultimately have to be put together again, as far as that is possible. The following sections try to suggest themes that will serve the former end while simultaneously signposting roads to the latter end.

The problem of 'uniqueness'

Breaking down the destruction of the Jews is not straightforward. Not only are there the ordinary, practical intellectual problems inherent to any investigation of the past: assessing the complex interrelations of factors and weighing variables. There is also a major artificial, philosophically constructed obstacle. I shall label this obstacle the 'Holocaust metanarrative', meaning the bundle of ideas and preconceptions handed down under the label 'Holocaust' that shapes the contours and parameters of our understanding of the subject. The Holocaust metanarrative has developed as part of 'consciousness' of 'the Holocaust' and is an obstacle to *historical* understanding of the destruction of the Jews because of its tendency to view those events from the latter-day perspective of the accomplished fact.

In one sense there is the very mundane problem presented for understanding from the point of view of posterity any historical episode as it developed. 'Intentionalism' in particular is characterised by this problem of teleology, as the genocidal outcome of Nazi *Judenpolitik* is traced backwards wholly to its roots in Hitler's rhetoric, irrespective of the intervention of a multitude of circumstantial factors, both within and beyond Hitler's control, between his pre-war antisemitic statements and the extermination process. Even the much more sophisticated survey by Saul Friedländer of Nazi Jewish policy from 1933 to 1939 contends that 'no historian can forget the end of the road ... the heavy shadow cast by what happened during [the war years] so darkens the pre-war years that a historian cannot pretend that the later events do not influence the weighing of the evidence'.[7] This is really no more than honesty about the way the historian's perspective is inevitably shaped by knowledge of what ensued, yet the 'shadow' of the wartime genocide has become so overwhelming as to seriously endanger proper historical contextualisation and explication of its occurrence.

Though related to the generic issue of reading the past teleologically, the Holocaust metanarrative presents a specific problem, and one encountered with increasing frequency even within academia. This is the widespread perception of the Holocaust as a particularly 'special', indeed 'unique' or even 'uniquely unique'[8] historical episode. While in itself an acceptable contention for a historian to make (if not necessarily a useful one), 'uniqueness' can never be more than a contention for the simple reason that it is not provable. It is a matter of opinion, not fact. And yet it has become an article of faith for many Holocaust survivors and not a few Holocaust scholars.

The concept of uniqueness gained particular currency with the rapid expansion of Holocaust studies from the late 1970s, as differentiated from the burgeoning interest in Germany in Nazism *per se* in the 1960s and early 1970s.[9] It can be seen partly as an attempt to justify focus on what had thereto been a neglected subject, notwithstanding the early post-war studies by Leon Poliakov and Gerald Reitlinger and Raul Hilberg's 1961 masterpiece *The Destruction of the European Jews*.[10] Lucy Dawidowicz stated the case plainly in 1981 in a self-explanatory article 'The Holocaust was Unique in Intent, Scope and Effect'. The totality of Nazi murderous intent has also been at the root of the claims to uniqueness by historians such as Yehuda Bauer and Michael Marrus and philosophers such as Emil Fackenheim.[11] Bridging the two perspectives is the work of Steven Katz, which adopts a case-by-case study of other instances of mass killing in history to establish that the Holocaust 'is phenomenologically unique'. In distinguishing the Holocaust from manifestations of 'traditional Christian antisemitism', for instance, Katz seizes upon the 'Nazi racial imperative that *all* Jews must die, and that they must die here and now'.[12]

But since the intent and extent of the killing are the salient issues both in judging 'uniqueness' and indeed in establishing genocide, at what point, we are entitled to ask, did genocide become genocide and this uniqueness thereby manifest itself? Thousands of Jews had already perished under Nazi rule, particularly in the Polish ghettos, before the beginning of the 'final solution' as many historians have understood it (that is, before the invasion of the Soviet Union crystallised or precipitated mass direct killing as a policy tool). And even when killing of Soviet Jews on a genocidal scale had demonstrably begun – say by the end of August 1941 – did this equate to the sort of total, utterly all-encompassing genocide that Bauer and Katz have in mind in their *ex post facto* judgements? What of the Jews of Jedwabne in northwest Poland, slaughtered by local Poles seemingly on their own initiative in July 1941 in an episode immortalised in Jan T. Gross's

Neighbors:[13] are they Holocaust victims? This is the problem of dealing with metanarratives: while the broad outlines are clear, while there was a more-or-less definable end as Nazism was defeated, and a pattern of expansion which by some point (say the middle of 1942) was more-or-less predictable and thus in some way 'characteristic', identifying 'a beginning' as such is impossible, as the seemingly endless attempts to locate a time of 'decision' for the 'final solution' are beginning to illustrate. On closer inspection the Holocaust metanarrative has significant frayed edges that prevent the murder of the Jews being lifted cleanly out of its historical, developmental contexts and held up as a unitary and self-sufficient whole for simplistic comparison and encapsulation in the fashion of Katz's 'phenomenological' analysis.

Michael Marrus identifies the extermination camps as an important index of uniqueness in the work of George Kren and Leon Rappaport, *The Holocaust and the Crisis of Human Behavior* (1980).[14] Elie Wiesel also has written of his absolute refusal 'to compare the Holocaust of European Judaism to events which are foreign to it. Auschwitz was something else. The Universe of concentration camps, by its dimensions and its design, lies outside, if not beyond, history.'[15] The same theory is implicit in the title of David Rousset's *L'univers concentrationnaire*,[16] even though he was talking about the whole camp system rather than just Auschwitz. Part of the supposed connection between the camps and uniqueness lies in the victims' experience of that bizarre and horrific enclosed existence, though it fails to account for the variety of experiences available within and between even extermination centres. The other part of the connection is that the camps seem emblematic of both the totality of killing and of a very particular killing mentality. Robert Lifton has extrapolated the notion of a Nazi 'biomedical vision' from the Auschwitz experience and the role of Nazi doctors in the camp both in the 'selection' process for the gas chambers and in medical experiments on the inmates. In this 'vision', the skills and mentality of the doctor are brought to bear on a biological problem in a way that is detached, quintessentially 'modern' and also scientifically logical in terms of 'treatment'.[17]

Yet the Nazis did not simply arrive at the point of industrial murder as a logical conclusion to their antisemitism. No matter what the demonic imagery conjured up by Hitler, the obsessive nature of his hatred, the murder of the Jews cannot itself be couched in the metaphysical terminology of the 'demonic', as used by Daniel Goldhagen.[18] Statements to the contrary are all intrinsically intentionalist, irrespective of the precise attitude of their authors towards the 'timing' issue: 'intentionalist', that is, in terms of their overarching emphasis on the motive consistency of ideas. Nevertheless, so often the history of the Holocaust is written from the hindsight of Auschwitz, and not just as metonym or representational device, as in Theodore Adorno's dictum that 'after Auschwitz, one can no longer write poetry', but with Auschwitz as somehow the 'true' essence of the killing process. Dan Diner writes that

> The singular slaughter of millions took place in an extremely short period of less than four years; and if the industrial mass destruction is taken as the actual core of Auschwitz ... then the actual span of the Holocaust is contracted still more ...
>
> Characterizing Auschwitz as an administrative and industrial event entails far more than just condemning it as particularly reprehensible. To classify the murder in this way is to emphasize the *standardized* nature of death, a repetition of one and the same action for weeks, months, and years.[19]

The image here is of Auschwitz-Birkenau, the largest, most technologically advanced killing centre, operating at full capacity, supplied by railway lines from all over Europe, its murderous business facilitated from Berlin by the men of Adolf Eichmann's Jewish desk scouring the continent with relentless efficiency: all in all, a centralised, bureaucratised, industrialised, all-embracing killing process, the logical expression of the ideology of 'total biologism'[20] from which it stemmed – and the very essence of the claims to 'uniqueness'. This totality, this 'oneness', has then been projected inexorably backward by the rhetoric of uniqueness.

If Auschwitz, and indeed Eichmann's ideological-bureaucratic activities, have *become* the Holocaust, this extrapolation from one – though obviously vital – ingredient of the process is at considerable cost to the representation of the full scope of Nazi *Judenpolitik* and, indeed, to the experiences in the Nazi period of Jews themselves. It is common knowledge that mass shootings of Jews *in situ* by Einsatzgruppen killing squads and other SS and police forces, some collaborator forces and independent Romanian units pre-dated the establishment of the killing centres. Some 1.8 million Jews were murdered in this fashion, up to half of those before the first mass gassing took place.[21] It is less well known that included in this 1.8 million were nearly 530,000 Jewish victims in Eastern Galicia (approximately one in eleven of the total number who perished in the Holocaust), that province annexed to Generalgouvernement Poland when in 1941 Germany overran the 1939 German-Soviet demarcation line. Some of these Jews were murdered in Belzec in the Lublin district, but the majority continued to be shot, even after the establishment of all three 'Operation Reinhard' extermination centres – Sobibor and Treblinka, alongside Belzec – by mid-1942.[22] About the same proportion of Jews perished of starvation, disease or exposure in the 'temporary' ghettos,[23] primarily in formerly Polish territories, many while the precise long-term disposition of their communities was still a matter for decision.

Auschwitz, in Eastern Upper Silesia, an area of south-western Poland annexed to the Reich in 1939, may well have become the epicentre of the Holocaust by 1943–44. However, the peak killing period of the genocide had already passed by that time. As Dieter Pohl reminds us, the seven weeks from the end of July until mid-September 1942 witnessed the most extensive killing of all. During that period, primarily in shooting massacres and in the Reinhard centres, daily death tolls regularly approximated to the nearly 34,000 Jews killed in the infamous Babi Yar massacre in Kiev over two days in late September 1941.[24] The eleven months from mid-March 1942 to mid-February 1943 accounted in total for over half of the Jewish death toll.[25]

It is unlikely that Auschwitz would have achieved its singular notoriety had it not on the one hand left a relatively large number of survivors and had it not on the other hand been the destination for the final, most public, and arguably most avoidable national killing operation of the 'final solution', the destruction of the Hungarian Jewish community in mid-1944. This 'Aktion' resulted in the murder of more than 400,000 Jews at Auschwitz-Birkenau, out of approximately 960,000 Jews killed there overall (with the numbers of Poles, Romanies and Soviet prisoners of war bringing the total of people murdered at the Auschwitz complex as a whole to around 1.1 million). Even then, the death toll of Jews at the 'Reinhard' camp Treblinka was comparable, at possibly in excess of 900,000.[26]

The geographical centres of gravity of the Holocaust before

Auschwitz were firstly the western territories of the Soviet Union and secondly the Generalgouvernement. The majority of Holocaust victims died in these regions – virtually four-fifths, adding together the death tolls from formerly Polish and Soviet regions. They were not transported across half a continent; they were not Anne Frank, nor Meryl Streep's character in the film *Sophie's Choice*, nor the Weiss family from the television mini-series *Holocaust*; nor were they the (Americanised) Hungarians presented to us recently in Spielberg's documentary *The Last Days*. They were primarily Yiddish speakers from in and around the Pale of Settlement, murdered in the lands of their birth. The build-up of antisemitic legislation in Germany in the 1930s would have meant little to them, again showing the inadequacy of approaching the 'final solution' as an undifferentiated whole, or along a single chronological avenue. Few of their deaths can be attributed directly to Eichmann's staff: they were preponderantly murdered by mobile SS and police killing squads with regional remits, the staff of local police posts and, in the case of the Reinhard centres, personnel organised – again on a regional basis – under the Lublin province SS and police leader Odilo Globocnik.

The larger point, though, than that of representational precision is that in no way was the murder of the Jews a necessary outcome of Nazi (or German or occidental) antisemitism as of the year 1933. This is obvious yet needs to be continually re-stated. The logic of the view to which Hitler and many of his coterie subscribed, of Jews as a defiling and subversive 'racial' element, *was* always their exclusion from the 'Aryan', and particularly German community, but exclusion did not instantly equate to murder. 'Auschwitz' developed out of a process, not the other way around: the process did not happen as a prelude to Auschwitz, irrespective of claims about the 'totality of [Hitler's/Nazi] ideology and of its translation of abstract thought into planned, logically implemented total murder'.[27]

The twisted road to total murder

Exclusion could mean a number of things, as the practice of the Nazi period showed. First, it would mean an attempt to exclude Jews from positions of prominence in society, to prevent them acting out their supposed subversive agenda. Alongside this, via the various pieces of racial legislation introduced from 1933, particularly the Nuremberg laws of 1935, exclusion meant officially defining the Jews, thereby creating a clear social space between them and non-Jews – a process of excluding them *within* Germany. Secondly, it came to mean excluding Jews *from* Germany, by means of emigration, enforced and encouraged by economic sanction, further social stigmatisation, and, particularly from 1938, state-sponsored violence. Thirdly, exclusion from Germany and the areas annexed to it developed into a specific form of spatial displacement. Alongside the development of a policy of increasing brutality in occupied Poland from 1939, Jews were scheduled for deportation to specific destinations in that territory, and even, in a more fantastic scheme, to the island of Madagascar. With the invasion of the USSR, the area of the Gulag archipelago, the lands to the north beyond the Urals, were slated as the new dumping ground after the predicted swift defeat of the Red Army. This third form of exclusion fed into the fourth and most radical type – outright murder.

This formula is merely meant to problematise the equation of Jew-hatred with a plan for murdering Jews. It is in itself simplistic, for it suggests that there were clearly defined phases in the development of Nazi *Judenpolitik*. These phases are actually only distinct with hindsight, and should not suggest that on this or that day it was decided upon to accelerate or expand the persecution policy in clearly definable ways.[28] Indeed, one of the problems of much of the existing scholarship has been to delineate too sharply between one type of 'solution' and another. Incarceration of ever larger numbers of Jews with minimum provision in unsustainable ghettos or designated regions – the 'territorial solution', to use Uwe Adam's term[29] – necessarily entailed the death of huge numbers by 'attrition', and formed part of the race-utopian vision of the Nazi new European order, as Peter Longerich in particular has emphasised.[30] A territorial solution was by no means incompatible with physical destruction.

Conversely, as Christopher Browning has recently re-stated, no matter the broad theoretical consistency on the principle of 'radical exclusion' of the Jews between the territorial solution from 1939 and outright murder, there is still a qualitative moral difference between the two, a psychological barrier of sufficient magnitude to call into question the notion of a clear policy continuum.[31]

Deciding between the two positions is likely to remain a matter of intuitive preference as much as of the weighing of facts. Browning's position is corroborated by the snowballing speed with which the practice of direct mass murder spread after it began in the second half of 1941 at the beginning of the crucial ideological conflict with the Soviet Union in late June. Longerich's interpretation finds substantiation in the facts that mass killing did not instantly equate to total killing, that total killing in one place was not necessarily accompanied by total killing elsewhere, and that aspects of the 'territorial solution' persisted for at least several months after that point in early autumn 1941 that Browning sees as decisive in expanding the killing 'solution' to the whole of Europe.

Should we for instance see the killings by the Einsatzgruppen of Jewish leaders and Jewish men of arms-bearing age from immediately upon the invasion of the USSR in June 1941 as the crystallisation of a general policy of killing, beyond which only tactical decisions about expansion of the murder programme were to be made? The classic intentionalist accounts support this view, as does the more qualified analysis of Richard Breitman.[32] Or were these killings qualitatively different from the later massacres – from the end of July, but particularly from August through October 1941 – of women and children alongside men, and then of entire communities?[33] Were the earlier episodes expressions, as Christoph Dieckmann and Ralf Oggoreck would have it, of a racist and paranoid security policy that increasingly lent itself to genocide but was not intrinsically genocidal, being directed instead at putative ideological standard-bearers of Bolshevism in an attempt to bring the Soviet system crashing down?[34] If so, as seems likely, what caused the expansion of killing? And were there separate decisions to kill all Soviet Jews and then – in autumn 1941 – to expand the genocide to the rest of Europe, as Browning and Hilberg maintain?[35] Or should we insert an intermediate stage, as Bogdan Musial suggests, when the Jews of Generalgouvernement Poland were singled out for annihilation, in early October 1941?[36] And to what extent did the decision of mid-September to begin deporting Jews from the 'Greater Reich' and the Protectorate of Bohemia and Moravia (and thereafter all remaining western European Jews) require further unfolding of the war situation up to December before it was transformed into a

73

'basic decision' to kill these Jews outright, as Christian Gerlach and L. J. Hartog think?[37] Or is all of this thinking simply too schematic?

Consider for a moment Operation Reinhard, the chief means by which Musial's putative intermediate decision was enacted. After Operation Reinhard had been identified, after some initial confusion in the post-war trials and early scholarship, it came to be agreed that it was the name for the programme of murdering and plundering the Jews of the Generalgouvernement.[38] And this it was, albeit that it has also been accepted that some Romanies and western and central European Jews died in the Reinhard camps along with some Jews from other formerly Polish regions, particularly Bialystok. The essence of the interpretation should not be altered by the recent discoveries that the processing of the loot from the campaign also involved Majdanek and very possibly Auschwitz.[39] Yet the epithet 'Reinhard', given in honour of the SS security chief Reinhard Heydrich after his assassination at the end of May 1942, was only attached to the programme when the expansion of the killing in the Generalgouvernement was well under way, and here is the crux of the problem. For, as has until very recently been typical, the best-known account of the Reinhard killing programme, by Yitzhak Arad, effectively used the attachment of the *ex post facto* programme name, and the facts that the three killing centres were under the same command structure, operating in the same geographical region and attacking contiguous pools of victims, to infer teleologically an *a priori* totality of intent in the establishment of the centres that is actually belied by the different chronologies of construction of Belzec, Sobibor and Treblinka (the decision for construction of the final camp was taken in mid-April 1942).[40] Arad in effect viewed the killings as an all-encompassing operation just awaiting a name: thus, 'Operation Reinhard set the guidelines and directives for the deportations'. He made little enquiry into the nature or timing of the decision-making process, simply asserting without supporting documentation – 'plans for Operation Reinhard began to take shape' – that only Belzec was at first constructed because the authorities had no idea how many camps would be needed for the task.[41]

As in the Auschwitz-centric view, there has been an understandable tendency to equate the introduction of 'industrial' killing technology with the mindset of and design for total, clinical, relentless killing. As Zygmunt Bauman put it, in a theory that has received much wider acceptance than his general, more challenging thesis on modernity,

> Like everything else done in the modern – rational, planned, scientifically informed, expert, efficiently managed, co-ordinated – way, the Holocaust left behind and put to shame all its alleged pre-modern equivalents, exposing them as primitive, wasteful and ineffective by comparison. It towers high above the past genocidal episodes in the same way as the modern industrial plant towers above the craftsman's cottage workshop, or the modern industrial farm, with its tractors, combines and pesticides, towers above the peasant farmstead with its horse, hoe and hand-weeding.[42]

But the preparation of dedicated killing centres in Poland (at Belzec from late October 1941 and Chelmno in the 'Reichsgau Wartheland' from around the same time) and their opening of operations (at the turn of the year 1941–42) did not automatically signal that a fundamental decision had been made to kill all Jews everywhere as soon as possible. Like gassing centres considered at the end of 1941 in Riga and in Mogilev near Minsk,[43] they may have been in the first instance 'improvised' local 'solutions' established in reception areas for deported central European Jews, used in a sort of horrific 'cull' of the *arbeitsunfähig* ('incapable of work') indigenous Jewish population to accelerate the 'Germanisation' of the regions in question – as with Globocnik in Lublin – or to create space for newcomers.[44] This would simultaneously get Jews out of the Reich and into confined ghettos or even concentration camps where they would undoubtedly perish over a shorter or longer period, and continue the already overtly genocidal assault on the eastern Jews.

The chief ramifications are not at the moral level. If anything, though, it is even more horrific than the notion of monumental, manichean decisions, whether taken before the war or amid the 'euphoria' of early victories over the USSR,[45] that the Reich authorities could approve initiatives for the creation of gas chambers as piecemeal killing measures. For just as the policy jump was thus smaller than previously imagined outside of extreme functionalist circles, so we can assume that the moral jump was correspondingly easier, indeed one might say more mundane, an upping of the ante rather than an expression of 'demonic' total intent. Conversely, this also suggests the survival well into the lifespan of the actual policy of extermination of a spatial basis to Nazi practices (rather than the exclusively 'existential' basis underpinning the 'uniqueness' argument) which is far from incomparable in the history of genocide and 'ethnic cleansing'. Put more clearly, it was obviously enough even for Hitler even late in the day that Jews be removed from the German sphere without an absolute guarantee that they would be killed. And even when the point had been passed that Jews within that sphere were all to be murdered over the medium term, some perhaps after the final military victory, the extermination process had yet to undergo acceleration throughout 1942 for reasons pertaining as much to occupation politics and logistical issues as anything else, as we shall see shortly.

Despite their fundamental differences, both 'intentionalist' and 'functionalist' interpretations, and also the synthesis positions of Christopher Browning and Philippe Burrin, effectively still search for a critical moment or phase of policy crystallisation, a time when 'the Holocaust' was decided – or stumbled upon – and became 'policy'. A more differentiated, flexible notion of a 'policy' of intended genocidal destruction seems to be called for by Longerich in particular. This 'policy' was constantly underpinned – *contra* the functionalists – by explicitly exterminationary ideology but within it mass killing and designs for mass death could substantially precede, and would in fact feed into, official radicalisations. Conversely, within the 'policy', even after the most radical measures had become official, mass immediate killing could co-exist perfectly consistently with less direct measures of decimation such as a modified 'territorial solution'. And, one might go even further than Longerich, and extend this picture of flexibility right up to the final war years, as Hitler himself approved the importing of scores of thousands of Jews into concentration camps back in the Reich (!) to work for German industry in a desperate attempt to stave off defeat.[46] In short, we should understand the functional development of the 'final solution' much as the development of many everyday policies embarked upon by more everyday regimes, and perhaps other programmes of genocide embarked on elsewhere. Intention was ideologically fixed but the nature and extent of implementation were subject to external circumstances. (This, indeed, is a very similar conclusion to the one I have independently arrived at concerning the complex development of the Armenian genocide – a historically very different case but nevertheless one in which the nature and timing of decision-making have long been a bone of contention.[47]) Rather than Diner's vision of standardised killing, which may have been appropriate for the views from both the perpetrators' and victims' sides within the camp of Auschwitz, Nazi *Vernichtungspolitik* as a whole was variable in terms of tactics and method. In terms of comprehending the Nazi system, the picture is no 'better' or 'worse' than Goldhagen's 'demonic' depiction or the popular logical-totality vision of Katz, it is just different.

Rhetoric and racist rationality

Another problem shared by intentionalists and functionalists is their difficulty with Nazi language. Famously, stripping away Nazi euphemism is considered a prerequisite for understanding the true essence of Nazi policy, and this remains obviously true for such abominable camouflage as 'special treatment'. Yet it is apparent, as recognised at the beginning of two impressive recent bestsellers on the 'final solution',[48] that up to a point in the destruction process, other expressions famously considered outright misnomers – 'deportation', 'evacuation', etc. – could, like the 'final solution' itself, have different meanings to different actors at different times, even perhaps into March 1942,[49] albeit that from late 1941 there must have been full awareness that each of them spelt some form of death over at most the medium term.

Intentionalists, such avid students of Hitler's pronouncements in *Mein Kampf* and his pre-war speeches, suddenly lose their faith in literalism when it comes to documents suggesting anything other than the inexorable implementation of total genocide, happy simply to label these as euphemisms or at most tactical shifts. This mirrors the earliest attempts to address the expansion of the killing when at the Nuremberg trial of Einsatzgruppen leaders the judges ignored the very clear evidence of the early discrimination between categories of victims and declared that 'the reference to individual categories of Jews is only macabre window dressing because ... *all* Jews were killed regardless of antecedents'.[50]

Functionalists, on the other hand, have been so used to treating

Hitler's rhetoric as just that, that they overlook or discount key pronouncements that strongly suggest concrete intent. One example is Hitler's 30 January 1939 pronouncement to the Reichstag in which he announced that should international Jewry again precipitate world war, the result would not be the Bolshevisation of the world and a triumph for the Jews 'but rather the annihilation of the Jewish race in Europe'. This speech has been key in various ways to the theses of Longerich, Gerlach and Hartog, and it reflects a mindset that Burrin has actually traced back to 1935 at least. (The idea being that Jews were always seen as fair game, should another war materialise, for use as hostages or for collective reprisals. This, parenthetically, has only opened up further questions of nuance, with Hartog and Gerlach arguing that 'world war' was not signified by Operation Barbarossa, but instead only by the entrance of the USA into the conflict, making it genuinely global.[51])

One outcome of intensive regional and case studies has actually been to show that the words and rationales used by German leaders and officials need to be given more credence within their own terms of reference. Even a superficial knowledge of Hitler's antisemitism suggests that however cynically he may have exploited situations, he bought in completely to the associations that were widespread in Europe in the inter-war period of the intimate connection between Jewry and Bolshevism. Allowing for an internal consistency in his belief system, and that passed on to the Einsatzgruppen leaders, it is wrong to concur with the Nuremberg court that such designations as 'partisan', 'commissar' and 'saboteur' were always just cynical codes for murdering innocent Jews, though they were often that too. (Naturally the depiction of Jews as potential military threats to Germans could become a self-fulfilling prophecy as a few took to arms in the face of the slaughter of their brethren, just as the preposterous *a priori* notion of Jews as carriers of typhus was also realised when they were crowded into unsanitary ghettos.[52])

Equally, on the economic side, the assumption of Governor Greiser of the Warthegau that the establishment of the Lodz ghetto at the end of 1939 would make Jewish 'hoarders' cough up their wealth in exchange for food is absurd to the ear of the non-antisemite, but this is not to suggest that it was not seriously meant.[53] Likewise labelling the Jews of the Generalgouvernement black marketeers had some basis in fact, though it was a fact of German making. Since Jews were on the lowest rations of all population groups, they were forced in disproportionate numbers into the black market to subsist. This in turn destabilised an already fragile economy and lent a material rationale to authorities already concerned with overpopulation in Poland and with procuring as much food as possible for Germany for the murder of more Jews in the immediate term.[54] The self-inflicted nature of this 'problem' and the ideologically based nature of its 'solution' should not therefore suggest that it was an imaginary or even 'convenient' problem. It also provides a further dimension to Nazi *Judenpolitik*, one which was intrinsically bound up with the war effort, occupation politics and the memory of mass German starvation and the collapse of the home front in the First World War, and which, therefore, certainly cannot lend itself to an interpretation based purely on a self-referential, self-rationalising and self-enclosed antisemitic escalation of murder.

One need not go as far as Götz Aly's and Suzanne Heim's *Vordenker der Vernichtung* (recently translated as *Architects of Annihilation*)[55] in detecting a subjective 'rationality' in aspects of Nazi genocide to determine the imprecision of Diner's description of 'a policy of extermination beyond all economics, [in which] work served as a mere masquerade of usefulness, camouflaging the literal purposelessness of the murder'.[56] One need not even go as far towards the 'final solution' in such terms as does Michael Burleigh towards the 'euthanasia' programme in his *Death and Deliverance*. But it is worth noting not only that Burleigh uncovers an economic impetus to murder inhabitants of institutions that in its emphasis on the First World War experience and maximising provision for the German 'racial community' in the Second World War bears striking similarities to some of the findings of Gerlach and Dieckmann on Jewish policy in the east, but also that Burleigh's interpretation has not been remotely controversial.[57] Diner's judgement on 'work' reflects a commonplace misapprehension in the canon of 'uniqueness', one shared to differing degrees by Goldhagen, Wolfgang Sofsky, Benjamin Ferencz and the representatives of survivor groups that have pressed in recent years for financial compensation for slave labour.[58]

The Nazi expression '*Vernichtung durch Arbeit*' ('extermination through work') has been widely adopted as indicating an explicit

Nazi policy designed to reconcile the ideological dictates of extermination with practical labour considerations. And clearly for much of the Holocaust period a policy of working Jews to literal exhaustion over the short to medium term was entirely compatible with killing others outright by bullet or gas. Indeed, the complementary policies co-existed for longer than is generally realised: though Jewish labour was rarely of paramount importance to the Nazis in quantitative terms, at all times during the war years some Jewish labour was being used, and the overall numbers run into hundreds of thousands of people. Thus at the infamous Wannsee conference of 20 January 1942, the convenor, Heydrich, alluded to using some 'capable' Jews for road-building projects in 'the east'. The conditions of such work, he judged, would entail an additional 'natural reduction' of the population.[59] Again we have the juxtaposition of real euphemism – 'natural reduction' – with something that has only lately been revealed as genuine: deportation to labour projects was not just a cover for deportation to extermination centres. One such project was the 'Durchgangstrasse IV', designed to be a vital transport link through Eastern Galicia to the Eastern Front, as well as a main conduit for the mass deportation of the eastern European populations in the interests of German 'living space'.[60] Ultimately, around 20,000 Jews died on its construction.[61]

The Majdanek concentration camp in Lublin is also an interesting example of the phenomenon of 'extermination through work'. Though almost universally cited as one of the six Nazi mass-extermination facilities of the 'final solution', alongside the Reinhard camps, Chelmno and Auschwitz-Birkenau, it is less well publicised that systematic mass gassings there were only a feature from autumn 1942, after experiments in May on Soviet prisoners of war (POWs) and sick inmates. Before that time mass executions, albeit on a smaller scale, had been conducted by shooting. From early 1942, in the framework of what would become Operation Reinhard, Majdanek received mass transports of Jews from the Polish ghettos, including therefore western European Jews and also some Greeks, though Jews did not form a majority of the victims of the camp. Overall, the majority of the indeterminate number of inmates that perished (with a minimum of 215,000), both Jews and non-Jews, did so as a result of the internal conditions in the camp rather than mass, orchestrated killing. As

Czeslaw Madajczyk put it, Majdanek became 'the model of a ... camp of gradual annihilation combined with a camp of immediate extermination'.[62]

But 'extermination through work' could mean different things at different times to different German authorities, with the emphasis on either of the contingent nouns.[63] Thus up to the end of 1943, amidst the murderous mayhem of Operation Reinhard, the disposition of skilled Jewish labourers in forced labour camps in Generalgouvernement Poland – particularly in trades in Eastern Galicia, and in the Radom province, where armaments production was concentrated[64] – remained the subject of fierce debate between the Wehrmacht, the civil authorities and the SS.[65] That these disputes were ultimately resolved in favour of instant murder, when inmate revolts at Sobibor and Treblinka late in 1943 caused Himmler to assert by final massacres the complete primacy of 'security' concerns over labour concerns in the Generalgouvernement,[66] should not obscure the real issues at stake. Even after the November massacres, several thousand Jewish labourers survived in other incorporated parts of Poland, particularly the Upper Silesia region.[67] Moreover, in the best-known instance of the use of Jewish labour, as slaves for German state and private industry from late 1943 onwards, the pressure for immediate extermination had to a limited extent to give way to pragmatic concerns voiced by Albert Speer's Armaments Ministry and even sections of the business-administration office of the SS.[68]

In some cases now the formula 'extermination through work' equated to a rationalisation of the prolongation of life for working Jews (and others). The doctrine in itself did not necessarily condemn the workers to death, for their fate on civilian work sites was often the responsibility of individuals who had to operate within the parameters of the racial hierarchy but did not subscribe to the letter of Nazi policy.[69] It is also the case that in work, towards the end of the war, the fate of Jews and non-Jews converged to a greater degree than in any other area of Nazi policy, as Jews were to an extent integrated into the same systems as other slave and forced labourers.

Besides, we should not extrapolate from the clear limitations on initiatives for the use of Jewish labour that there was an absence of economic criteria. In certain circumstances economic considerations acted to accelerate the murder process, as was the case in the Generalgouvernement from 1942. Then, work needs were not the primary issue, since they were fulfilled by using Polish forced labour in the Reich. The chief economic concern was supplying Germany with food from these lands that were deemed to be overpopulated even before the war, including by Polish leaders.[70] At the bottom rung of the Nazi hierarchy, and living in disease-wracked, overcrowded ghettos, Jews were targeted ever more intensively by civilian officials in the occupation government as Hermann Göring's Office for the Four Year Plan increased its requisition demands on the region, in full knowledge of what this would mean. (The only partial exception being the slave labourers 'important for the war effort'.) The fate of the Jews was further accelerated as requisitioning was on the brink of starving the larger Polish population and therefore, the Germans feared, of inspiring Polish resistance; since artificial famine was seen as too large and complicated a policy for Poland while the war was still under way, Jews were killed at an accelerated rate in the interests of raising the calorie intake of the rest of the population.

Some similar patterns existed in Belarus, while in Lithuania the need to supply the army led even earlier to the murder of 'useless' Jews.[71] And as Pohl puts it with regard to the Reichskommissariat Ukraine, 'the further the Wehrmacht pushed eastwards, the less industry it encountered, and the less labour power was consequently needed',[72] presumably giving further 'legitimation' to the pre-existing idea that these lands were overpopulated. Finally, as Aly and Heim observe, if this logic was accepted, then transporting Jews *en masse* to their deaths, or killing them on the spot, was not a piece of irrational murder in the face of labour and military transport needs, but rather a saving in terms of the number of supply trains that would have otherwise been needed to feed the ghetto inhabitants.[73] Which all returns us to the flaws in the Holocaust metanarrative.

Parenthetically, despite the flaws in the metanarrative and in overly determinist or teleological readings of the genocide, with which the concept of 'uniqueness' has been closely if not exclusively or inevitably linked, the general thrust of the early scholarship of exceptionalism did have clear merit. In a world which was reluctant to privilege Jewish suffering even while the 'final solution' was under way, and which from the post-war trials onwards had tended to subsume the Jewish fate within the larger tragedy of war,[74] the scholarship from the 1970s onwards has performed the valuable historical, intellectual service of differentiating Nazi racial policies. Had that not been done, it would be the duty of present-day historians of the period to do it. The Jews had a paramount and peculiar place in Nazi ideology and the relentlessness of the 'final solution' when it was under way *was* unquestionably greater than in other Nazi programmes. None of that should be gainsaid. The intellectual problem that we now face, however, is that the process of differentiation has gone too far, developing its own momentum and resulting in a loss of contextualisation.

The effects of the distortion can be divided into two broad categories, one historical, in terms of the contexts and understanding of the perpetration of genocide, the other concerning the wide array of philosophical, representational, communal and memorial responses to it. The large and growing cross-disciplinary and also non-academic body of literature emanating from the latter category owes much to the uniqueness approach, but issues of space prohibit examination of it here. Let it suffice to refer to the first chapter of this book, where Tony Kushner illustrates some of the issues affecting survivor writing on the Nazi experience by the construction of a literary genre of 'Holocaust testimony'. The remainder of this chapter seeks to address the more tangible historical questions.

The 'final solution' amid other racial policies

Beyond what Karl Schleunes called *The Twisted Road to Auschwitz*,[75] a road with even more twists than he allowed for, the next obvious complexity of the relationship between antisemitism and the 'final solution' lies in the widely varied levels and qualities of Jew-hatred in Germany and Europe around the Nazi period. While there can be little question in the light of recent research that the Nazi hierarchy and important SS and police sections had fully internalised Nazi antisemitism, if the question is why 'ordinary' Germans did not protest against *Judenpolitik* and in many cases allowed themselves to be implicated in its execution, the answers are not as simple.

One problem can be summed up by the proposition that people other than Germans killed Jews, and Germans killed others than

Jews. The 'Schutzmannschaften', composed of Lithuanian, Latvian, Ukrainian and Belarussian auxiliaries operating within the 'Reichskommissariat Ukraine' and the 'Reichskommissariat Ostland', the major belt of German civilian-administered imperial territories east of Poland, numbered at their peak some 45,000 men, many of whom were involved in guarding and shooting Jews. Ukrainians outnumbered the German personnel in the ranks of guards at Belzec, Sobibor and Treblinka. Catholic Croatian fascists also butchered Jews, as did Romanian and Hungarian units acting independently of their German ally. The list could go on.

Goldhagen's *Hitler's Willing Executioners* most obviously elides the problem of the scope of German killing. Yet the same is also true of more recent, more subtle restatements of the antisemitic basis for killing, such as Yaacov Lozowick's study of Eichmann's Jewish desk, which is discussed in greater detail later. Despite his closing call to listen to 'the screams' of the Jewish victims, at no point does Lozowick account in his analysis of SS antisemitism for the fact that Eichmann's office was also responsible for the deportation to their deaths of several thousand Romanies.[76]

The Einsatzgruppen have been the subject of considerable interest in what one popular study has awkwardly titled *The Invention of the Holocaust*, another *The Genesis of the 'Final Solution'*.[77] Yet it has been of virtually no interest, and only a little more scholarly enquiry, that they also killed freely the patients of psychiatric institutions in Poland and the USSR,[78] or at least those patients who had survived the Wehrmacht's regimen of deliberate underrationing in order to 'free up' bed space for wounded German soldiers.[79] (These victims rarely figure at all, even in the limited popular perceptions of the Nazi campaigns of 'eugenic' murder. While an approximate figure of 80,000 dead in the 'euthanasia' campaign has gained general currency, this number stems only from those German citizens killed in the semi-official German programme. The death toll of physically and mentally 'handicapped' needs to be raised by perhaps 50,000 for the German children and adults killed in secret outside the official 'euthanasia' campaign, and for those killed in Polish and Soviet territory.) SS and police squads also murdered Romanies wherever they met them, as part of a broader killing policy pursued with only a fraction less rigour than that against the Jews and which extended to mass gassings in the extermination camps. Between 200,000 and 500,000 in total were killed, the uncertainty about the numbers casting light on how easily Europe gave up these people, how little the loss has been addressed, and why this was the least abhorred of all Germany's genocidal operations. Despite some clear parallels between the Nazi pursuit of the Romanies and the 'final solution', one has to search through the small specialist literature of Nazi *Zigeunerpolitik* for substantive detail on that genocide.[80]

These historiographical lacunae tell us more about the priorities of latter-day scholarship, about the way that the murder of the Jews has been promoted to obscure so much of the rest of the Nazi record of atrocity, than they do about the relative significance of the historical issues at stake. Here once again, the popular representation of the Holocaust has worryingly superseded the historical actuality of 1939–45. The politicisation of the memory of Nazi genocide over the last three decades has certainly warped our understanding of the whole racial project, as a glance at the roll-call of victims at public commemorations such as Britain's annual Holocaust Memorial Day suggests.[81] To take but one example, one of the first groups generally invoked as primary victims of Nazism is gay men. Yet of the presumably several millions dwelling under Nazi control, estimates suggest that between 5,000 and an absolute maximum of 15,000 gays perished in the concentration camps, with the actual number likely to be much nearer the lower figure.[82] Without belittling such terrible atrocities, and while recognising that the fates of any who died for simple membership of a collective are equally worthy of commemoration, at the elementary quantitative level – which is after all important – these numbers are dwarfed by death tolls from other groups. And at the more sophisticated level of Nazi intent – which we have already seen is so crucial in the attention devoted to the 'final solution' – gays fell victim less to an orchestrated higher policy of total murder than to the arbitrary, homophobic-sadistic behaviour of individual guards and camp regimes.[83] In terms of sheer scale, however, the most noteworthy hole in popular comprehension is the fate of non-Jewish eastern European civilians.

Had Germany consolidated its rule over eastern Europe, literally tens of millions of the Slavic populations would have perished under the so-called Generalplan Ost as part of a calculated policy of starvation by way of providing for the material needs of first the German army and then the new settler empire.[84] Massive forced population movement would certainly have followed as the 'racial reordering' begun in western Poland in 1939 was fully extended to formerly Soviet territories up to and perhaps beyond the Ural mountains. The idea was to maintain a thinned-out helot population of Slavs under German overlordship, to replace urban areas and nascent industries with arable land, and to dump the remainder of the population outside the borders of the German sphere and into Siberia, the Ural-border to be protected by a huge *Ostwall* and garrisoned, in Himmler's fantasies, by 'racially pure' SS warrior-farmers.

The depredations that were actually inflicted in the east were in any case on a scale that almost defies belief. Around two million non-Jewish Poles were murdered from September 1939. (The three million figure that is often quoted conflates this two million with others killed by Stalin.) Precise numbers are unobtainable of Soviet civilians killed outwith the laws of war in aerial bombardments, brutal sieges such as that of Leningrad, indiscriminate anti-partisan 'reprisals' and hostage-takings, scorched-earth campaigns, executions based on arbitrary suspicions, and forced labour either for the Wehrmacht or German industry. Some estimates of total Soviet dead during the war reach in excess of twenty million people, around seven million of whom were civilian. Within the former USSR, for instance, Belarus lost 1.7 million of its pre-war population of 9.2 million people. More than 1.1 million of these were non-Jews. A further 380,000 were dragged into the Reich as forced labourers. The cities were largely obliterated and up to three million people were left homeless, industrial capacity was reduced virtually to zero, and livestock was reduced by about 80 per cent.[85] One particularly noteworthy instance of mass death is the treatment of the mass of Soviet prisoners of war who fell into German hands in the early months of the war. Approximately 3.3 million were either killed or simply allowed to die from thirst, starvation or exposure in huge open air camps, most within the first year of Operation Barbarossa.[86] Others were worked to death. Without wishing to reduce such massive human tragedies to crude numbers, the total of POWs thus perishing is about equal to the combined numbers of Armenians, Cambodians and Rwandan Tutsis killed in twentieth-century genocide. In a modified form, this was the only part of the starvation plan intrinsic to the Generalplan Ost that actually reached fruition, and the catastrophe was permitted because the POWs were viewed as racial enemies.[87]

The purpose here is not simply to bombard the reader with a list of atrocities, nor just to reinforce the point that with such a vast 'mosaic of victims'[88] and killers broader explanations and contexts for the genocide of the Jews must be allowed. It is also to suggest very real interconnections between the different episodes. The 'euthanasia' technique of gas chamber murder is one obvious developmental model for the 'final solution', one in which Heinrich Himmler and Heydrich were very interested.[89] The staff who directed that euthanasia programme were seconded to Odilo Globocnik in Lublin to operate the Reinhard camps. The first extermination centre of the 'final solution' to begin killing on a mass scale was Chelmno, in December 1941. The technique of killing there, the gas van, and the personnel operating it, the 'Sonderkommando Lange', led by the SS officer Herbert Lange, were both on hand in the 'Warthegau' because they had been busy murdering the inhabitants of psychiatric and other institutions in the region.[90] The first group of deportees to Poland to be gassed at Chelmno was the survivors of five thousand Austrian Romanies recently deported through Eichmann's facilitation to the Lodz ghetto.[91] Auschwitz and Majdanek and all the 'orthodox' concentration camps in 'Greater Germany' were staffed by a regime that had perfected its brutal practices – the de-humanisation of the inmates, the form and psychology of 'punishment' beatings – in Dachau in the early 1930s more on the bodies of political and 'asocial' inmates than on 'racial enemies'. Many of the Einsatzgruppen leaders had learned to kill by murdering Poles in 1939–40. The infamous sterilisation experiments conducted on inmates of Auschwitz were to have a wider utility in preventing the reproduction of 'inferiors' and entire Slavic peoples.[92]

The carnage wrought in Poland, the mass murder of the Polish elite and of the 'handicapped' since 1939 each constituted what Browning calls the crossing of a 'moral rubicon'. Mentalities and technologies of killing had been honed. Moreover, to the extent that the Nazi leadership was concerned with international and German public reaction to its extreme policies, it would surely have been gratifying that the slaughter of Poles at least, though not the 'euthanasia' programme, raised barely a ripple. The same was true of the murder of the Soviet POWs and civilians, and is an important comparative factor in assessing world responses to the 'final solution'. As for the German population, it is no surprise at all that they took it in their stride, for while antisemitic indoctrination had been the main official stock-in-trade since 1933, Germans had centuries of anti-Slav chauvinism and eastward-looking imperial aspirations to fall back upon.

A growing body of evidence points to the influence on German opinion of the First World War experience in eastern Europe, as soldiers returned from the warzone with stories of the poverty and backwardness of the Tsarist borderlands. Their accounts, coloured by the state of war and turmoil in which they were shaped, nevertheless concretised for many Germans who had never been there traditional stereotypes of 'the east' as a great space waiting to be properly exploited, the people as primitives whose lives were not only cheaper but who would benefit from civilising German overlordship. The Great War also provided a brief experience of actual colonial rule in northern Poland and the Baltic states, as the military dictatorship of Erich Ludendorf planned and began to enact programmes of cultural and linguistic Germanisation.[93]

These traditional chauvinisms were not identical to Nazi imperial goals but they could accommodate them and in turn be accommodated by Hitler. Some of the geo-political underpinnings of expansionism remained constant: the abortive Brest-Litovsk treaty of 1917 indicated the extent of radicalised German ambition; and the oil of the Caucasus and the wheat fields of the Ukraine remained prime targets, albeit that the earlier aims of economic dominance of eastern and south-eastern European structures were replaced with infinitely more radical and ruthless change of the socio-economic infrastructure. And in ideological terms, a disproportionately large number of early members of the Nazi party (the 'old fighters') were drawn from the ranks of right-wing paramilitary volunteer organisations (the 'Freikorps'), which continued an unofficial war with Bolshevik forces in the old Tsarist border territories after the armistice, as well as fighting communists on the streets of Germany.

It can be posited further that since the First World War experiences bolstered a perception that 'the east' was not of Europe, it was easier to accept Hitler's argument that the ideological war against Bolshevism should not be fought according to the (occidental) laws of war. Certainly recent studies show how diaries kept by Wehrmacht soldiers from 1941 echo the accounts of their predecessors in the Reichswehr with their fulsome belief in the subhumanity of the Slavic populations, the imagery of filth and degradation recurrent, complemented now with anti-Bolshevism, merged thoroughly with racism, though antisemitism was not necessarily everpresent, or at least not explicitly so.[94] The mass influx to Wehrmacht custody of Soviet POWs in the summer of 1941 thus posed an almost identical quandry to the German occupiers as the worsening situation of the Polish ghettos established the previous year. The problem of a mass of ('sub')humanity enclosed in prison conditions and making potentially huge demands on the German supply infrastructure was solved wholesale in the most radical way – with the death of the inmates – in the POWs' case first, before similar principles were applied to the ghettos.[95]

But perhaps the most significant linkage between different Nazi population programmes and genocide has been forged by the work of Aly. His *Final Solution* builds on the work of Browning and Robert Koehl, and on strands of the classic 'functionalist' analyses of Broszat and Mommsen. Like Sybille Steinbacher's less-publicised work on Eastern Upper Silesia, *Final Solution* describes the courses and frictions of the movement in different directions in and around the formerly Polish territories of on one hand 'ethnic Germans' and on the other Poles and Jews, and it correlates policy developments in both.[96] This multi-faceted programme was exemplified in the Reichskommissariat für die Festigung deutschen Volkstums (RKFDV; Reich Commissariat for the Strengthening of Ethnic Germandom) and in the Race and Settlement Office of the SS. The RKFDV, the more important of the two, was created under Himmler on a Hitler directive shortly prior to the invasion of Poland, and its establishment gave Himmler the authority to mastermind Nazi population policy.[97] Initially, deportation of Jews and Poles and 'relocation' of *Volksdeutsche* were conducted by the same office and personnel within the RKFDV.[98] Indeed, in both the RKFDV and the Reich Security Head Office (RSHA), the other main organisation involved in resettlement policy, the early focus was primarily on simultaneous movement of Poles and Germans. Jewish policy only achieved priority as the twin strategy faltered logistically, as it had shown signs of doing since the early days of occupation in Poland. The extermination of the Jews materialised as policy as expulsion eastwards was delayed because of the Wehrmacht's failure to obliterate Soviet forces in the summer and autumn of 1941. Thus, for instance, the consensus reached on the necessity of mass murder in Lublin between Globocnik and Himmler in September–October 1941, the former acting in his capacity both as SS and police leader for Lublin and as Himmler's regional RKFDV plenipotentiary with responsibility for 'Germanising' the territory.[99]

While the precise relationship between Hitler's antisemitic rhetoric over time and the development of substantive designs for 'solving' the 'Jewish problem' remain the subject of debate, his intentions as regards a more general ethnic/racial 'restructuring' of central and eastern Europe were actually spelled out more clearly well in advance of the war. As Aly, Browning and Steinbacher have shown, paradoxically the inability to carry out the latter contributed significantly to the radicalisation of measures for the former. So, irrespective of the *relatively* limited enactment of plans of mass movement for non-Jews, they provide a fundamental hermeneutical context for the 'final solution'.

Central Europe too was a focus of projected population engineering. The famous 'Hossbach memorandum', detailing a meeting in November 1937 with the German service chiefs, records Hitler's ruminations contingent on the future overthrow of Czechoslovakia and Austria. He posited that this 'annexation ... would mean an acquisition of foodstuffs for 5–6 million people on the assumption that the compulsory emigration of 2 million people from Czechoslovakia and a million people from Austria was practicable'.[100] In a speech in Prague's Czernin Palace in October 1941 Reinhard Heydrich distinguished between short-term measures and the 'final solution' (*'Endlösung'*). Concerning the 'Protectorate of Bohemia and Moravia', that rump of Czech territory remaining after the removal of the Sudetenland and Slovakia, he declared that 'this territory must once more become German', lest history be again proved correct, and the Reich suffer 'further stabs-in-the-back' from the treacherous inhabitants. The subject of his animus was not, however, the Jewish population but Czechs themselves. The 'final solution' of the Czech question, Heydrich declared, was only to be postponed until after the war

insofar as Czech labourers were needed for German war industries.[101] According to a 1940 report by the German army commander, official policy towards the 'Protectorate' was actually
formalised as follows by Hitler in the autumn of 1939, thus providing the context for Heydrich's dichotomy of immediate and
longer-term measures: 'Assimilation of the Czechs ... in so far as
this is of significance in view of its value from a racial or other
standpoint ... The remaining half of the Czech nation must be
deprived of its power, removed and deported ... This is particularly true of the section which is racially Mongolian and of the
majority of the intellectual class.'[102]

It is so clear as to be self-evident that Nazi policy towards ethnic
Czechs was not as phobic or destructive as that towards Jews,
though it was on an anti-Slavic continuum the endpoint of which
was visceral hatred of Poles and 'Russians'. And in the scheme of
things, since Germany was defeated and was thus not in a position to act out its designs, the non-Jewish Czech population got
off relatively lightly under occupation, discounting the humilia-
tions routinely inflicted on all Germany's subject populations and
large individual atrocities such as the destruction of the village of
Lidice in 'reprisal' for Heydrich's assassination in May 1942. Nevertheless Heydrich's language in Prague – the 'final solution',
'long-term' and 'short-term measures', the temporary use of undesirables for labour – was no mere coincidence of terms with that
of the 'Jewish question'. Nor was such language the sole property
of Nazism, as we shall now see.

An international context for Nazi genocide

Ethnic or national 'questions' dominated the population politics
of many a central and eastern European state from the late nineteenth century onwards, and gained in prominence with the
wartime break-up of the European land-empires and the establishment of new, unstable and competing nation-states from 1918.
Some of the most vivid examples of the 'solutions' to these questions actually occurred on the eve of the First World War, in the
1912–13 Balkan wars when ethnic groups on the 'wrong' side of
any border were used alternately as recruiting grounds for ir-
regular warfare and targets for collective reprisals, and 'alien'
populations in lands coveted and conquered by the participants

were subjected to ethnic cleansing, terrorisation or forced assimilation. As Rogers Brubaker writes, these wars were conducted in the interests of 'unmixing' peoples, 'at the high noon of mass ethnic nationalism, undertaken by states bent on shaping their territories in accordance with maximalist – and often fantastically exaggerated – claims of ethnic demography and committed to moulding their heterogeneous populations into relatively homogeneous national wholes'.[103] These processes continued into the Great War itself as the Russian, Habsburg and Ottoman lands became theatres of war and internal strife.

It was a well-established nationalist paranoia that concentrated minority populations could serve as the basis for separatist movements manipulated externally, and irredentism was frequently used as a weapon in struggles for national expansion. The fear of ethnically defined fifth columns found expression in the Tsarist wartime deportation of Jewish, Polish, German, Latvian and Lithuanian groups, as well as assaults on Chinese and Koreans, and on Muslim populations in the Caucasus and central Asia. The most famous case of forced population movement from the First World War occurred on the very borders of Europe, when the ruling Turkish 'Committee of Union and Progress' (CUP) perpetrated the genocide of some one million Armenians under the influence of an explosive mixture of late Ottoman chauvinism and half-digested ideological imports from the west, radicalised by the prospect of the imminent collapse of the empire. That genocide itself was part of a larger exercise in population engineering in the pursuit of Turkish population homogeneity (and owing to wartime upheaval) as in and around the First World War approximately one-third of the pre-war Anatolian population of more than 17 million people, including Kurds and other non-Turkish Muslims, were subject to 'relocation'.[104]

The nationalist's concern with security of borders and 'territorial integrity' coincided dangerously with the ethnic-essentialist's obsession with population homogeneity and the social Darwinist's belief in inter-group struggle to produce a panoply of explosive and paranoid chauvinisms in east-central and south-eastern Europe and the Near East. If, like antisemitism, general racist thought had gained a respectable pedigree amongst European elites over the previous decades, these newly emerged, intolerant nationalisms could shade into outright racism. It may in fact be appropriate to talk of a general 'racialisation' of European nationalism since the late nineteenth century, and even earlier.[105] Internalising a bastardised version of Darwin's theories, or, like the Turkish CUP, adopting the prevalent sociological positivism of thinkers like Auguste Comte[106] – the idea that human affairs were governed by scientific laws and were appropriate for scientific solutions – did not require a fully fledged racial theory, but the malign influence of such trends is clear.

After 1918, dominant ethnic groups in Poland, Hungary, Romania and Czechoslovakia, to name but four, sought to marginalise minorities, particularly those related to dominant groups in neighbouring states and regions, by harassment, ethnic cleansing, coercive dispersion or cultural assimilation, the latter usually forced to one degree or another. A portentous variation was provided by the orchestrated 'population exchanges' in 1923–26 between Greece and Turkey, in the aftermath of war between the two. In often brutal circumstances, and with a high death toll on either side, some 1.25 million Greeks and 356,000 Turks (by no means all of whom of either group would have defined themselves as such) exchanged countries with the approval of all the signatories to the Lausanne peace treaty.[107] These episodes, and Stalin's population policies in the 1930s, certainly shaped the perception of what was possible for the likes of Aly's and Heim's demographic intellectuals, the 'architects of annihilation'.[108] There is anecdotal evidence that they also made an impression on Hitler. In a series of interviews given early in the 1930s, when he was still thinking of the Jewish question as a problem of space,[109] Hitler noted both his intentions towards population relocation and his belief in the national vigour resulting from ethnic 'purification':

> We must already be thinking of the resettlement of millions of men from Germany and Europe ... We must colonize the East ruthlessly
> ...
> We intend to introduce a great resettlement policy; we do not wish to go on treading on each other's toes in Germany. In 1923 little Greece could resettle a million men ... and remember the extermination of the Armenians. One eventually reaches the conclusion that masses of men are mere biological modelling clay.[110]

There is a vital caveat to associating these other themes and episodes with the murder of the Jews without due regard to the particular history of European antisemitic fantasies both ancient and

modern. Seemingly alone amongst them there was no real inter-
active dynamic in the Holocaust. While there were discernible
mutually antagonistic political dynamics of some sort at various
times between, for instance, Serbs and Croats, Greeks and Turks,
Russians and Poles, Germans and Poles, and Germans and Russians, the same cannot be said for Jews and Germans. Such a
German–Jewish dynamic as did exist did so only in Nazi minds.
And yet this very absence of concrete grievances lent Nazi
antisemitism, like other conspiracy theories, extra force in the portrayal of Jewish subversion and clandestine power networks. As
Omer Bartov puts it, the Jews became 'elusive enemies'.[111] The in-
flation of the 'Jewish problem' to the point where, unlike other
minority 'problems' or other states' 'Jewish problems', it was not
solely a question of the Jewish presence in one discrete territory,
meant limitlessly increasing the number of potential 'grievances'
and 'provocations'. Nowhere was this more clearly illustrated
than when in mid-September 1941 Alfred Rosenberg, figurehead
of Hitler's 'Eastern Ministry', suggested that the deportation of
central European Jews begin as a reprisal for the recently announced Stalinist deportation of the Volga Germans (as a supposed ethnic fifth column).[112]

It is testament to the power of Hitler's fantasies that Nazi policies could be made according to belief in the universal power of
Jewry, despite all evidence to the contrary. He seems for instance
genuinely to have regarded the Jews under German control as
hostages to determine Jewish-influenced American behaviour
during the war, and considered that Jews could be blamed for
Allied bombing.[113] At the same time, however, the other side of the
antisemitic coin, the Judeo-Bolshevik stereotype, was considerably more than just a Nazi belief, even in western Europe, as well
as among the ranks of prospective collaborators of Germany in
formerly Soviet-controlled regions of eastern Europe, including
the Jedwabne killers.[114] The difference between Nazism and other
forms of antisemitism in this regard was the degree to which the
supposed connection influenced action.

The book chiefly responsible for the German '*Historikerstreit*'
('historians' debate') in the 1980s on the historical
contextualisation of Nazism was Ernst Nolte's *Der europäische
Bürgerkrieg 1917–1945: Nationalsozialismus und Bolschewismus.*[115]
This erroneously described the crimes of Bolshevism as '*Vorbild*'

and 'Schreckbild' – both a model and a sort of terrible precedent – for the crimes of Nazism, and has been suitably called to account.[116] The earlier examination of the RKFDV and the schemes of population re-ordering in eastern Europe suggest that Nazi genocide owes much more to the legacy of nationalist ethnic cleansing over the previous decades than to any crimes stemming from corruptions of communism, as also arguably do the Stalinist deportations of 'suspect' nations such as the Volga Germans, alongside Muslim nationalities, Armenians and many others, during the Second World War.[117]

It is clearly a delicate issue to insert full-scale Nazi genocide at least partially into a continuum of ethnic cleansing and demographic politics in eastern and central Europe. Yet this has been made immeasurably harder by the insistence on a phenomenological approach to the Holocaust that is concerned more with its difference and 'uniqueness' than its immediate historical contexts beyond the one context of racialised antisemitism. A strand of German historiography has rightly been criticised for seeming to create an equivalence between, for instance, the 'final solution' and the expulsion of ethnic Germans from eastern Europe at the end of the war. Andreas Hilgrüber's contribution to the *Historikerstreit*, *Zweierlei Untergang* (a 'twofold collapse'), left itself dangerously open to attack by appearing to do just that concerning the flight before the Red Army from 1944.[118] Different exact causation operates in each case, and simplistic conflation of one event with another is profoundly anti-historical. It is clear, for instance, that the mass expulsions of Germans from Poland and Czechoslovakia at the end of the Second World War were stimulated in part by fear of future German manipulation of the minority question and revenge for German occupation. Nevertheless, they were also pursuant to the chauvinist logic that had been actively present since before the Second World War about the necessity for national stability of population homogeneity.[119] The eviction of more than 200,000 ethnic Germans from Hungary from 1945, conducted by many of the same Hungarian personnel as had helped deport Jews in 1944, had been envisaged by the then regent Admiral Miklos Horthy as part of a reciprocal exchange as early as 1934, and had been discussed with the Nazis during the war.[120] (On a smaller scale, the end of the Second World War also saw an organised Hungarian–Slovak population exchange at the behest of the re-formed Czechoslovak state.[121])

Each of these instances of post-war population engineering met with the same resigned acceptance by the western allies as the Greco-Turkish exchanges and the abuse of the minorities clauses in the 1920s and 1930s elicited from Britain: in each case the logic was treated as inevitable.[122] And while the moral questions too are different in these cases, this is not to deny attention to the 12 million Germans uprooted in 1944–48, by no means all of whom had been complicit in the German structures of domination in Europe, and at least 1.5 million of whom perished during the exodus.[123]

Further evidence of the conceptual and even causal link between Nazi genocide and other instances of 'cleansing' and forced 'homogenisation' is provided by the wartime actions of countries allied to Germany and conquered by Germany. One of the basic principles of German rule in the east was dividing the ethnic elements of a country against each other, if indeed encouragement was needed. Germany was not always immediately successful with the strategy amongst its allies. Hitler had to cajole Slovak leaders out of their initial reticence to secede from the doomed Czechoslovak state in the late 1930s. Even the introduction of antisemitic measures, Germany's foremost racial priority, was not always satisfactory to the Reich authorities. Bulgaria, Romania, Finland and Hungary acted at their own paces with the enactment of antisemitic legislation. Then they proceeded, like France, to kill or deport Jews (or not) in accordance with their own priorities, whether related to the citizenship status of particular groups of Jews or to the repercussions for their economies of the mass removal of Jews. This only serves to underline Gross's recommendation to comprehend 'a society's experiences of war [as of] occupation as if they were endogenous' rather than the result simply of 'external, imposed circumstances'.[124]

Even in Poland, the country whose inhabitants arguably had least room for manouvre under Nazi occupation, to the extent that not even collaborationist organisations were allowed to exist, the pre-existing state of Polish–Jewish relations determined the general absence of solidarity with the Jews. But the matter is more complicated still, for Polish–Jewish relations did not form a self-enclosed cultural-political dynamic separate from other inter-ethnic relations and socio-economic concerns. This is what makes all the more perplexing Gross's bestseller *Neighbors*. Contrary to Gross's earlier and more sophisticated work on occupation, collaboration and ethnic politics in Poland (and downplaying the exceptional nature of the massacre),[125] this effectively becomes a simple story of antisemitism let loose, stripped for the most part of the detailed interrelations over the longer and shorter term between Poles, Jews, Lithuanians, Belarussians, Russians, Ukrainians and Germans. In terms of contextualising the German occupation within the Polish and European context, it is of interest, for instance, that perhaps 10 per cent of the approximately 13.5 million inhabitants of eastern Poland were deported eastwards into the Soviet interior during the Soviet occupation of 1939–41. Around 140,000 of the deportees were Jews who had already fled from the German zone. Moscow was also happy to 'repatriate' some 128,000 *Volksdeutsche* in agreement with Germany (people whose houses would be used to accommodate evacuees from the new security zone adjacent to the German–Soviet border), and remained suspicious of those ethnic Germans who elected to stay put in eastern Poland.[126]

To the south of Jedwabne a 'homogenisation' process was conducted on the changing Polish–Ukrainian borders from 1942 with Poles as the chief victims, as for instance in the murder of some 40,000 Volhynian Poles in 1943–44,[127] and then, from the close of the Second World War, with mutual violence.[128] The cleansing of Germans from Poland at the end of the Second World War, meanwhile, was only the final chapter in a centuries-long battle to establish ethnic primacy in Poland's western borderlands. Prior to 1918, Germany had been exporting colonisers and trying to 'Germanise' local Poles; thereafter, the process was reversed. In that inter-war period, German protests against the treatment of the very large, embattled German minority in Poland were based on real grievances, as to a lesser extent was the case with the Germans of Czechoslovakia, with the vicious conflicts over the disposition of Upper Silesia being a prime source of ill-will. Such concerns led not only to Germany paradoxically becoming an upholder of the Versailles minority protection clauses,[129] but it also led to the formation of radical and sometimes brutalised ethnic German militias – another characteristic of some of the ethnic conflicts during the First World War[130] – that would become co-perpetrators of Germany's racist crimes during the occupation,[131] as would similar units formed from other national minorities in the occupied territories.[132]

Each country had its own dynamics, both ethnic and geo-political, and its own pattern of interaction with Germany.[133] Like Italy, Romania and Hungary had gone down their paths of alliance with Germany in good part because of bitter disappointment at the territorial terms of the Versailles treaty. The war for them was a means of expansion or re-expansion. In Hungary, the swinging territorial losses of 1918–19 left the large Jewish minority exposed in the rump of what had previously been a multinational polity, and subject to radicalised Magyar opinion. Prevailing Hungarian antisemitism was not inherently genocidal, as the comparative security of Hungarian Jews up until the German occupation in 1944 showed – though non-Hungarian Jews within the kingdom's borders were killed and deported from 1941 onwards. It did, however, demand at least the economic marginalisation of Jews to the end of ethnic Magyar control.[134] It bore some similarities to pre-war Polish desires to reduce the 'excess' Jewish population by deportation – possibly to Madagascar – in the interests of economic advancement in an 'overpopulated' region.[135] Pre-war Romanian nationalists also seriously entertained thoughts of deportation.[136] And each programme echoed aspects of Ottoman policy up to and during the First World War, as Greeks and Armenians were targeted for expropriation in the interests of creating a Turkish 'national economy'.[137] Each episode in turn provides a vital contextualisation for Nazi policies of 'Aryanisation' – another point at which economic and ideological calculations intersect.[138]

Elsewhere the threads of inter-war society swiftly unravelled just as comprehensively, and no more obviously than in Yugoslavia. The Croatian Ustasha fascists who murdered Jews also murdered Serbs; in fact they killed more Serbs than they did Jews. And Serbian right-wing royalist partisans, the Chetniks, carried out revenge massacres, as well as killing some Jews. And both Serbs and Croats killed Yugoslavian Muslims, who themselves were not entirely passive, since a group of Bosnian Muslims joined the Waffen-SS to form a regiment known as Handschar. The Second World War and the wilfully immoral and violent nature of Nazi rule only served to exaggerate and give free rein to pre-existing nationalist, irredentist and secessionist tendencies. Thus, crudely, the Serbo-Croat dynamic that exploded in 1941 can be traced back to Croatian fears of Serbian ethnic dominance in the early decades of the Yugoslav state, just as pre-1939 Polish rule over regions of the western Ukraine led to bloody recrimination after the Nazi advance. Even Belgium witnessed fratricide as Flemish nationalists turned on their Francophone compatriots.[139]

Little of this was clear-cut in terms of allegiance to the Axis cause, just as the large number of volunteers of different nationalities who joined the Waffen-SS did so in furtherance of their own political and ideological ambitions.[140] The Organisation of Ukrainian Nationalists that was a main organ of Ukrainian collaboration with Germany and the chief agent in Eastern Galicia of the murder and ethnic cleansing of Poles sided with the power which appeared (falsely) most likely to pave the way to independent Ukrainian statehood and liberation from Soviet rule. Even in the ostensibly more stable, long-established nation-state of France defeat and occupation brought massive internal tensions to the fore – between population groups to a degree but primarily between different visions of what sort of country France should be. The political influence that manifested itself as the Vichy government was the right-wing that inherited the mantle of the anti-revolutionary tradition and of the persecution of Alfred Dreyfus in the 1890s. They too clearly partook of antisemitism, yet of a different form from that of the Nazis. The deportation of many foreign and some French Jews to the extermination camps was not so much an expression of French antisemitism as of straightforward French collaboration. The infamous anti-Jewish legislation (the *statuts*) derived, on the other hand, from Vichy's conservative, religious tradition.[141]

As well as being a coercive presence Nazism was thus a facilitating force for older, broader and more diverse exclusionary tendencies across the continent. Indeed Nazism itself would not have been conceivable without the history of generally right-wing European nationalisms obsessed with national 'space' and borders and with 'alien' minorities, and prepared to wage war in each connection. And though the peculiar history of Europe's relationship to its Jews renders the nature of the 'Jewish question' in turn somewhat anomalous in this comparative context, the idea of violent 'solutions' to population problems was by no means novel, and was applied by Germany to Jews and many other groups besides.

Equally, the paramount place of antisemitism within Nazi ideology did not necessarily equate to a prescription for genocide: there was no pure 'logic' of antisemitism leading from definition of 'the Jew' to the gas chambers, no pure 'policy' of murder fully untainted by economic or logistical concerns. However, at some point genocide began, and the questions therefore are of how it could begin and how it could be conducted. How did the Nazis and Nazism shape the German people into perpetrators and quiescent onlookers for their specific racist aims? What combination of factors determined the extremity to which those aims would be pursued? And how were the resources of the state deployed in the interests of genocide? These issues are taken up in chapter 3.

Notes

1 Richard Rubenstein, *The Cunning of History: The Holocaust and the American Future* (New York, Harper Colophon, 1978), pp. 12–16.

2 Zygmunt Bauman, *Modernity and the Holocaust* (Ithaca, N.Y., Cornell University Press, 1989), p. 52.

3 Norman Cohn, *Warrant for Genocide: The Jewish World Conspiracy and the Protocols of the Elders of Zion* (London, Serif, 1996).

4 Ian Kershaw, *The Nazi Dictatorship: Problems and Perspectives of Interpretation* (London, Edward Arnold, 1989), p. 90.

5 Helen Fein, *Accounting for Genocide: National Responses and Jewish Victimization during the Holocaust* (New York, Free Press, 1979). Cf. Wolfgang Seibel, 'Staatsstruktur und Massenmord: Was kann eine historisch-vergleichende Institutionenanalyse zur Erforschung des Holocaust beitragen?', *Geschichte und Gesellschaft*, vol. 24 (1998), pp. 539–69.

6 As cited on the inside cover of William Sheridan Allen, *The Nazi Seizure of Power: The Experience of a Single German Town 1930–1935* (New York, New Viewpoints, 1973).

7 Saul Friedländer, *Nazi Germany and the Jews: The Years of Persecution, 1933–1939* (New York, HarperCollins, 1997), pp. 4–5.

8 See the discussion in Pierre Papazian, 'A "Unique Uniqueness"?', *Midstream*, vol. 30, no. 4 (1984), pp. 14–25.

9 On the German historiography, see Ulrich Herbert, 'Vernichtungspolitik', in Ulrich Herbert (ed.), *Nationalsozialistische Vernichtungspolitik 1939–1945: Neue Forschungen und Kontroversen* (Frankfurt am Main, Fischer, 1998), pp. 9–66, here pp. 13–15.

10 Gerald Reitlinger, *The Final Solution* (London, Vallentine Mitchell, 1953); Leon Poliakov, *Harvest of Hate* (London, Elek, 1956); Raul Hilberg,

The Destruction of the European Jews (New York, Harper, 1961) – subsequent references to Hilberg's work are to the revised, three-volume edition (New York, Holmes and Meier, 1985).

11   Lucy Dawidowicz, 'The Holocaust was Unique in Intent, Scope, and Effect', *Center Magazine*, vol. 14, no. 4 (1981), pp. 56–64; Yehuda Bauer, 'The Place of the Holocaust in Contemporary History', *Studies in Contemporary Jewry*, vol. 1 (1984), pp. 201–24; Emil Fackenheim, 'Why the Holocaust is Unique', *Judaism*, vol. 5 (2001), pp. 438–47. See also the sources detailed in the lengthy footnote in Steven T. Katz, *The Holocaust in Historical Context, vol. 1: The Holocaust and Mass Death before the Modern Age* (New York, Oxford University Press, 1994), p. 27.

12   Katz, *The Holocaust in Historical Context, vol. 1*, p. 580.

13   Jan T. Gross, *Neighbors: The Destruction of the Jewish Community in Jedwabne, Poland* (Princeton, Princeton University Press, 2001).

14   Michael Marrus, *The Holocaust in History* (London, Penguin, 1993), pp. 19, 23.

15   Cited in A. Dirk Moses, 'Conceptual Blockages and Definitional Dilemmas in the "Racial Century": Genocides of Indigenous Peoples and the Holocaust', *Patterns of Prejudice*, vol. 36, no. 4 (2002), pp. 7–36, here p. 12.

16   David Rousset, *L'univers concentrationnaire* (Paris [1946]), interestingly translated into English as *A World Apart* (London, Secker and Warburg, 1951).

17   Robert Jay Lifton, *The Nazi Doctors: Medical Killing and the Psychology of Genocide* (London, Macmillan, 1986).

18   Generally, Daniel Jonah Goldhagen, *Hitler's Willing Executioners: Ordinary Germans and the Holocaust* (London, Little, Brown & Co., 1996). For the 'demonic' assessment, see Daniel J. Goldhagen, 'A Reply to My Critics', *New Republic*, 23 December 1996, pp. 37–45, here p. 41, cited in A. Dirk Moses, 'Structure and Agency in the Holocaust: Daniel J. Goldhagen and his Critics', *History and Theory*, vol. 37 (1998), pp. 194–219, here p. 213. Moses' article also discusses relevant issues. On the 'demonic', see also Lucy Dawidowicz, *The Holocaust and the Historians* (Cambridge, Mass., Harvard University Press, 1981), pp. 20–1.

19   Dan Diner, 'Varieties of Narration: The Holocaust in Historical Memory', in Jonathan Frankel (ed.), *Studies in Contemporary Jewry: The Fate of the European Jews, 1939–1943* (Oxford, Oxford University Press, 1997), pp. 84–100, here pp. 89–92.

20   The title of the final chapter of Götz Aly's *'Final Solution': Nazi Population Policy and the Murder of the European Jews* (London, Arnold, 1999).

21   Thomas Sandkühler, 'Die Täter des Holocausts', in Karl Heinrich Pohl (ed.), *Wehrmacht und Vernichtungspolitik: Militär im*

nationalsozialistischen System (Göttingen, Vandenhoeck and Ruprecht, 1999), pp. 39–65, here p. 47.

22 Dieter Pohl, *Nationalsozialistische Judenverfolgung in Ostgalizien 1941–1944* (Munich, Oldenbourg, 1996); Thomas Sandkühler, *'Endlösung' in Galizien: Der Judenmord in Ostpolen und die Rettungsinitiativen von Berthold Beitz 1941–1944* (Bonn, J. H. W. Dietz, 1996).

23 Hilberg, *Destruction*, vol. 3, pp. 1212, 1219.

24 Dieter Pohl, 'Die Ermordung der Juden im Generalgouvernement', in Herbert (ed.), *Nationalsozialistische Vernichtungspolitik*, pp. 98–121, here pp. 98–9.

25 Christopher Browning, *The Path to Genocide: Essays on Launching the Final Solution* (Cambridge, Cambridge University Press, 1992), p. ix.

26 On Auschwitz death tolls, Franciszek Piper, *Die Zahl der Opfer von Auschwitz* (Oswiecim, Panstwowe Muzeum, 1993); on Treblinka, Sandkühler, 'Die Täter des Holocausts', p. 47.

27 Bauer, 'The Place of the Holocaust', p. 202.

28 The best problematisation of the notion of distinct decisions, and a convincing argument for the idea of phases of policy acceleration, and of a more fluid, general 'policy of destruction', which could be altered in terms of short-term methods in accordance with prevailing circumstance, is Peter Longerich, *Politik der Vernichtung: Eine Gesamtdarstellung der nationalsozialistiche Judenverfolgung* (Munich, Piper, 2000).

29 Uwe Dietrich Adam, *Judenpolitik im dritten Reich* (Düsseldorf, Droste, 1972), pp. 303–13.

30 Longerich, *Politik der Vernichtung*.

31 Christopher Browning, *Nazi Policy, Jewish Workers, German Killers* (Cambridge, Cambridge University Press, 2000), pp. 29–30.

32 For a summary of the intentionalist views in the context of the intentionalist–functionalist debate of the 1970s–1980s, see Christopher Browning, *Fateful Months: Essays on the Emergence of the Final Solution* (New York, Holmes and Meier, 1991), ch. 1; also on these debates, Kershaw, *The Nazi Dictatorship*, ch. 5. For Breitman's position, focusing on March 1941, see Richard Breitman, *Architect of Genocide: Himmler and the Final Solution* (Hanover, N.H., Brandeis University Press, 1991).

33 For the most up-to-date analyses of the killing patterns of the Einsatzgruppen, see Peter Klein (ed.), *Die Einsatzgruppen in der besetzten Sowjetunion 1941/42: Die Tätigkeits- und Lageberichte des Chefs der Sicherheitspolizei und des SD* (Berlin, Edition Hentrich, 1997).

34 Christoph Dieckmann, 'Der Krieg und die Ermordung der litauischen Juden', in Herbert (ed.), *Nationalsozialistische Vernichtungspolitik*, pp. 292–329, here p. 301; Ralf Oggoreck, *Die Einsazgruppen und die 'Genesis der Endlösung'* (Berlin, Metropol, 1996). For a slightly different interpretation, see Peter Longerich, 'Vom Massenmord zur "Endlösung". Die Erschießungen von jüdischen Zivilisten in den ersten Monaten des Ostfeldzuges im Kontext des nationalsozialistischen Judenmords', in Bernd Wegner (ed.), *Zwei Wege nach Moskau: Vom Hitler–Stalin-Pakt zum 'Unternehmen Barbarossa'* (Munich, Piper, 1991), pp. 251–74.

35   Browning, *Nazi Policy*, ch. 2; and his earlier summary of his and Hilberg's positions in *Fateful Months*, ch. 1. See also for studies with some common ground in terms of timing, if not necessarily in terms of explanation of context, Adam, *Judenpolitik im dritten Reich*, pp. 303–12, 355–61; Peter Witte, 'Two Decisions Concerning the "Final Solution to the Jewish Question": Deportations to Lodz and Mass Murder in Chelmno', *Holocaust and Genocide Studies*, vol. 9 (1985), pp. 318–45; Philippe Burrin, *Hitler and the Jews* (London, Arnold, 1989).

36   Bogdan Musial, *Deutsche Zivilverwaltung und Judenverfolgung im Generalgouvernement: Eine Fallstudie zum Distrikt Lublin 1939–1944* (Leipzig, Harrassowitz, 1999), pp. 193–200, 343.

37   Christian Gerlach, 'The Wannsee Conference, the Fate of German Jews, and Hitler's Decision in Principle to Exterminate all European Jews', *Journal of Modern History*, vol. 70 (1998), pp. 759–812; L. J. Hartog, *Der Befehl zum Judenmord: Hitler, Amerika und die Juden* (Bodenheim, Syndikat Buchgesellschaft, 1997).

38   Donald Bloxham, *Genocide on Trial: War Crimes Trials and the Formation of Holocaust History and Memory* (Oxford, Oxford University Press, 2001), ch. 3.

39   On Majdanek, Tomasz Kranz, 'Das KL Lublin – zwischen Planung und Realisierung', in Ulrich Herbert et al. (eds), *Die nationalsozialistischen Konzentrationslager: Entwicklung und Struktur*, 2 vols (Göttingen, Wallstein, 1998), vol. 1, pp. 363–89, here pp. 371–3; on Auschwitz, Bertrand Perz and Thomas Sandkühler, 'Auschwitz und die "Aktion Reinhard" 1942–5. Judenmord und Raubpraxis in neuer Sicht', *Zeitgeschichte*, vol. 26 (1999), pp. 283–316. Perz and Sandkühler make more extensive claims, but they have yet to be fully corroborated.

40   The Treblinka decision – made probably on a Himmler visit to Warsaw – has been used by Longerich to corroborate his thesis that at the end of April or the beginning of May the decision was made to kill all Jews immediately, as manifest in the extension of murder throughout the Generalgouvernement: *Politik der Vernichtung*, p. 504.

41   Yitzhak Arad, *Belzec, Sobibor, Treblinka: The Operation Reinhard Death Camps* (Bloomington, Indiana University Press, 1987), pp. 14–16, 23.

42   Bauman, *Modernity and the Holocaust*, p. 89.

43   On Riga and also possible consideration of a killing centre in

Lvov in Eastern Galicia, Peter Longerich, *Die Wannsee-Konferenz vom 20 Januar 1942* (Berlin, Gedenk- und Bildungsstätte Haus der Wannsee-Konferenz, 1988), pp. 24–5; on Mogilev, Christian Gerlach, 'Failure of Plans for an SS Extermination Camp in Mogilev, Belorussia', *Holocaust and Genocide Studies*, vol. 11 (1997), pp. 60–78.

44 Dieter Pohl, *Von der 'Judenpolitik' zum Judenmord: Der Distrikt Lublin des Generalgouvernements 1939–1944* (Frankfurt am Main, Lang, 1993), p. 101; Gerlach, 'Wannsee Conference', arguing for a 'fundamental decision' for total murder only after work had begun on Chelmno and Belzec; Ian Kershaw, 'Improvised Genocide? The Emergence of the "Final Solution" in the "Warthegau"', *Transactions of the Royal Historical Society*, 6th series, no. 2 (1992), pp. 51–78, also contains relevant argumentation, showing that the initial decision to kill 100,000 Jews from the Lodz ghetto was half of a 'bargain' struck by the Warthegau district chief and Himmler for the former's agreement to accept deportees from Germany. For a summary position, which extends the idea of this piecemeal killing even into spring 1942, Longerich, *Politik der Vernichtung*, esp. p. 488. Cf. the counter-argument of Musial, *Deutsche Zivilverwaltung*, pp. 207–8. Relatedly, see Martin Broszat, 'Hitler und die Genesis der "Endlösung": Aus Anlass der Thesen von David Irving', *Vierteljahreshefte für Zeitgeschichte*, vol. 25 (1977), pp. 737–75, on initiatives to use the high death toll in the ghettos as a way of 'helping nature take its course' when deportation further eastwards looked impossible because of the military situation.

45 The 'euphoria of victory' being the model propounded by Browning in *Nazi Policy*, as in *The Path to Genocide*.

46 Donald Bloxham, 'Jewish Slave Labour and its Relationship to the "Final Solution"', in John K. Roth and Elizabeth Maxwell (eds), *Remembering for the Future 2000: The Holocaust in an Age of Genocide* (London, Palgrave, 2001), vol. 1, pp. 163–86, here pp. 172, 178.

47 Donald Bloxham, 'The Armenian Genocide of 1915–16: Cumulative Radicalisation and the Development of a Destruction Policy', *Past and Present*, vol. 183, no. 1 (2003), pp. 141–91.

48 Peter Longerich, *The Unwritten Order: Hitler's Role in the Final Solution* (Stroud, Tempus, 2001); Mark Roseman, *The Villa, the Lake, the Meeting: Wannsee and the Final Solution* (London, Penguin, 2003), pp. 8–9.

49 Longerich, *Politik der Vernichtung*, p. 488, on the deportation to the Lublin province of German Jews in March 1942 with no evidence of intent to kill them in the immediate term.

50 Cited in Bloxham, *Genocide on Trial*, pp. 207–8. Emphasis in original.

51 Hans Mommsen, 'The Realisation of the Unthinkable: The "Final Solution of the Jewish Question" in the Third Reich', in Gerhard

Hirschfeld (ed.), *The Policies of Genocide* (London, German Historical Institute, 1986), pp. 93–144, here pp. 111–12. See the later statement of Mommsen's position in 'Hitler's Reichstag Speech of 30 January 1939', *History and Memory*, vol. 9, nos 1 and 2 (1997), pp. 147–61. Gerlach, 'Wannsee Conference', Hartog, *Der Befehl*, Longerich, *Politik der Vernichtung*, all passim.

52 Browning, *The Path to Genocide*, ch. 7.

53 Ibid., pp. 129–31.

54 Christian Gerlach, *Krieg, Ernährung, Völkermord: Forschungen zur deutschen Vernichtungspolitik im Zweiten Weltkrieg* (Hamburg, Hamburger Edition, 1998), pp. 167–257; Musial, *Deutsche Zivilverwaltung*, pp. 208–9.

55 Götz Aly and Suzanne Heim, *Vordenker der Vernichtung: Auschwitz und die deutschen Pläne für eine neue europäischen Ordnung* (Frankfurt am Main, Fischer, 1993).

56 Dan Diner, *Beyond the Conceivable: Studies on Germany, Nazism and the Holocaust* (Berkeley, University of California Press, 2000), p. 198. I thank Dirk Moses for this reference.

57 Michael Burleigh, *Death and Deliverance: 'Euthanasia' in Germany, 1900–1945* (Cambridge, Cambridge University Press, 1994). On Gerlach and Dieckmann's findings, see below.

58 Goldhagen, *Hitler's Willing Executioners*, pp. 283–323; Benjamin Ferencz, *Less than Slaves: Jewish Forced Labour and the Quest for Compensation* (Cambridge, Mass., Harvard University Press, 1979), e.g. pp. 18–23. Wolfgang Sofsky, *Der Ordnung des Terrors: Das Konzentrationslager* (Frankfurt am Main, Fischer, 1993), suggests that labour within the camps was only another manifestation of terror and ultimately annihilation. On the issues of survivor compensation, Bloxham, 'Jewish Slave Labour', pp. 163, 177–8.

59 Roseman, *The Villa*, p. 113.

60 The history of the Durchgangstrasse IV is detailed in Sandkühler, '*Endlösung*' *in Galizien*, pp. 146–59. Also Hermann Kaienburg, 'Jüdischer Arbeit an der "Strasse der SS"', 1999. *Zeitschrift für Sozialgeschichte des 20. und 21. Jahrhunderts*, vol. 11 (1996), pp. 13–39.

61 Pohl, *Nationalsozialistische Judenverfolgung*, pp. 169–70.

62 Helmut Krausnick and Martin Broszat, *Anatomy of the SS State* (London, Granada, 1982), p. 116; Hans Marsalek, *Die Geschichte des Konzentrationslagers Mauthausen: Dokumentation* (Vienna, Österreichische Lagergemeinschaft Mauthausen, 1974), pp. 162–3; Josef Marsalek, *Majdanek: The Concentration Camp in Lublin* (Warsaw, Interpress, 1986), pp. 128–9, Madajczyk quote taken from p. 142. On the indeterminate numbers of dead at the camp, see Sandkühler, 'Die Täter des Holocausts', p. 47.

63 See Bloxham, 'Jewish Slave Labour', p. 175. It has also been

The Holocaust

pointed out that the expression means different things to different historians: Jens-Christian Wagner, 'KL Mittelbau-Dora', in Herbert et al. (eds), *Die nationalsozialistischen Konzentrationslager*, vol. 2, pp. 707–29, here pp. 719–20. Christopher Browning has spoken, for instance, of extermination *and* work: 'Vernichtung und Arbeit: Zur Fraktionierung der planenden deutschen Intelligenz im besetzten Polen', in Wolfgang Schneider (ed.), *'Vernichtungspolitik': Eine Debatte über den Zusammenhang von Sozialpolitik und Genozid im nationalsozialistischen Deutschland* (Hamburg, Junius, 1991), pp. 37–52.

64   Pohl, 'Die Ermordung der Juden im Generalgouvernement', p. 106; Pohl, *Nationalsozialitische Judenverfolgung*, p. 406.

65   For example, Frauendorfer note, 22 June 1942, and Hänecke to the High Command of the Wehrmacht, 18 September 1942, respectively in Tatiana Berenstein et al. (eds), *Faschismus – Getto – Massenmord: Dokumentation über Ausrottung und Widerstand der Juden in Polen während des zweiten Weltkrieges* (East Berlin, Rütten and Loening, 1960), pp. 438–9, 444–6; Pohl, 'Judenpolitik', pp. 159–60. For a case of conflict over Jewish labour from the Baltic states, see Wolfgang Scheffler, 'Einsatzgruppe A', in Klein (ed.), *Die Einsatzgruppen*, pp. 29–51, here pp. 34, 37–8.

66   Thomas Sandkühler, 'Das Zwangsarbeitslager Lemberg-Janowska 1941–1944', in Herbert et al. (eds), *Die nationalsozialistischen Konzentrationslager*, vol. 2, pp. 606–35, on the Erntefest massacres as a logical conclusion of developments in the Generalgouvernement.

67   Alfred Konieczny, 'Die Zwangsarbeit der Juden in Schlesien im Rahmen der "Organisation Schmeldt"', in Götz Aly and Suzanne Heim (eds), *Sozialpolitik und Judenvernichtung: Gibt es eine Ökonomie der Endlösung?* (Berlin, Rotbuch, 1987), pp. 91–110, here pp. 106–7.

68   Bloxham, *Genocide on Trial*, pp. 215–16.

69   The discretion allowed to different industrialists is to be discerned in Thomas Sandkühler, 'Zwangsarbeit und Judenmord im Distrikt Galizien des Generalgouvernements', in Hermann Kaienburg (ed.), *Konzentrationslager und deutsche Wirtschaft 1939–1945* (Opladen, Leske and Budrich, 1996), pp. 239–62, here p. 261; Neil Gregor, *Daimler-Benz in the Third Reich* (New Haven, Yale University Press, 1998), pp. 216–17; William Manchester, *The Arms of Krupp 1587–1968* (New York, Bantam, 1970), pp. 535–66. See also Hermann Kaienburg, 'Wie konnte es soweit kommen?', in Kaienburg (ed.), *Konzentrationslager und deutsche Wirtschaft*, pp. 265–78, here p. 266; Wagner, 'KL Mittelbau-Dora', p. 724. The Auschwitz subcamps also featured different qualities and amounts of food and accommodation: see Irena Strzelecka and Tadeusz Szymanski, 'Die Nebenlager Tschechowitz', *Hefte von Auschwitz*, vol. 18 (1990), pp. 189–224, here pp. 197, 199, 210; Emeryka Iwaszko, 'Nebenlager Brünn', *Hefte von Auschwitz*, vol. 18 (1990), pp. 225–45, here

106

p. 234. See also Hans Mommsen and Manfried Grieger, *Das Volkswagenwerk und seine Arbeiter im dritten Reich* (Düsseldorf, Econ, 1997), pp. 766–99, 863–902, 922. For more on this point, see the final section of chapter 3.

70   On which see Aly and Heim, *Vordenker der Vernichtung*; Michael G. Esch, *'Gesunde Verhältnisse': Deutsche und polnische Bevölkerungspolitik in Ostmitteleuropa 1939–1950* (Marburg, Verlag Herder Institut, 1998); Magnus Brechtken, *'Madagaskar für die Juden': Antisemitische Idee und politische Praxis 1885–1945* (Munich, Oldenbourg, 1997), e.g. p. 82.

71   Gerlach, *Krieg, Ernähung, Völkermord*, ch. 3; Musial, *Deutsche Zivilverwaltung*, p. 195; Christian Gerlach, *Kalkulierte Mord: Die deutsche Wirtschafts- und Vernichtungspolitik in Weißrußland 1941 bis 1944* (Hamburg, Hamburger Edition, 2000); Dieckmann, 'Der Krieg und die Ermordung der litauischen Juden'.

72   Dieter Pohl, 'Schauplatz Ukraine', in Norbert Frei, Sybille Steinbacher and Bernd C. Wagner (eds), *Ausbeutung, Vernichtung, Öffentlichkeit* (Munich, Saur, 2000), pp. 135–73, here p. 144.

73   Aly and Heim, *Vordenker der Vernichtung*, ch. 8. Also for some of Aly and Heim's related arguments, 'Die Ökonomie der "Endlösung": Menschenvernichtung und wirtschaftliche Neuordnung', in Aly and Heim (eds), *Sozialpolitik und Judenvernichtung*, pp. 7–90. The reader should also bear in mind the comments in the introductory chapter, contrary to Holocaust mythology, about the low priority given by the Reich railway authorities to 'Jewish' trains, and the relatively tiny number of trains that were actually dedicated to the deportations. See Alfred C. Mierzejewski, 'A Public Enterprise in the Service of Mass Murder: The Deutsche Reichsbahn and the Holocaust', *Holocaust and Genocide Studies*, vol. 15, (2001), pp. 33–46, here pp. 35–6.

74   Tony Kushner, *The Holocaust and the Liberal Imagination* (Oxford, Blackwell, 1994); Bloxham, *Genocide on Trial*.

75   Karl Schleunes, *The Twisted Road to Auschwitz* (Urbana, University of Illinois Press, 1970).

76   Yaacov Lozowick, *Hitlers Bürokraten: Eichmann, seine willigen Vollstrecker und die Banalität des Bösen* (Munich, Pendo, 2000), especially the conclusion, 'Auf die Schreie Hören'.

77   Richard Rhodes, *Masters of Death: The SS Einsatzgruppen and the Invention of the Holocaust* (New York, Perseus, 2002); Oggoreck, *Die Einsatzgruppen und die 'Genesis der Endlösung'*.

78   A. Ebbinghaus and G. Preissler (eds), *Die Ermordung psychisch kranker Menschen in der Sowjetunion: Dokumentation: Beiträge zur nationalsozialistischen Gesundheits- und Sozialpolitik, Bd 1* (Berlin, Rotbuch, 1985), pp. 75–107.

79   Hans-Walter Schmuhl, 'Vergessene Opfer: Die Wehrmacht und die Massenmordean psychisch Kranken, geistig Behinderten und "Zigeunern"', in Pohl (ed.), *Wehrmacht und Vernichtungspolitik*, pp. 115–39, here pp. 124–5.

80 On the murder of the Romanies, Michael Zimmermann, *Rassenutopie und Genozid: Die nationalsozialistische 'Lösung der Zigeunerfrage'* (Hamburg, Christians, 1996); for a wider context, amongst other works of theirs, Donald Kenrick and Grattan Puxon, *The Destiny of Europe's Gypsies* (London, Heinemann, 1972). There are also some clear differences between Nazi policy towards the two groups, but such differences are overstated in e.g. Guenter Lewy, *The Nazi Persecution of the Gypsies* (Oxford, Oxford University Press, 1999).

81 Donald Bloxham, 'Britain's Holocaust Memorial Days: Reshaping the Past in the Service of the Present', in Sue Vice (ed.), *Representing the Holocaust* (London, Frank Cass, 2003), pp. 41–62, here pp. 53–7.

82 Richard Plant, *The Pink Triangle: The Nazi War against Homosexuals* (New York, Henry Holt & Co., 1986), p. 154; cf. Donald Niewyk and Francis Nicosia (eds), *The Columbia Guide to the Holocaust* (New York, Columbia University Press, 2000), p. 50.

83 Rüdiger Lautmann, 'The Pink Triangle: Homosexuals as "Enemies of the State"', in Michael Berenbaum and Abraham Peck (eds), *The Holocaust and History: The Known, the Unknown, the Disputed and the Reexamined* (Bloomington, Indiana University Press, 1998), pp. 345–57, which contrasts the persecution of homosexuals with the extermination of the Jews.

84 See Gerlach, *Krieg, Ernährung, Völkermord*. Additionally the work of Aly and Heim has illustrated how, though the Jews were Hitler's primary ideological enemies, and were slated as those who would be first to suffer and die as the war progressed, the giant schemes of 'racial' and economic reorganisation of the 'east' envisaged – and to an extent realised – suffering and death for non-Jews on an vast scale. See Aly and Heim, *Vordenker der Vernichtung*. For a comprehensive documentary history of the various population schemes referred to under the title 'Generalplan Ost', see Czeslaw Madajczyk (ed.), *Vom Generalplan Ost zum Generalsiedlungsplan* (Munich, K. G. Saur, 1994). It is interesting to note the extent to which Germany had been reliant on grain and other exports from these lands before the war, in accord with Soviet–German agreements. See Edward E. Ericson III, *Feeding the German Eagle: Soviet Economic Aid to Nazi Germany, 1933–1941* (Westport, Ct., Praeger, 1999).

85 Gerlach, *Kalkulierte Morde*.

86 Christian Streit, *Keine Kameraden: Die Wehrmacht und die sowjetischen Kriegsgefangenen 1941–1945* (Bonn, J. H. W. Dietz, 1991); see also Reinhard Otto, *Wehrmacht, Gestapo und sowjetische Kriegsgefangene im deutschen Reichsgebiet 1941/42* (Munich, Oldenbourg, 1998).

87 Karel C. Berkhoff, 'The "Russian" Prisoners of War in Nazi-ruled Ukraine as Victims of Genocidal Massacre', *Holocaust and Genocide Studies*, vol. 15, (2001), pp. 1–32.

88 Michael Berenbaum (ed.), *A Mosaic of Victims: Non-Jews Persecuted and Murdered by the Nazis* (London, Tauris, 1990).

89 Charles W. Sydnor, 'Reinhard Heydrich and the Planning for the Final Solution', in Berenbaum and Peck (eds), *The Holocaust and History*, pp. 159–86, here pp. 167–8.

90 Browning, *Fateful Months*, pp. 3–4.

91 Hans Safrian, *Eichmann und seine Gehilfen* (Frankfurt am Main, Fischer, 1995) pp. 119, 122.

92 Aly and Heim, *Vordenker der Vernichtung*, ch. 13.

93 Vejas Gabriel Liulevicius, *War Land on the Eastern Front: Culture, National Identity, and German Occupation in World War I* (Cambridge, Cambridge University Press, 2000).

94 On the First World War, Liulevicius, *War Land on the Eastern Front*. On the Second World War, Klaus Latzel, *Deutsche Soldaten – nationalsozialistischer Krieg? Kriegserlebnis – Kreigserfahrung* (Paderborn, Ferdinand Schöningh, 1999). Omer Bartov perhaps goes further than Latzel in his *Hitler's Army: Soldiers, Nazis and War in the Third Reich* (Oxford, Oxford University Press, 1992), as does Walter Manoschek in his more selective collection of soldiers' letters from the eastern warzones, *'Es gibt nur eines für das Judentum: Vernichtung': Das Judenbild in deutschen Soldatenbriefen 1939–1944* (Hamburg, Hamburger Edition, 1995).

95 A point made in Safrian, *Eichmann und seine Gehilfen*, p. 141; Musial, *Deutsche Zivilverwaltung*, p. 210; and much more extensively by Gerlach, *Krieg, Ernährung, Völkermord*, ch. 1.

96 Aly, *Final Solution*; Browning, *The Path to Genocide*, ch. 1; Robert L. Koehl, *German Resettlement and Population Policy, 1939–45* (Cambridge, Mass., Harvard University Press, 1957); Sybille Steinbacher, *'Musterstadt' Auschwitz: Germanisierungspolitik und Judenmord in Ostoberschlesien* (Munich, K. G. Saur, 2000). Deborah Dwork and Robert Jan Van Pelt, *Auschwitz 1270 to the Present* (London, Norton, 1996), p. 197, covers some of the same ground as Steinbacher. See also Hans Mommsen, 'Umvolkungspläne des Nationalsozialismus und der Holocaust', in Helge Gräbitz, Klaus Bästlein and Johannes Tuchel (eds), *Die Normalität des Verbrechens* (Berlin, Edition Hentrich, 1994), pp. 68–84.

97 On the SS Race and Settlement Office (Rasse- und Siedlungshauptamt), see Isabel Heinemann, '"Another Type of Perpetrator": The SS Racial Experts and Forced Population Movements in the Occupied Regions', *Holocaust and Genocide Studies*, vol. 15 (2001), pp. 387–411.

98 As for the Generalplan Ost, the versions prepared after 1940 in preparation for the attack on the USSR, and the development of the plan during the first months of the invasion, were not explicitly concerned with Jewish policy. On the divergence, see Madajczyk (ed.), *Vom Generalplan Ost*, pp. xiv–xvi. Nevertheless, planning for the two related policies does seem still to have had some connections in terms of key decisions. See Witte, 'Two Decisions', pp. 329–30.

99   Musial, *Deutsche Zivilverwaltung*, p. 203.

100   J. Noakes and G. Pridham (eds), *Nazism 1919–1945: A Documentary Reader, vol. 3* (Exeter, University of Exeter Press, 1988), doc. 503.

101   Safrian, *Eichmann und seine Gehilfen*, pp. 105–6.

102   Noakes and Pridham (eds), *Nazism, vol. 3*, doc. 618.

103   Rogers Brubaker, *Nationalism Reframed: Nationhood and the National Question in the New Europe* (Cambridge, Cambridge University Press, 1996), p. 154.

104   Bloxham, 'The Armenian Genocide of 1915–16'.

105   On which see the discussion of the work of Paul Gilroy in the conclusion to this book. See also Eric Hobsbawm, *Nations and Nationalism since 1780* (Cambridge, Cambridge University Press, 1990), pp. 106–10; and one of the general arguments of Eric Weitz in *A Century of Genocide: Utopias of Race and Nation* (Princeton, Princeton University Press, 2003).

106   Feroz Ahmad, *The Young Turks: The Committee of Union and Progress in Turkish Politics 1908–1914* (Oxford, Clarendon Press, 1969).

107   Aviel Roshwald, *Ethnic Nationalism and the Fall of Empires: Central Europe, Russia and the Middle East, 1914–1923* (London, Routledge, 2001), pp. 185–6; Norman M. Naimark, *Fires of Hatred: Ethnic Cleansing in Twentieth-Century Europe* (Cambridge, Mass., Harvard University Press, 2001), pp. 52–6 on the significance of the agreement.

108   Aly and Heim, *Vordenker der Vernichtung*, ch. 13.

109   See, for example, Browning, *The Path to Genocide*, ch. 1.

110   Cited in Rhodes, *Masters of Death*, pp. 86–7.

111   Omer Bartov, *Mirrors of Destruction: War, Genocide, and Modern Identity* (Oxford, Oxford University Press, 2000), ch. 3.

112   Burrin, *Hitler and the Jews*, pp. 122–3. Burrin suggests that this proposal could only have played a minor part in Hitler's decision-making, as does Longerich in *Politik der Vernichtung*. Roseman, *The Villa*, p. 41, attaches more weight to it, illustrating Hitler's 'vengeful' nature. On the deportation of the Soviet Germans, which eventually totalled 1.2 million out of a population of 1.5 million, see Naimark, *Fires of Hatred*, pp. 88–9.

113   Gerlach, 'Wannsee Conference', p. 787; Witte, 'Two Decisions', pp. 323–6.

114   Gross, *Neighbors*.

115   Ernst Nolte, *Der europäische Bürgerkrieg 1917–1945: Nationalsozialismus und Bolschewismus* (Frankfurt am Main, Propylaen, 1987).

116   Richard Evans, *In Hitler's Shadow: West German Historians and the Attempt to Escape from the Nazi Past* (London, Tauris, 1989), ch. 2.

117   Robert Conquest, *The Nation Killers* (London, Sphere, 1972); Naimark, *Fires of Hatred*, ch. 3, arguing that the Stalinist deportations of the Chechens-Ingush and the Crimean Tatars during the Second World War qualify fully as instances of 'ethnic cleansing'. See pp. 88–92 on the Soviet leadership's focus on 'national enemies' as opposed to class enemies during 1936–37.

118   Andreas Hillgruber, *Zweierlei Untergang: Die Zerschlagung des deutschen Reiches und das Ende des europäischen Judentums* (Berlin, Siedler, 1986), as critiqued in Evans, *In Hitler's Shadow*, chs 3, 4 and 5. Equally tendentious is Alfred M. de Zayas, *A Terrible Revenge: The Ethnic Cleansing of the East European Germans, 1944–1950* (New York, St Martin's Press, 1994).

119   Philipp Ther and Ana Siljak (eds), *Redrawing Nations: Ethnic Cleansing in East-Central Europe, 1944–1948* (Lanham, Md., Rowman and Littlefield, 2001), parts I and II; Naimark, *Fires of Hatred*, ch. 4.

120   Christian Gerlach and Götz Aly, *Das letzte Kapitel: Der Mord an den ungarischen Juden* (Stuttgart, Deustche Verlags-Anstalt, 2002), pp. 425–33.

121   Brubaker, *Nationalism Reframed*, p. 157.

122   Mark Kramer, 'Introduction', to Ther and Sijak (eds), *Redrawing Nations*, pp. 1–41, here pp. 4–7, on the Greco-Turkish and post-Second World War exchanges. On responses to the breaches of the League of Nations minority treaties in the inter-war period, see Mark Mazower, *Dark Continent* (London, Allen Lane, 1998), pp. 54–5. See also Tony Judt, 'The Past is Another Country', in Istvan Deak et al. (eds), *The Politics of Retribution in Europe* (Princeton, Princeton University Press, 2000), pp. 293–323, here p. 298.

123   Kramer, 'Introduction', pp. 4–7.

124   Jan T. Gross, 'Themes for a Social History of War Experience and Collaboration', in Deak et al. (eds), *The Politics of Retribution in Europe*, pp. 15–35, here p. 15.

125   Jan T. Gross, *Revolution from Abroad: The Soviet Conquest of Poland's Western Ukraine and Western Byelorussia* (Princeton, Princeton University Press, 1988); Jan T. Gross, *Polish Society under German Occupation: The Generalgouvernement, 1939–44* (Princeton, Princeton University Press, 1979). For a sound critique of some of Gross's arguments in *Neighbors*, see Dariusz Stola, 'Jedwabne: Revisiting the Evidence and Nature of the Crime', *Holocaust and Genocide Studies*, vol. 17 (2003), pp. 139–52.

126   Martin Dean, *Collaboration in the Holocaust* (New York, St Martin's Press, 2000), pp. 4–6. See more generally Gross, *Revolution from Abroad*.

127   Tadeusz Piotrowski (ed.), *Genocide and Rescue in Wolyn: Recollections of the Ukrainian Nationalist Ethnic Cleansing Campaign against the Poles* *during World War II* (London, McFarland & Co., 2000); idem, *Poland's Holocaust* (London, McFarland & Co., 1998).

128   Part I of Ther and Siljak (eds), *Redrawing Nations*.

129   Carol Fink, '"Defender of Minorities": Germany in the League of Nations, 1926–1933', *Central European History*, vol. 5 (1972), pp. 330–57.

130   For the formation of 'self-defence' groups on various sides in the Caucasus and the Ottoman empire during the First World War, see Bloxham, 'The Armenian Genocide', section II.

131   Christian Jansen and Arno Weckbecker, *Der 'Volksdeutsche Selbstschutz' in Polen 1939/40* (Munich, Oldenbourg, 1992), for crimes against Poles. This organisation consisted of more than 100,000 men. See also Valdis O. Lumans, *Himmler's Auxiliaries: The Volksdeutsche Mittelstelle and the German National Minorities of Europe, 1933–1945* (Chapel Hill, University of North Carolina Press, 1993), on the attraction of the German minorities to Nazism.

132   Raul Hilberg, *Perpetrators, Victims, Bystanders* (London, Lime Tree, 1993) ch. 8.

133   For the most recent research on eastern Europe, see Christoph Dieckmann, Christian Gerlach, Wolf Gruner et al. (eds), *Kooperation und Verbrechen: Formen der Kollaboration im östlichen Europa 1939–1945* (Göttingen, Wallstein, 2003)

134   Gerlach and Aly, *Das letzte Kapitel*, chs 2 and 4.

135   Brechtken, *'Madagaskar für die Juden'*, pp. 81–91; Aly and Heim, *Vordenker der Vernichtung*, passim.

136   Gerlach and Aly, *Das letzte Kapitel*, p. 422 on Romania.

137   Donald Bloxham, 'Determinants of the Armenian Genocide', in Richard Hovannisian (ed.), *Looking Backward, Moving Forward: Confronting the Armenian Genocide* (New Brunswick, Transaction, 2003), pp. 23–50, here pp. 30–1, 33, 38.

138   And as Hans Safrian shows, the establishment of the 'Vienna model' in 1938, so influential in the way that 'Aryanisation' was conducted in Germany itself, got much of its impetus from indigenous Austrian measures of expropriation of Jews. See Safrian's 'Expediting Expropriation and Expulsion: The Impact of the "Vienna Model" on Anti-Jewish policies in Nazi Germany, 1938', *Holocaust and Genocide Studies*, vol. 14 (2000), pp. 390–414.

139   On which see Martin Conway, *Collaboration in Belgium* (New Haven, Yale University Press, 1993).

140   Hans Werner Neulen, *Eurofaschismus und der Zweite Weltkrieg: Europas verratene Söhne* (Munich, Universitas, 1980).

141   Robert Paxton, *Vichy France* (New York, Columbia University Press, 1982).

3

Perpetrators and perpetration part II: radicalisation and participation

The progression from discrimination to full-scale annihilation was not straightforward: that much is clear. To borrow from the lexicon of economics, if racial antisemitism was the necessary factor in producing the 'final solution', it was not by itself sufficient. A number of explanations have been adduced as to the role of other factors, but a growing consensus points to the critical importance of Germany's wartime expansion in pursuit of 'living space' and continental domination, and particularly the cataclysmic conflict with the Soviet Union. Alongside wartime radicalisation, the peculiar dynamics of the Nazi political system have also been pinpointed. The system fostered by Hitler fed off the licence given to key Nazi interests and individuals, and to strands of discriminatory thought – many of which predated Nazism – against Germany's 'enemies'. Yet within this overarching and ideologically determined system, getting beyond imprecise terms like 'radicalisation' to understand the concrete development of Jewish policy can only be achieved with reference to specific institutional histories and practices, and the actions of particular individuals and agencies at particular times.

Then we come to address the real ramifications for Nazi Germany of the radicalisation process. Why did tens of thousands of people become agents of genocide? The answers are not all-encompassing. Not only were there different ideological impulses, different levels and qualities of hatred (and many perpetrators demonstrably did not hate as such, and certainly not their individual victims), there were and are more general obstacles to murder in all its guises which cannot be subordinated inevitably to personal or group disposition. One of these is legality, though that was not an important impediment during the Holocaust; quasi-legal endorsement was, however, significant in facilitating killing, as we shall see. The other obstacles are morality and sensibility, or perhaps sensitivity. These were of greater importance in the Holocaust and genocide generally than in pogroms or individual massacres, owing to the protracted nature of the 'final solution', which could not be dependent upon frenzied, heat-of-the-moment actions for its fulfilment. Morality was an issue right across the spectrum of perpetrators from bureaucrats to concentration camp guards, though the moral questions raised were slightly different in each case. At the moment of abuse or killing itself, sensibility came into the frame. Explaining how both obstacles were surmounted is as important as charting the role of Nazi antisemitism itself.

Nazis and Germans

Bearing in mind the relationship between antisemitism and ethnic nationalism in Europe, it is noteworthy that Nazi antisemitism was not a major factor in Hitler's partial electoral success. Notwithstanding the multiplicity of small far-right-wing parties in the 1920s and 1930s, Germany was not crying out for a programme of racist persecution. We may say that most Nazi voters (just over a third of the electorate in the last free elections) were not at all deterred by it, but that is a rather different matter, and there is in any case clear evidence that antisemitism was somewhat de-emphasised in the Nazi programme at the end of the 1920s.[1] This is not to suggest that there were not powerful or particularly virulent strands of antisemitism in German society, and it is written in full cognisance of Hitler's occasional tactical downplaying of Nazi antisemitism.[2]

Friedländer's concept of Nazi 'redemptive antisemitism' pinpoints some of its roots in the Bayreuth circle around the family of the composer Richard Wagner, the embodiment of a combination of racist-cum-mystical obsessions peculiar even in *fin-de-siècle* Europe: 'German Christianity, neoromanticism, the mystical cult of sacred Aryan blood, and ultraconservative nationalism'.[3] Peter Pulzer has also convincingly argued that the 'rise of political

antisemitism' in Germany from the 1880s onwards left a profound imprint upon German political life to the extent that it became almost a default position for conservative parties, one
which did not even need explicit expression in manifesto or campaign.[4] And there is broad historiographical consensus that general public attitudes towards Jews were poisoned by the rhetoric
and disinformation propagated around the so-called Jewish-elec-
tions (*Judenwählen*) of 1912, where the political left made substantial gains; the subsequent issues of putative war-profiteering and
draft-avoidance that culminated in the infamous Jew-count
(*Judenzählung*) amongst servicemen in 1916; the Bolshevik revolution, the brief Bela Kun regime in Hungary and the abortive post-
war communist coups in Berlin and Munich, all supposedly
suggestive of the extent of subversive Jewish influence; and
above all the collapse of the home front in 1918 when it seemed
that the military war, at least in the east, had been won, thus giving rise to the 'stab-in-the-back' myth.[5] In an unquantifiable way
these factors did matter. They entrenched stereotypes, probably
reduced the resistance of the German people to yet more extreme
antisemitism, and in all likelihood hardened the population to
some degree to the hardships that Jews would undergo from
1933.

The success of Nazism in power in marshalling identification of
the party with the state, and both of these with the *Volksgemeinschaft* (the ethnic-German national community), is one of
the striking features of the period. In the Nazi world-view, to be a
member of the German national community was by definition to
be non-Jewish, and thus Jews were instantly cast outside what
Fein calls 'the universe of obligation'.[6] Conversely, though, one
did not need to be a vehement antisemite or to identify fully with
all aspects of Nazi ideology to approve generally of Nazism, but
one was certainly more likely to go along with even extreme Nazi
policies if one had benefited from their other measures, and particularly if what the Nazis did was equated – as it came to be –
with the well-being of the German nation. For over and above
radical racism, the Nazis addressed a host of concerns common to
the far broader church of German nationalism, with promises of
economic and social renewal, a restoration of putatively German
values over 'degenerate' liberal/libertarian Weimar values, anti-
communism, anti-socialism, opposition to the terms of the

Versailles settlement and protection of German minorities beyond Germany's borders.

The sense of belonging to a collective was in fact enhanced by the persecution of 'others'. Irrespective of the precise causal linkage between the pre-war and war years, the earlier period provided conditioning for those who would unforeseeably participate directly and indirectly in the genocide.[7] The years 1933–38 saw a huge volume of racist propaganda directed against the Jews, on top of legalised social ostracisation. The language employed was often violent in the extreme, even if violence itself was employed less frequently than is sometimes thought in those years: the concentration camps in the Reich were only used for Jews in large numbers in the aftermath of the Kristallnacht pogrom; otherwise, the direct physical assaults that occurred, particularly in 1933 and 1935, were somewhat regionally variable, the product of pressure from below from SA and/or old Nazi party members seeking successfully to radicalise anti-Jewish policy. These persecutions were hugely significant for the whole Jewish community, for they indicated the reversal of the emancipation process that had been so hard fought for. But terrible though the 1933–38 persecutions were for the Jews themselves, and in that they provided a model of discriminatory legislation that could be swiftly superimposed on some of the occupied countries, they were at least as important in terms of the later 'final solution' – especially since the great majority of European Jewry did not experience Nazi rule during the period – in 'disciplining' the German people by binding them into a more tightly defined and exclusive national community.[8]

Looking retrospectively, the establishment of social space between Germans and German Jews was the key to minimising public discontent during the murder process. This would not only take place away from the eyes – if not always the ears[9] – of the German public, but the majority of victims were, as we have seen, not German or even other 'civilised' western European Jews with whom Germans might more easily identify. Even the Nazi leadership did not move smoothly into killing Jews from the Reich in the way that it authorised the mass murder – if not yet outright genocide – of Soviet Jews before the June 1941 invasion. (This distinction may have been predicated on the Nazis' fear of alerting and/or antagonising German opinion.[10]) As well as anti-Slavism and the 'Judeo-Bolshevik' stereotype attached to the Soviet Jews, the long-standing cultural stereotype of the alien, orthodox *Ostjuden* (eastern Jews) could also stymie public empathy, just as in France the authorities and population were more comfortable with the deportation of eastern European Jews. This should all be considered alongside the fact that the genocide was perpetrated when Germany was at war, with all the introversion, intensified nationalism and greater tolerance of extreme measures by the national leadership that that circumstance brought. Most Jewish victims were by their citizenship – if not their 'race' – cast as 'enemy nationals' in the war, since most came from Poland and the USSR. And given the *de facto* domestic acceptance of the brutality of German rule in Poland in 1939–41, not to mention of the abominations perpetrated in the Reich's concentration camps from 1933 onwards, there is no reason to think that any notion of shared humanity was strong enough to elicit protest at the 'final solution'.

It was a risky thing to maintain social ties with Jews still in Germany, or to lend them moral support, since such could bring social stigmatisation or even official suspicion. While helping Jews was a thankless task, doing nothing in the face of their persecution was not only the line of least resistance, it was also potentially rewarding. On the levels of both the ordinary shopkeeper and the big-businessman, for instance, the removal of economic competition from Jews was without doubt a bonus – capitalism was as important as racism in this sense.[11] Others might go even further and benefit directly from the theft of Jewish businesses and property that the 'Aryanisation' process entailed; then there was the prospect of the cheap purchase of the property of Jews who were forced out of Germany. Professionals, too, could benefit from the extra jobs made available by the banning of Jews from a long list of careers: the number of non-Jewish university lecturers, doctors, lawyers and civil servants who protested against the dismissal of Jewish colleagues was lamentably small. Longerich draws our attention to the clever use by the Nazi leadership of wartime language about solving the 'Jewish question' which, while not revealing details of the murder process, was calculated to implicate the German population in its enaction, therefore further binding the community together in the criminal war effort.[12] In between, on myriad everyday occasions ordinary Germans were drawn into the broad spectrum of complicity by an equally broad spectrum of incriminating acts, the least of which, but perhaps also the most important in terms of overall judgements on the German people during the period, was unprotesting witness.

For those within the Third Reich's universe of obligation, patterns of life prior to the war changed less than has sometimes been depicted. This was even true up to the final war years as the government succeeding in providing materially for the Reich at the expense of the occupied countries. Despite the quasi-militaristic regimentation of public life, mass mobilisation behind the Nazi party and its subsidiary organisations, ubiquitous propaganda, and the intrusion of the state into many private spheres, 'ordinary' Germans were subject to nowhere near the same disruptions as were, for instance, Soviet citizens during the 1930s and 1940s in that other 'totalitarian' state. Terror, for instance, was a near-universal experience in Stalin's USSR, with every citizen a potential suspect for the secret police. In the 'Third Reich' terror was only applied to select groups, and though there was the latent threat of the concentration camps for anyone moved to strident political opposition, as Eric Johnson has shown, the Gestapo proved itself to be very discerning in terms of the types of people and 'crime' that it pursued, anxious not to antagonise the 'desirable' majority.[13]

At the same time the changes wrought in German political and economic life brought substantial benefits at many levels to a majority of the population. Improved welfare provisions compensated for the encroachment on personal freedoms. As Burleigh and Wippermann have shown, there were 'positive' aspects to Nazi population policy for desirable Germans, particularly mothers, newly-weds and the young, albeit that these were all part of the calculation of 'racial' health.[14] The rejuvenated prestige achieved for Germany by Hitler's foreign and rearmament policies outweighed the erosion of political liberties, and the (brutally) successful clampdowns on crime and vagrancy eased any popular misgivings about inhumanities visited on the 'asocial'.[15]

A racist consensus

Many of these social trends had roots in pre-Nazi Germany and indeed western civilisation from the late nineteenth century.

Fears of population stagnation and national decline encouraged inter-war France, for example, in its pro-natalism.[16] Eugenic thinking, already popular in Europe, particularly Scandinavia, and in the USA, where mass, forced sterilisation of the 'unfit' was an accepted state practice,[17] provided the intellectual basis for the Nazi 'law for the prevention of hereditarily ill progeny' and the later 'euthanasia' campaign.[18] Each policy was pursuant to the social-biological notion of the nation as a body whose health could be treated in the same way as an individual body in pursuit of a healthy, homogeneous and productive nation-state.

This was not simply a metaphor. If social problems were perceived in a biological way, they were also ascribed to individual biologies, such that 'asocial' behaviour and forms of criminality alongside 'race' and illness were supposedly hereditary conditions. The 'political police' therefore came into play as 'doctors', alongside the whole state scientific, medical and nursing machinery, which was deeply implicated in Nazism's domestic crimes. And just as the Gestapo developed out of the Prussian secret state police, inheriting some of its operational and ideological precepts and manpower, so too the criminal police, the Reich detective service (Kriminalpolizei), brought with it from the pre-Nazi Prussian police a considerable crossover of personnel and notions of tackling 'degenerate' and 'inherited' criminality in radical new ways.[19] As their powers expanded in the Nazi years, and particularly from 1936, both of these organisations developed wide powers of 'preventive' arrest and incarceration in concentration camps, in what was now openly known as the 'racial-biological fight against crime'.[20] One of the criminal police's main victims was Germany's Romany community, the racialised understanding of 'crime prevention' and social hygiene now giving an explicitly racist and ultimately genocidal slant to centuries-old chauvinism.[21]

Destructive prescriptions for collective health and fitness had analogies at the pan-national level too. As Aly and Heim have shown, a host of German demographers, anthropologists, economists, agronomists, statisticians, regional planners and public health officials all addressed the supposed issue of overpopulation in eastern and south-eastern Europe and advocated the most radical solutions: mass death and mass population removal to render those regions economically viable. Both supporting and contributing to the Generalplan Ost, these planners took it for granted in their calculations that the Jews would 'disappear' from Europe. Aly and Heim quite rightly point out that while the connection between eugenics and Nazi population policy has been widely accepted, hardly any attention has been accorded to this equally prevalent contemporary 'scientific' obsession with over-population,[22] and therein lies the considerable strength of their thesis. However, establishing the existence of ideas such as those of the various 'technocrats' is not the same as ascribing causal importance to them in terms of the development of Nazi Jewish policy. Certainly they added yet another justification for the harsh treatment of the Jews and Slavs, but their contribution was part of a spiralling development, feeding back into the broader racist perceptions and permissive atmosphere that spawned them. The value of examining the role of these individuals is in spanning the breadth of collusion in the Nazi schemes of racial imperialism, and showing how eminently possible it was for ambitious individuals with no demonstrable personal extremism to contribute in a genocidal state by implicitly accepting that the moral ground for decision-making and initiative had shifted, and adjusting their own perspectives accordingly.[23]

Nazism gave vent to each of these tendencies unrestrained by the norms that would otherwise police even the implementation of fashionable 'scientific' doctrines. Or rather, a new set of norms governed, norms arbitrated by the Nazi understanding of the relationship between people as a whole under Germany dominion, the 'valuable' German 'national community' or *Volksgemeinschaft*, the German state, and the rule of law. At the beginning of the process, for those deemed outside the *Volksgemeinschaft*, the notion of the modern-day contract between loyal citizen and (nation-)state was one-sidedly torn up, with the latter not only withdrawing protection from the former's life and property but actually victimising and expropriating it. The extent to which radical racist and pseudo-scientific tendencies were accepted and encouraged on the official plane was on a different level from anything that had gone before in Germany.[24] In their adoption as official policy, their systematisation and codification, they exceeded anything that had theretofore been introduced in even the most antisemitic/racist of European countries – a club to which Germany did not belong before Hitler. During the Second

World War, they would outstrip all others in the quality and quantity of violence they brought forth.

However, the accession of 1933 did not instantly herald the establishment of the totalitarian racial state, nor yet Hitler's assumption of the presidency in 1934. The organs of state had still to be fully co-opted or, as the Nazi terminology had it, 'co-ordinated' with Nazi ideology and aims, notwithstanding the considerable identification of Germany's conservative elites with Hitler's nationalist, anti-leftist and authoritarian goals, and the belief prevalent amongst Germany's approximately 1.5 million civil servants that the Nazi government was an entirely legitimate one.[25] Pressure from Nazi party radicals for more extreme antisemitic measures had to an extent to be balanced over the short term with Hitler's tactical judgements about what established elites, and indeed the wider population and even the outside world, would accept while the Nazi grip on Germany was being consolidated and antisemitism ever more intensively propagated. Even the famous Nuremberg racial laws of 1935, defining who precisely the Nazis considered a Jew to be, and forbidding sexual relations between Jews and non-Jews, had something of this compromise character,[26] while the years 1936–37 have become labelled, entirely relatively, the 'quiet years' of antisemitic agitation, owing in part to Germany's prominence on the world stage with the Berlin Olympics.[27]

The year of 1938 was key simultaneously for the Nazi consolidation of power, the escalation of Hitler's foreign policy programme, and Jewish policy. It was the year of the beginning of 'compulsory Aryanisation',[28] of 'Kristallnacht', and the resultant sharp increase in emigration, as many Jews who had the means to emigrate, but who had been holding on to the hope that the storm would pass, finally gave up.[29] It was the year of the *Anschluss* with Austria and the takeover of the Sudetenland. Joachim von Ribbentrop replaced the conservative Konstantin von Neurath at the helm of the Foreign Office; Hjalmar Schacht was likewise replaced in economic and fiscal policy by Hermann Göring's Organisation for the Four Year Plan. In the military, meanwhile, Hitler appointed himself commander-in-chief of the armed forces, and the pliable Wilhelm Keitel to the head of the High Command of the Armed Forces.[30]

If not immediately externally obvious, 1938 was also marked by the full ascendance in Jewish policy of the security police (Sicherheitspolizei or Sipo, comprised of the Gestapo and the Kriminalpolizei) and the SD, the SS's intelligence agency, under Reinhard Heydrich. These 'political police' forces substituted the visceral but rather uncoordinated antisemitism of the party elite and the SA with a more systematised, bureaucratic-legalistic but no less ideologically committed approach to the persecution of Germany's 'enemies'. From September 1939 they would all be run under the aegis of Heydrich's newly created Reich Security Head Office (RSHA), which more than any other organisation illustrated the fusion of ideological/party functions with administrative/executive/state functions. The leaders of these police forces were a sort of technocratic vanguard of Nazism 'security' and racial policy, equipped with modern surveillance techniques and under the leadership of one of the most ambitious and ruthless men in the Reich. As opposed to the open violence and destruction up to and during Kristallnacht, which had engendered some public unease, though often simply because non-Jewish property was destroyed, these men were responsible for the subsequent incarceration of around 30,000 Jews in concentration camps. This measure was designed to terrorise Germany's remaining Jews into emigration as part of an accelerated and more streamlined policy of making the Reich 'Jew-free'.[31]

The Nazi penetration of the state machinery opened up opportunities for rapid career advancement for comparatively young, ideologically committed bureaucrats. Men like Wilhelm Stückart and Roland Freisler became vastly influential state secretaries in the Ministries of the Interior and Justice.[32] The same was true of entry into even the ordinary German police forces, where upon the Nazi accession preference was swiftly given to Nazi party, SA or SS applicants, and 'uncooperative' individuals were removed, and this on top of the general police bias towards the political right during the Weimar years, as the Freikorps were tolerated and even integrated into the police structure.[33] Many 'cooperative' pre-Nazi officials of course remained in post, and influential. With German territorial expansion and the relative brevity of Nazi rule, there was inadequate time for complete takeover of the bureaucracy, and still a need for trained officials in the established ministries, certainly below the highest, 'Nazified' civil service ranks.[34] These bureaucrats became bound to the Nazi project by their acquiescence in the racist restructuring process, in the same way, but to a greater degree, than ordinary Germans, particularly as the 1933 Law for the Re-establishment of the Professional Civil Service implicated them in their own 'self-cleansing'.

The traditional ministries did not provide the core of 'desk murderers' for the 'final solution'. Nevertheless, institutions such as the Justice and Interior Ministries lent vital expertise and legitimacy to matters such as the legal definition and expropriation of Jews, while the Foreign Office was important in pressurising other governments to surrender their Jews. Ironically, despite Nazi suspicion of what was seen as an overly legalistic, conservative civil service, that very narrow legalism paved the way for the participation of some of these bureaucrats in the process of genocide. The German legal tradition was based not on what was seen as a confusing Anglo-Saxon combination of common law precedents and statutes passed by the legislature, but instead almost solely on the clarity of explicit legislation initiated by the government. It reflected and emphasised the traditional strength of the state rather than individual rights within the state.[35]

But since genuine identification with radical Nazi goals was important in Hitler's scheme, it should not be surprising that the real manpower and machinery for genocide was to be found in new organisations created from 1933 to supplement and compete with existing state organs, and those created from 1939 to run the conquered territories. Pre-eminent in the former category was the SS; in the latter category, the various forms of administration appointed in occupied eastern Europe. When we add to these organisations the wartime ascendancy in the Nazi economy of the 'new power centres' such as Albert Speer's Armaments Ministry,[36] and, earlier, of Göring's Organisation for the Four Year Plan, we begin to see the extent to which bureaucracy in the genocidal phase of the Third Reich was far from 'traditional' or apolitical.

The personnel staffing key Nazi institutions represent in some ways a radical microcosm of the most enthusiastic Nazi constituencies. As a simplification, the most aggressive, nationalist elements in inter-war Germany can be divided into two groups: first, those who were deeply impressed by the First World War 'front-experience' (*Fronterlebnis*) and took this militaristic ethos back into civilian life, whether through simply supporting anti-Weimar parties or even joining right-wing paramilitary organisations such as the Freikorps; second, those who were too young to join the actual First World War 'battle community' (*Kampfgemeinschaft*) but were socialised and educated in the bitter aftermath of defeat, imbibed the mythology of the war, identified strongly with the embattled German 'ethnic community' (*Volksgemeinschaft*) shaped by the earlier generation, and sought their opportunity to avenge Germany's loss.[37] These related models of the German community promised a society where class distinctions were downplayed in the interests of a larger whole, but which did not go down the universalist road of communism.

The first category produced most of the early members of the Nazi party, the so-called 'old fighters' (*älte Kämpfer*), some of the longest-standing antisemites of conviction, many with personal ties of loyalty to Hitler, from whom were drawn the class of Nazi regional leaders, or *Gauleiter*.[38] These also went on to provide the leadership of civil occupation governments, men such as Hinrich Lohse, head of the Reichskommissariat Ostland, Erich Koch of the Reichskommissariat Ukraine and the Bialystok district,[39] and Arthur Greiser of the Warthegau. The same age and experience cohort provided a generation of front-line military officers from 1914 to 1918, men who would enter the Second World War as staff officers determined not to allow a repeat of the 'stab in the back' by 'Judeo-Bolshevism'.[40] Finally, the milieu also produced a high proportion of the higher SS and police leaders (HSSPFs), a select group established by Himmler in 1937 to orchestrate joint police operations within their respective geographical spheres, and some of the most enthusiastic murderers in the Nazi occupation hierarchy.[41]

The second age category provided what Ulrich Herbert describes as 'the nucleus of the Nazi policies of persecution and genocide', the leadership corps of the RSHA. This group consisted at the beginning of the war of about 300 men, and went on to constitute the leadership of the Einsatzgruppen, and, after the establishment of civilian administrations in the occupied countries, of the political police outposts, including the vital positions of commander and commander-in-chief of the security police and SD. Through the RSHA's 'Jewish office' within the Gestapo and under Adolf Eichmann, they also coordinated the deportations of the western, central and southern European Jews. As well as being younger than the other elites of the Third Reich, they were better educated than party leaders and from more elevated social backgrounds: in 1939, two-thirds of the top Gestapo and SD leaders were under 36, and almost as many had university degrees, with a concentration in law.[42]

The predominance of lawyers – as they had predominated in the traditional German civil service – was not simply a smokescreen or legal fig leaf, the Nazi suspicion of legal strictures notwithstanding. Many welcomed the career prospects opened up by these new organisations after the huge academic unemployment of the Weimar years, and became enthusiastic recruits to the Nazi cause. Legal mechanisms were important to the concerted state assault on Nazism's 'internal enemies', even within the SS, which was to become an extra-legal organisation. In so far as it is possible to identify a developed political philosophy of Nazism it is in the writings of these young Nazi jurists, as well as of more advanced if equally misdirected theorists such as Carl Schmitt, an assailant of the principle of equality of nations under international law.[43] Perhaps the key SS theorist, a fundamental influence on the shaping of the SD and the RSHA, was Werner Best (1903–89).

Best's was not necessarily a 'Nazi' world-view as such. He preferred '*Volk*' over the more nebulous, international 'race' as a fundamental philosophical concept, and did not always support the prioritisation of the 'final solution' over other considerations, as for instance during the early months of his period in charge of the German administration in Denmark from November 1942. He was nevertheless entirely open to co-optation by Nazism given the shared common ground and his respect for Hitler's dynamic leadership. He was also convinced that the Jews were injurious to the German national body and needed at the least to be removed from the German sphere, and was himself implicated in the murder process in Poland from September 1939 and France from mid-1941. Like so many others of his generation and educational background he had set himself against the perceived injustices of the Versailles settlement, rejecting the international order and fledgling international law. He sought to render domestic law wholly into an instrument of the will of an appropriately aligned leader, whose role in turn would be to protect the German *Volksgemeinschaft*, including those millions of eastern Germans separated from the fatherland by the post-First World War settlement. The role of the 'political police' in all of this was to guard the 'health of the German national body', to quell threats to that health by any means necessary and without the need for any formal 'statutory legitimation'. Perpetual struggle between competing peoples was envisaged, and the recognition of that struggle, and of the cool ruthlessness needed to wage it, without irrational hatred but with 'objective' judgement of the national interest, constituted Best's self-avowed 'heroic realism'.[44]

As an aside, it is noteworthy how many of the Nazi perpetrators originated from peripheral or 'lost' German or Habsburg lands, the regions with whose Germanic inhabitants Best so keenly identified. Peter Black notes the disproportionate representation of Austrians in Nazi ranks, including of course Hitler himself, but also other notables such as Eichmann, Ernst Kaltenbrunner, Heydrich's successor as RSHA chief, and Rudolf Höß, commandant of Auschwitz.[45] Austrians were also highly represented in the occupation administration in Poland.[46] To cite but a few other indicative examples, Globocnik was from multinational Triest, Rosenberg from the Baltic region and Greiser from Posen (Poznan), a region lost to Poland after the First World War, and to which he was returned as head of the Nazi administration in October 1939.[47] In the comparative connection, the importance of these constituencies from outside Germany's pre-1938 borders was mirrored at the time in radicalised Magyars from lost Hungarian territories, and was foretold decades earlier by the makeup of the murderous Young Turk elite, many of whom too were drawn from lost or threatened Ottoman lands.

A vital part of understanding the development of the 'final solution' is thus understanding that policy-making and implementation increasingly fell to the most extreme elements in the 'Third Reich', in a process that was partially self-selecting. Michael Mann's study of 1,500 biographies of camp staff and doctors, 'euthanasia' killers, Einsatzgruppen and other security police members and party perpetrators only confirms this: that on the 'cutting edge' of Nazi genocidal policy too, perpetrators were drawn disproportionately from 'core' Nazi socio-economic constituencies. Two-thirds of his sample were long-established party members, one-third had been pre-war extremists, many criminals, and, unsurprisingly, there was a correlation between length of involvement in the cause and commitment to its policies.[48] But the selection process was not governed by depth of ideological commitment alone. Other characteristics were important, particularly drive, ambition, ruthlessness, initiative, and also an eye for the main chance.

Jeremy Noakes and Ian Kershaw have respectively illustrated the importance of some of these qualities with reference to one particular document, a record of a 1934 speech by one Werner Willikens, a state secretary in the Agriculture Ministry. Hitler's charismatic – and therefore aloof – ruling style, the informal and unstructured nature of his governance, and his dislike of formal channels and modes of decision-making, led Willikens to conclude that

> everyone with a post in the new Germany has worked best when he has, so to speak, worked towards the Führer. Very often and in many spheres it has been the case ... that individuals have simply waited for orders and instructions ... but in fact it is the duty of everybody to try to work towards the Führer along the lines he would wish. Anyone who makes mistakes will notice it soon enough. But anyone who really works towards the Führer along his lines and towards his goal will certainly both now and in the future one day have the finest reward in the form of the sudden legal confirmation of his work.[49]

The same point was made equally well in William Sheridan Allen's 1965 study of the Nazi seizure of power in the central German town of Thalburg. While concluding that 'Hitler, Goebbels, and the other Nazi leaders provided the political decisions, ideology, national propaganda, and, later, the control over the government which made the revolution possible', he also made clear that 'Thalburg's Nazis created their own image by their own initiative, vigor and propaganda. They knew exactly what needed to be done to effect the transfer of power to themselves in the spring of 1933, and they did it apparently without more than generalized directives from above.'[50] And though neither of these instances concerned Jewish policy *per se*, they provide an insight into what is now generally accepted as the rough model of how policy developed almost by consensus, with actors at the geographical and/or power 'periphery' not only accommodating initiatives from the power centre, but also anticipating them and looking to 'improvise'[51] new measures thought to be in accord with the general policy thrust.

One result of the importance in a competitive sense of Nazi *Judenpolitik* was the involvement in it of men who might otherwise have pursued their careers in other directions. Some, like Best, had obvious ideological commitment to Nazi goals but were not obsessed with Jewish policy; others, like Heinrich Müller, head of the Gestapo, and Martin Luther, head of the Foreign Office department containing its 'Jewish desk', seem to have been more motivated by opportunism.[52]

Establishing a genocidal system

The quest for the imprimatur of interpreter of the Führer's will led to competition between individuals and organisations even at the highest levels. This was further encouraged by the Hitlerian government system. Peter Hüttenberger labelled it 'polycratic', owing to the number of different power centres effectively pitted against each other in the absence of clearly delineated jurisdiction over policy spheres and lines of authority.[53] Such competition was not in itself novel, being a feature of authoritarian systems as diverse as Byzantium and Imperial Germany,[54] but the rationale was perhaps different, being less of simple divide and rule, and more a physical expression of the doctrine of social Darwinism, with its emphasis on struggle for survival. A glance at the rise of the SS gives an impression of how the system functioned.

By 1936 the SS had established centralised authority over the concentration camp network and all German police organisations, including the regular 'non-political police' or Ordnungspolizei. The former had been achieved over competition from the SA, which had established a series of its own camps in 1933–34; the latter was achieved in the face of Göring, who had tried early on to maintain control of the Gestapo in Prussia, and of the Interior Ministry, which wished to subordinate the political police in the larger police network that up to 1936 was under its jurisdiction.[55] Control of the police also made the *Gauleiter* more dependent on the SS for intelligence.[56] Himmler was now positioned *de jure* within the Ministry of the Interior but the Minister (Wilhelm Frick) had no *de facto* control over him; in 1943, Himmler would himself be appointed minister anyway. The SS was becoming a 'state within a state', increasingly powerful and independent of the requisites of legislation and normal legal recourse, as the political police's mandate for 'preventative incarceration' showed. (One response from the Justice Ministry was to advise judges to put more people in 'preventive detention' themselves to avoid being outdone by the police.[57]) This was graphically illustrated in a wartime agreement between Himmler and the Reich Justice Minister, Thierack, to transfer 'asocial' elements from prison to the concentration camps for 'extermination through work'.[58]

Himmler's personal authority expanded yet further when upon the invasion of Poland Hitler appointed him RKFDV, and then again in March 1941 when Hitler assigned him the 'special tasks' accompanying the forthcoming invasion of the Soviet Union.[59] He was not, though, to find the other agencies establishing themselves in the east as accommodating as the Justice Ministry in surrendering their assumed prerogatives, particularly not Hans Frank's regime in the Generalgouvernement.[60] Nevertheless, whether it be in the first instance denying the civil administrations in Poland in their desire to have their territories rendered *'Judenrein'* by deportation further east, as the movement of *Volksdeutsche* was temporarily given priority, or, later on, murdering skilled Jewish labourers required by the Generalgouvernement and Wehrmacht authorities, the SS stamped its authority on Jewish policy. Beyond this, the war years saw Himmler mount a significant challenge to the military monopoly of the army as the Waffen-SS grew exponentially and took its place alongside the regular army on the Third Reich's battlefields.[61]

Himmler's success in internecine competition was replicated within the SS itself. The Wannsee conference is a case in point. As well as its function in orchestrating the ongoing 'final solution', the conference was an attempt by the convenor Heydrich simultaneously to implicate the civilian agencies of the Third Reich and to establish the authority of his office in the process; hence his ostentatious reference in the invitations to Göring's written authorisation of that authority on 31 July 1941.[62] However this was not just a question of asserting the SS over, for instance, the Reich Chancellery, the Four Year Plan Organisation, Rosenberg's Eastern Ministry or Luther's department in the Foreign Office, but also over other SS offices such as the 'Race and Settlement Office', which had its own stake in Jewish policy,[63] and perhaps also over the HSSPFs, who were making headway of their own in 'solving the Jewish question', as with Globocnik in Lublin, and others – of whom more shortly – in the USSR.

Heydrich's vigorous leadership of the political police forces had already seen him become first among equals among Himmler's immediate subordinates. The RSHA's rise had been meteoric, from its establishment in 1939 to its foremost role in 'security' policy in the USSR and Heydrich's commission by Göring. This was all tacitly accepted, for instance, by Kurt Daluege, the head of the Ordnungspolizei, despite his parity in rank with Heydrich, and the fact that they were both leaders of SS head offices (*Hauptämter*). The importance of the personal factor in Third Reich politics was again illustrated as Heydrich was assassinated. Under the leadership of the less driven Kaltenbrunner, from December 1943, the RSHA fragmented somewhat[64] and lost ground relatively in the SS power-play to the SS Business-Administration Head Office (Wirtschafts- Verwaltungshauptamt; WVHA) under Oswald Pohl, which controlled the rapidly expanding concentration camp network.

Himmler had long been cognisant of the tendencies of the various SS head offices to in-fighting and empire-building, and anyway feared losing control of a rapidly growing organisation.[65] In 1937 he created the institution of the HSSPF with the intention of establishing a direct line of control over the SS and police forces operating within their respective regional remits. The success of this measure varied directly with the extent and strength of the pre-existing power structures within the relevant region, thus the HSSPFs in Germany developed nowhere near the influence of those in newly invaded territories where they could establish themselves on virgin political territory.[66] (Paradoxically, some of the SSPFs in the Generalgouvernement then went on to pursue their own mini empire-building agendas, sometimes on the back of Jewish labour.[67] Himmler in turn sought to bring any Jews that were not immediately killed in Operation Reinhard into a closed, WVHA-run concentration camp economy.[68])

The HSSPFs were assigned authority in joint actions of different police agencies during invasion and occupation. They played a pivotal role in the aggregate of individual shootings and in the expansion of the killing programme, and signpost the direct involvement of Himmler in the development of the 'final solution'. In many locales their murder tolls vastly exceeded those of the

Einsatzgruppen. Thus the conglomerate forces of Friedrich Jeckeln, HSSPF for the southern Soviet Union (based in Kiev), murdered 44,125 Jews in August 1941 alone. He began to murder all Jews, irrespective of age or sex, even before the Einsatzgruppe (C) in the vicinity.[69] So influential was he in the developing murder process that in October 1941 a sub-section of Einsatzgruppe C, Einsatzkommando 4a, anxiously reported back to Berlin that it too had been involved in the killings, which were not the achievement of the HSSPF alone.[70] Pohl's study of Einsatzgruppe C in fact reveals that the squad 'had nowhere near the significance for the war of annihilation in the Ukraine that is often attributed to it': of the approximately 1,400,000 Jews murdered there, the Einsatzgruppe claimed to have accounted for approximately 118,000, all except 45,000 of whom were killed in conjunction with Jeckeln's forces.[71]

Jeckeln's counterpart in the central area of the occupied Soviet Union, HSSPF Erich von dem Bach-Zelewski, was equally important in the development of the 'final solution'. As with Jeckeln, when the murder of Soviet Jewry intensified from mid-July 1941, the turning point from the killings of the initial racist 'security policy' to almost total killing in that sphere, he was accorded regional authority over the vastly increased SS and police manpower then assigned to the USSR.[72] The context or at least pretext for this increase in manpower was a Hitler announcement that in the consolidation of German rule in the newly conquered territories it was fortunate Stalin had made his 3 July call for partisan warfare against the invaders. This gave Germany the opportunity to annihilate all hostile elements: 'in this vast area, peace must be imposed as quickly as possible, and to achieve this it is necessary to shoot anyone who even looks oddly at us'. (Similarly, the actions of Tito's partisans in Yugoslavia from the early summer of 1941 'legitimated' the rapid intensification of anti-Serbian and particularly anti-Jewish measures.) One vital consequence was the delegation to Himmler and his plenipotentiaries of responsibility for all security-related matters in the USSR.[73]

Overall, from mid-July, 5,500 order policemen were posted to the USSR, alongside a larger build-up in the General-gouvernement. Added to these were the 25,000 men of Himmler's personal murder battalions, the Kommandostab Reichsführer-SS,[74] composed of Waffen-SS men, and also a large number of local auxiliaries.[75] Together these forces greatly exceeded the 3,000-strong Einsatzgruppen whose numbers were inadequate for 'policing' the huge space assigned to them.[76] Each would participate in Nazi genocide and population policy, as would many Wehrmacht soldiers. As civilian governments were established in the 'pacified' Soviet territories, and the policy of murder spread back westwards into the formerly Polish territories, and also into Serbia, the murder machinery was further augmented from outwith the ranks of the SS and police.[77]

What does this vision of the Nazi system tell us? The murder of the Jews has sometimes been represented as a bureaucratic affair, most famously by Hilberg, Zygmunt Bauman and Arendt, and in a slightly different way by Martin Broszat and Hans Mommsen. Unlike the latter two, the first three were concerned less with locating immediate initiative for genocide in the middle ranks of the executive than with making theoretical statements about the potentialities of modern bureaucracy. The stimulating nature of these analyses notwithstanding, it may be more helpful to conceptualise the destruction process in the terms of the business rather than the administrative world. This gets us away from the idea of a disinterested, apolitical bureaucracy, which much of the bureaucracy of the Third Reich was not, and it is more appropriate for the incorporation of extra-legal, overtly ideological executive organs such as the SS. It also introduces the idea of competition and even conflict, both of which were certainly present in Nazi *Judenpolitik*, and yet are less conspicuous in classic conceptions of bureaucracy.

Where in the free marketplace the ground-rules of capitalist competition are self-evident, the aims of profit-making implicitly accepted, in the 'racial state' of the Third Reich the same was true of racist assumptions. Thus Aly and Heim are incorrect to regard their 'architects of annihilation' as amoral technocrats, even though that may be how these Germans perceived themselves. Instead, they were operating according to very particular ideological tenets: namely that Jews and Slavs were at the bottom of the racial ladder, and were therefore fair game as subjects for their schemes. Similarly, the civilian officials in the Generalgouvernement who opted to lower rations for ghettoised Jews did so because it was an unwritten assumption that Jews should be the first to go without, something which the literal reading of documents alone from the period does not always transmit. Browning's study of two managers of the Polish ghettos illustrates how these men, 'neither hard-core party activists nor fanatic anti-Semites', who had once laboured to make the ghettos productive, self-sustaining economic units, obediently adapted their outlook when it was clear that extermination was now the overall aim. As Browning writes, 'they never questioned that there was a Jewish question that had to be solved, and they never believed that the ghetto was the ultimate solution ... When signals came from Berlin that a new policy was at hand ... their acceptance of and accommodation to this new policy was a foregone conclusion.'[78] The same pattern can be observed in the Foreign Office Jewish desk late in 1941.[79]

Whatever competition and conflict there was in the system over other matters, the principle of anti-Jewishness was accepted by everyone that mattered. To use an expression from the marketplace, Jewish policy was one of *the* growth areas. Owing to the importance attached by the regime to the 'Jewish question' in 1933–45, the prize of influence in the area was correspondingly great. In the system Hitler created, or, more appropriately, encouraged to grow up around him, authority was not the indisputable possession of any given person or office. Power was there to be fought for, and was the prize for the most dynamic element. In a very real sense, business loved competition in Nazi Germany and, without taking the metaphor too far, it is no coincidence that Germany's post-war economic miracle was founded upon the dynamism and inventiveness of industrialists and businessmen socialised under Nazism. Amid shifting factions and power bases, as in business competition, innovation was the name of the game: the provision of new 'solutions' to the 'Jewish question'.

Beyond this potential for radicalisation in the Nazi system, more purely contingent circumstance also played a key role in developing Jewish policy: the shifting world situation of the 1930s, for instance, or the course of German military campaigning in 1939–42. Yet though these did not always present opportunities or problems that Hitler had clearly anticipated, they were pursuant to an intertwined foreign and racial policy that had as its basis the related notions of revising the terms of Versailles, securing 'living space' and the raw materials to supply that living space, and racially reordering the territory accruing to the Reich. Conquests prepared the ground for leaps of the Nazi imagination as new vistas opened up in terms of the sheer space conquered and the reality of vastly extended power, while at the same time exacerbating logistical and conceptual problems regarding what to do with the ever-increasing number of Slavic and Jewish 'undesirables' under Nazi rule.

The east was a playground for the most extreme racial fantasies, as the Generalplan Ost showed. The sensibilities of the 'inferior' populations mattered not at all to the occupiers, with anti-Slavism arguably just as strong as antisemitism for many Germans. The Nazis sought to import into Europe the settler colonialism that the European nations had hitherto reserved for the extra-European world, alongside the sort of racist contempt for the local peoples that had hitherto been reserved for non-whites.[80] The effects of settler policies had already been shown to be catastrophic for native peoples in the Americas, Africa and Australasia in terms of direct and indirect killing by the settling powers – and all this even without the extremes of Nazi ideology coming into play. In the specific case of Wilhelmine German imperialism, Jürgen Zimmerer for one has sought to establish a close link in terms of occupation mentality and the 'breaking of a taboo' between Nazi occupation in eastern Europe and the genocide from 1904 of at least 65,000 Hereros by the German army in southwest Africa.[81] It is well known that Hitler spoke of making the Ukraine into Germany's India, and, indeed, Rosenberg's Eastern Ministry was supposedly modelled on the British India Office.[82] Of the Generalgouvernement, Black writes that it 'served as *the* laboratory for the implementation of both Nazi annihilation and resettlement policies ... where the police-colonial culture of which the SS claimed to be the exponent would be planned, conceived, and hatched'.[83]

Displacement of all the Polish Jews was inevitable on the invasion in September 1939. One of the Einsatzgruppen then deployed – the 'Einsatzgruppe von Woyrsch' – instantly began trying to terrorise Jews into fleeing over the Soviet–German demarcation line, and pursued this policy until the Soviets closed the border.[84] As early as October, groups of Reich Jews were deported to the Lublin district on the demarcation line in pursuance of the 'Nisko plan' to concentrate all Jews under German rule in a reservation in the Generalgouvernement. When the plan had to be radically curtailed owing to the RKFDV's movement of ethnic Germans, it was replaced briefly in some minds on the defeat of France by the mooted scheme to deport to the French colony of Madagascar.[85] Whatever the destination – and on Operation Barbarossa attention was turned to the vast Russian spaces – the Polish ghettos constructed in 1940 were supposed to be temporary collection points for Jews on the way out of the German sphere.

The invasion of the Soviet Union set the tone for yet more extreme racial policy given the scope of the Einsatzgruppen's initial killing orders and the Wehrmacht's understanding of its task as fighting an 'ideological war' outside the normal laws of war and civilisation. This greater moral permissiveness was not, however, initially matched in the Reich and the Polish territories by 'progress' in ridding those areas of their Jews, except in Eastern Galicia, the province attached to the Generalgouvernement in July 1941, where mass killing instantly began, and which provided a sort of policy 'bridge' between the Soviet and Polish territories. The design to deport the Jews to beyond the Urals could, inherently, only be enacted at the end of the German–Soviet war. It was predicated upon *Blitzkrieg* victory facilitated by the encirclement and annihilation of the bulk of the Red Army before they could retreat into the interior and regroup, thus also isolating Britain within Europe and concluding the war before the USA might join.[86] None of these ends was achieved.

Not only were the self-imposed supply and disease problems of the Polish ghettos continually exacerbating, they were compounded by pressure from the German *Gauleiter*, from Greiser in the Warthegau, and from the authorities in the Protectorate, to fulfil their mandates to free their areas of Jews, while at the same time Hans Frank was vigorously opposed to allowing more into the Generalgouvernement. If the decision to begin deporting the central European Jews in mid-September 1941 was due to revived 'euphoria' amid Wehrmacht progress towards Kiev, that optimism was lost by the beginning of December and the failure of the assault on Moscow.[87] If the post-war 'territorial solution' was now a long way off, the 'Jewish question' now had to be answered *in situ* in the eastern areas under German control, either in one fell swoop or, as was contended earlier, more likely at first in a series of more-or-less parallel, piecemeal regional measures, as in

Lithuania initially, then Galicia and the Warthegau.[88]

Therefore Hitler not only set the general ideological tone but also provided the military and expansionist context for further radicalisation. Himmler provided more direct and precise management from the power centre. In November 1941, he rebuked Jeckeln, now HSSPF for the northern USSR region, for ordering the shooting in Riga of 1,000 Jews arriving from the Reich, disregarding his instructions and those of the RSHA.[89] Clearly at that point the wholesale slaughter of deported German Jews was still too sensitive a matter,[90] perhaps because of concerns over the effect on German public opinion and even in some quarters a residual sense of cultural connectedness, but the importance here of the episode is to illustrate that the parameters and progress of Nazi *Judenpolitik* were still policed from the power centre. On occasion, Himmler was not above rearranging his personnel for maximum effect, as when at the beginning of 1942 he replaced some of the SS and police leaders in the Generalgouvernement whom he considered insufficiently extreme.[91] There is increasing evidence, gleaned in part from the discovery of his appointments diary in the Moscow 'special archive', of Himmler's direct involvement in driving the murder process, often after meetings with Hitler.[92] This was repeatedly manifest in visits to the eastern killing grounds to cajole and encourage the SS and police killers as well, of course, as maintaining his stamp on this most important ideological project.

On 12 August 1941, for instance, he met with Jeckeln, and at the beginning of October toured the Ukraine, both times to urge expansions of the circle of victims.[93] On 17 April 1942, he ordered the killing of western European Jews in the Lodz ghetto.[94] It is of particular significance that on Heydrich's assassination he personally took over the RSHA, from June to December 1942.[95] In this capacity he made some of the seminal decisions of the 'final solution'. On 19 July 1942, after meetings with Hitler and at the end of a tour of Polish killing centres, he ordered HSSPF Krüger of the Generalgouvernment to complete the murder of the region's Jews by the end of the year – the date that was to mark the end of his tenure at the RSHA helm. Three days later, deportations began to Treblinka from the largest ghetto, that of Warsaw, and by the beginning of September 310,000 of the surviving 380,000 ghetto inhabitants had been murdered. Himmler also contrived in that fateful half year to accelerate vastly the deportation of western European Jews from France, Belgium and the Netherlands to the extermination centres.[96]

This acceleration in killing from the time of Himmler's takeover of the RSHA corresponds approximately to that identified by Longerich over the course of May–July 1942.[97] It would also explain the significance of naming the murder of the Generalgouvernement's Jews 'the Reinhard action' if at the time of Heydrich's death there was a discernible radicalisation of the killing policy rather than just a continuation of pre-existing practice. In more general terms, interventions such as these from the power centre did not make the regional players wait for instructions – they were not automata. Quite the opposite: the atmosphere of ever-expanding killing and permissiveness encouraged local initiative in what Wendy Lower has aptly termed 'anticipatory obedience'.[98] The Einsatzgruppen leaders for one had been carefully selected by Heydrich in collaboration with Himmler on the basis of their initiative and independence.[99] The technical leadership of the WVHA also developed a belief in what Michael Thad Allen describes as the 'double-edged' nature of their subordinates' duties, which 'demand submission to large, impersonal institutions but also bestow the power to control and exploit the capacity of concerted organisation'.[100]

The term 'cumulative radicalisation' was coined by Mommsen in the context of his functionalist interpretation of Nazi policy-making.[101] It remains appropriate, if in a somewhat modified form, in assessing the way in which *Judenpolitik* developed. We should think of it as describing the momentum built up in a partly self-selecting, partly self-driven Jewish policy underpinned by a general racist consensus, unchecked by opposing views in the state, and feeding off foreign policy developments that increased its ambit and freed it ever more from 'moral' restraint. Further, at key points, initiatives from the very highest Reich authorities showed the way forward, often by Himmler's personal example.

There was little capital to be made anywhere in the system by suggesting more lenient treatment for Jews, and it was almost impossible to maintain consensus in other than a negative direction given the underlying assumption of hatred at the highest level and the premium put on finding ever more extreme expressions of that hatred. Thus the in-built limitations on projects such as the use of Jewish slave labour, which had a constructive potential (in purely instrumental terms),[102] or on the idea, which was taken very seriously from mid-1942 onwards, of exchanging specific Jews for Germans outside the German sphere of influence.[103] Although Jewish policy developed somewhat unevenly in different spheres and in different regions of occupied Europe, it nevertheless reached the same endpoint by these different routes, and not as a result of value-free bureaucratic problem solving, but because of the pro-activity of individuals and institutions with personal and professional and, if by no means always, ideological stakes in radicalism.

Some perpetrator types

As Thomas Sandkühler has written, the perpetration process was *'arbeitsteilig'*, or based on a division of labour. Such were the variety of functions involved that no all-embracing explanation of perpetrator motive will suffice. Perhaps the one common factor was the knowledge of each perpetrator in each Nazi genocide that they were involved in a project that was tacitly state-sanctioned and thus in at least some narrow sense 'legitimate'. This is at the heart of the application of the famous 'Milgram test' to the question of participation.

In the Milgram tests, the eponymous psychologist illustrated the extent to which obedience to authority and group conformity are instilled through socialisation and evolution. His naive subjects participated in a 'learning experiment' where at the behest of a supposed scientific authority they were to apply increasingly powerful electric shocks to a victim actor according to his responses. The increasingly pained (fake) reactions of the 'victim' were played through to the naive subjects, who nevertheless in two-thirds of the cases tested continued to inflict pain up to the extreme level.[104] Paying attention to historical context only serves to reinforce the applicability of what might otherwise be dismissed as a piece of pop psychology.

It is not to subscribe to stereotypes of German authoritarianism to observe that deferential and/or patriotic obedience, the imperative to 'obey orders', was significantly greater in a central European ethnically defined society in the 1940s in the course of a world war, when the authority figures were representatives of a radical state, than in the increasingly pluralistic USA in the 1960s when the authority figure was a scientist. Nationalistic loyalty, 'my country right or wrong', has thankfully lost some of its force since the Second World War, but in the fifty years or so from the late nineteenth century it was the single most potent social bond, and as the example of Germany (alongside the other warring powers) for most of the First World War showed, it had the capacity to transcend class and most party-political boundaries even under the severest pressure.

Though it may have been taken to extremes by German civil servants and by men like Best, the belief in positivism, in the state as bearer of ultimate authority in a moral as well as a legal sense, would not be properly challenged anywhere on the world stage until the post-war Nuremberg trials.[105] Perpetrators at all stages of the hierarchy could take direction and psychological comfort from the existence of 'higher orders' or permissiveness.[106] This is only to plead for historical understanding, not moral or legal mitigation, nor to accept the totalitarian caricature of the Nazi system provided by both defence *and* prosecution at Nuremberg.[107] An individual's 'inward' focus upon what was in the perceived interest of the state (and/or him or herself as well) rather than simply an 'outward' focus on the hatred of Jews may explain firstly why so many perpetrators killed at all, and secondly why so many killed others as well as Jews.

A few other generalisations may also be made about the killing machine. The first concerns the mentality characterising German personnel posted to the east. The civil authorities of the Polish and Soviet territories lived in what Pohl has called an 'occupation climate', where feelings of ethnic or racial superiority were compounded by a siege mentality of living among enemy populations during wartime and a sense of being the German frontline in an ideological war. They provided a general stimulus to specific criminal acts.[108] A counter-example which tends to prove this point negatively is Browning's study of an order police unit stationed in Upper Silesia. These men, atypically, were drawn from populations in or near the area, and were less swiftly barbarised than parallel units elsewhere. Being acquainted with the area and often the people over whom they were supposed to be wielding the power of life and death, they were less inclined to dehumanise the Jews.[109]

The civilian regimes in the east would often endorse the murder process and even exhort greater speed in making their areas Jew-free. At the Wannsee conference Generalgouvernement State-Secretary Josef Bühler requested priority for the 'final solution' in that region on Hans Frank's behalf; and throughout the acceleration of the killing process there in 1942, German civil officials were at the forefront in pressing for 'unproductive' Jews to be killed and cooperated in orchestrating the deportations.[110] The role of Greiser's civil administration in the Warthegau was even more significant, for there he played perhaps the foremost role in driving the extermination process. The authorities of Rosenberg's Eastern Ministry were just as deeply implicated, even though they only established themselves after the 'first sweep' of Einsatzgruppen and police killings in the summer of 1941.[111]

Beyond the highest ranks, two further generalisations can be made. Firstly, the staff of the civil administrations were appointed because they already shared the ideological priorities of the regime, even if some only volunteered because they saw an opportunity for rapid career advancement. Secondly, as Pohl suggests, their qualifications for administrative responsibilities, at least on the scale they faced in post, diminished from western to eastern Europe. Those appointed to Eastern Galicia from July 1941, for instance, had failed to prove themselves in the Generalgouvernement. Yet they were still charged with the enactment of what – in the early days at least – was only a vaguely defined, if extreme Jewish policy, in an atmosphere free from moral restraint and traditional social ties and networks and the stability they bring. Corruption was also rife, lending motivation to some involved in expropriating Jews, and contrary to another stereotype of the frictionless murder machinery; the Generalgouvernement ('GG') was known colloquially in Nazi circles as the 'Gangster-Gau'.[112] The administrators in the east were often also few in number, particularly in rural areas; thus even with the SS and police build-up in the Generalgouvernement during the first half of 1942, other local agencies – railway police and officials, customs officials and Wehrmacht units – were solicited for assistance, which they frequently provided out of a 'perverted spirit of cooperation'.[113]

The colonial administrators rather blur the distinction between bureaucrats and direct executioners. Nevertheless, the majority of the actual work of killing everywhere was done by military, and particularly paramilitary and police units, as in fact is true of most 'modern' genocides. The political police, the Waffen-SS, the order police and local auxiliary forces made up the main contingents of killers, and it is to them we now turn. About them, too, we can make certain statements of broad if not total applicability concerning the governing ethos of the institutions in which they served.

The German army is an interesting case because of the latter-day sensitivity among the German public about the complicity in genocide of this pre-Nazi organisation that was in its self-image apolitical, and in which 15–18 million people served. There is actually little space for legitimate historical debate about military complicity. Under the terms of an agreement of spring 1941 between the High Command of the Wehrmacht and the SS, the Einsatzgruppen were given freedom of operation in the army's sphere of authority in Serbia and the USSR, unlike in Poland.[114] The squads were under the administrative control of the army, however, and the latter supplied them with logistical support, protection, and sometimes also manpower in the massacres. Some army units also periodically undertook 'Jew-hunts' of their own. The military was prepared to open up POW camps to the Einsatzgruppen which combed the population for 'politically suspect' elements who were then shot, and it shot many such individuals itself. We have already seen that it was implicated in the starving of Soviet POWs, the murder of institutional patients and Romanies, and a brutal, criminal anti-partisan conflict. 'Partisan warfare' everywhere from the time of Operation Barbarossa would be met with extreme violence, as later in Greece and Italy, but it was probably most pronounced in Serbia and Belarus where, alongside massive atrocities against the non-Jewish populations, the anti-Jewish actions of the army shaded almost completely into genocide.[115]

Given the scope of this violence and the different types of victim, we are instantly obliged to say that antisemitism cannot have been the whole story as regards motivation for the military. Any explanation must begin with the recognition that for the army 1941 was a more important turning point than 1939, much more clearly so than in Jewish policy as a whole. Alexander Rossino's study of Wehrmacht involvement in anti-Jewish atrocities in

1939–40 adduces insufficient evidence that this was anything other than localised and relatively infrequent,[116] and there are indeed indications that the army protested against the brutality of the SS and police,[117] hence the clear Hitlerian pronouncement on the SS's increased powers in 1941. (Perversely, and reinforcing the image of inter-agency competition, when the army managed to entrench its authority *vis-à-vis* the SS in France from 1940, it was then obliged to institute what became genocidal policies in order to maintain its primacy.[118]) The army's involvement in Jewish policy in the Generalgouvernement was more focused on exploiting Jewish labour, sometimes fighting the SS for the preservation of 'its' Jewish workforce.[119]

This is not to suggest that the army was not becoming increasingly 'Nazified'. Omer Bartov has uncovered extensive evidence of the political subversion of military norms and even military organisation, and of the extensive indoctrination of the troops.[120] This was only strengthened by the racist and even downright genocidal exhortations of commanders such as Field Marshal Walter von Reichenau.[121] Moreover, we have already seen that Hitler's 1938 changes in the leadership of the Wehrmacht were designed to 'coordinate' the institution with Nazism. The differences between war in the Polish and Soviet theatres were, however, manifold. For a start, Poland was swiftly and totally pacified; the war against the much larger and more formidable Soviet Union, a war seen as a matter of life and death for Germany, went on until the German collapse. A second factor is the explicitly ideological nature of the highly propagandised 'anti-Bolshevik' war. In this propaganda, the purported Judeo-Bolshevik connection was strongly emphasised.

For Christian Streit, a more 'traditional' fear of communism amongst the military elite, spilling over into antisemitism, rather than total conformity with Hitler's brand of antisemitism, was the chief motivation behind the army's ruthless conduct of the war in the east.[122] Hannes Heer, however, suggests that the army completely bought into the Judeo-Bolshevik connection, not least because of the strength of the stab-in-the-back myth from the First World War,[123] a paranoia given spurious legitimacy by Stalin's order for partisan warfare and by the actions of Tito's communist partisans. The cynical equation of male Jews with partisans certainly provided the backdrop to the army's actions in Serbia and

Belarus from the autumn of 1941, albeit in the context of the imperative for occupation authorities to 'solve' their Jewish questions themselves, just as it did for the killing of Romanies, who were also accused of spying – a libel with a long pedigree.[124] The Jew–partisan equation can be seen as an attempt to provide a military (and therefore 'honourable') rationale for mass slaughter of civilians. Overall, however, the length and intensity of the conflict on one hand and the ideological background on the other exaggerated the inherently brutalising nature of warfare, inuring the troops to atrocity and encouraging radical orders from the command staff.

Barbarossa was in fact preceded by a pair of orders that underlined the nature of the conflict and encouraged even greater exhortations towards atrocity. The first, the 'commissar order', removed POW status from communist functionaries ('commissars') in the Red Army and any of those considered hostile in the civil administration, and prescribed execution. The 'Barbarossa jurisdiction decree' removed Wehrmacht actions against Soviet citizens from the jurisdiction of military courts (the same was applied to Yugoslavia),[125] and advocated collective reprisal for anti-German action against whole settlements. In this, the Nazis were, whether consciously or not, building once again on foundations established in European colonial wars outside Europe. There, the laws of war had never been deemed applicable to 'savage' populations, and collective reprisal, including against women and children, was *de rigueur*,[126] as were other collective punishments and 'pre-emptive' measures including scorched earth policies, 'free-fire zones' and land clearances, all of which were practised in eastern Europe from 1941 to 1945.[127] Particularly in the military context, with its premium on disciplined obedience, these orders provided the all-important legitimisation for, indeed obligation to, extra-ordinary violence that had been missing in the Polish campaign. Though not in all cases, this may well have been sufficient motivation for men such as Field Marshal Erich von Manstein, one of Germany's celebrated, apolitical 'military professionals', who nevertheless went on to endorse and even amplify von Reichenau's antisemitic orders.[128]

The Einsatzgruppen squad leaders were drawn predominantly from the higher ranks of the political police, particularly the SD.[129] As such, it may be assumed as previously intimated that their adherence to Nazi ideology, including virulent antisemitism, was relatively very strong. The same might be said of much of the rank and file, particularly those drawn from the ranks of the Waffen-SS, and therefore also of the Kommandostab Reichsführer-SS. Even if some members of these organisations did not have pre-dispositions to ideological extremity at the time of their joining (and joining the SS in the absence of such conviction suggests at least an amoral ambition that could admit participation in immoral acts), prolonged exposure to the SS and police ethos would have had a profound affect on their world-view, not least in the induction to a closed, self-perceived elite community.[130] The same can be said for the leaders of political police outposts in the east, though research remains to be conducted on the interaction between these radicals and the often 'ordinary' police forces under their authority.[131]

As for the regular (non-reserve) order police, which supplied 500 men to the Einsatzgruppen and several thousand more in the form of separate police battalions, these men were not subject to the same vetting as the SS forces. Nevertheless, we have already seen how through recruitment Germany's non-political police forces had become increasingly Nazified from 1933. From 1937 and particularly 1940 the order police were also subjected to institutionalised indoctrination. By 1941, 30 per cent of all officers in the regular order police were SS members, and 66 per cent belonged to the Nazi party, in comparison to a party membership level of 9 per cent amongst the wider German population. They were also increasingly militarised. In accordance with a directive of autumn 1936 for training to be based on a 'military foundation', personnel released from the Wehrmacht were permitted direct entry into police ranks at corporal level.[132]

Many regular order police battalions were drafted into full military service alongside the Wehrmacht and Waffen-SS in the Second World War. Those fighting on the eastern front, as in Edward B. Westermann's case study of battalion 310, a study claiming to illustrate the importance of ideological commitment to the Nazi cause amongst the killers, appear to have been thoroughly 'barbarised'[133] by the brutal combat in which they sustained heavy losses, as well as inflicting massive casualties during and outside battle against Soviet soldiers and civilians. This is the context in which battalion 310 partook fulsomely of executions and round-ups of Jewish communities in the USSR in 1942, and it should not be forgotten that prior to their involvement in the 'final solution' they had been involved in 'partisan hunts' and 'collective reprisals' against whole Russian settlements, where the massacres regularly included large numbers of women and children.[134] This is another example of perpetrators accepting the legitimacy of attacking a variety of groups falling within a general *'Feindbild'*, or vision of Germany's enemies.

At the same time, of course, other order police squads were assigned to killing duty immediately upon their entry into Soviet territory, without battlefield experience in the ideological war. The record of police battalion 322, operating in Belarus from July 1941 onwards, showed that the vast majority of its members killed Jews (and others) in accordance with orders, and never really questioned the legitimacy of those instructions. Only a few refused on principle, and their refusals were tolerated, but at the other end of the spectrum only a few exceeded the scope of their orders in participation through acts of sadism (the so-called *Exzeß-Täter*, or 'perpetrators of excessive crimes') and/or by presenting themselves as committed volunteers for shootings.[135]

The only certain conclusion that can be drawn from the case of battalion 322 is that Germany could rely on large numbers of its citizens to participate directly in genocide, but this is nothing new. Whether or not the key motive for participating – or perhaps it would be better put for 'not refusing to participate', given the prevailing general onus on militaristic obedience in Nazi-German ranks during wartime – was the extent of identification with the ideological goals of the Nazi leadership can only really be hinted at by examination of a slightly different group of killers whose record nevertheless bears some resemblance to that of battalion 322.

Moving beyond the Wehrmacht and the more militarised, ideological vanguards of the SS and police, we encounter the reserve order police, a group of whom formed the focus of Browning's study *Ordinary Men: Reserve Police Battalion 101 and the Final Solution in Poland*. Unlike the regular order police these reserve battalions were recruited from population sections not yet subject to conscription. In some cases they were men deemed unfit for military service anyway. Most were too old to have spent their formative years under the Nazi regime of indoctrination. As for

Browning's chosen battalion, many were drawn from socio-economic backgrounds and a regional milieu (Hamburg) that produced lower-than-average Nazi partisanship. The official indoctrination they received in Germany and Poland was decidedly feeble, its specifically antisemitic content low. Yet when called upon in mid-July 1942 to murder 1,500 Jews of the Lublin village of Josefow, all but a dozen of these 500 policemen participated, and this despite the fact that their commanding officer had expressly invited any of the older men who did not feel up to the task to step out – a choice not offered to battalion 322. After the Josefow massacre and a brief hiatus as the policemen recovered psychologically, killings resumed with much less friction.

The participation of battalion 101 in genocide was surely in part influenced by the 'occupation climate', but since this particular group had not been involved in combat, wartime barbarisation could not have played a part. Other, more mundane circumstantial factors seem to have been at least as important, as some of them were in the case of battalion 322: a predictable inclination to obey state directives; concern for their future careers in the order police; and a pressure to conform and not to appear 'weak', not least to 'muck-in' and share the burden in an unpleasant task which would have to be performed irrespectively. That, as Goldhagen argued in pursuit of his thesis on German antisemitism, such men became barbarised and accustomed to killing, and that some showed signs of sadism, should not obscure the fact that this was not how they started out, nor that only a minority went down the road of the sadists, nor that sadism may have been used in some cases as a coping strategy.[136]

One ostensible message of Browning's case study might be the popular wisdom that people can get used to anything. Nevertheless the process did rely on hardened, more 'professional' killers to a certain extent, hence in the largest massacres the security police and auxiliaries from the formerly Soviet states took over the shooting responsibilities, with battalion 101 consigned to guard duties. And it seems that the policemen did devise mechanisms over time to minimise their human contact with their victims (and thus the psychological burden upon themselves), and that a number of individuals took opportunities when unobserved to avoid killing.[137] Josefow clearly changed things, however, which suggests the importance of the availability of such rich testimony on the first real 'engagement' of any sort for a killing squad, as well, of course, as Browning's skill in exposing it. The survivor Jean Améry wrote of the 'first blow' he received in the concentration camps and its seminal effect, instilling in him the reality of his desperate position outside the guards' contract of reciprocal humanity.[138] Is it too much to suggest that the first kill performed the same function in reverse for battalion 101, as perhaps did 'initiation rituals' used the amongst concentration camp SS?[139]

The staff of the concentration camps and extermination centres were not a homogeneous group. Beneath the SS management level, the small Operation Reinhard camp staffs were comprised of SS auxiliaries from the western Soviet territories, of whom more below, and a select band of German 'euthanasia' specialists seconded to Globocnik. Whatever the skills of the latter, in the light of their treatment of Germany's 'handicapped' it is probably safe to concur with Dick de Mildt that:

> among the best suited [to the job] … were the so-called 'burners', whose daily job had consisted of dragging the corpses to the incineration ovens of the extermination centres. To these utterly desensitized figures, their transfer to the Polish annihilation camps merely constituted a change of scenery. For others, such as the former 'T-4' desk clerks and photographers, the transition may well have required slightly more efforts to adjust, but even they had, of course, already grown thoroughly accustomed to the routine of mass murder.[140]

The much larger concerns of Auschwitz and Majdanek were established under the authority of the WVHA. These shared personnel, therefore, with the more 'conventional' concentration camps established in Germany from 1933, employing men who had learned their trade in courses at Dachau where they perfected the systematic brutalisation and dehumanisation of inmates.[141] Though it is certainly true that when Jews were incarcerated in the German camps they were treated worse than the many other prisoner groups, simply by the great predominance before 1938 of 'political' and 'asocial' inmates in these institutions, the guards were routinely associated with atrocities against a variety of 'enemies'. Some of these guards, including a number of important future camp commandants, temporarily broke off their concentration camp careers to serve in the Waffen-SS 'Death's Head' units in Poland and France, and then the USSR where they suffered disproportionately high death rates and perpetrated considerable atrocities.[142]

As the Second World War and the 'final solution' progressed, and as Auschwitz developed its explicitly genocidal function, while simultaneously the WVHA was attempting to build up the economic side of the concentration camps, stratification of the inmates became still clearer. The 'new breed' of commandants that took over many of the key camps from 1942 had fully imbibed the SS doctrine of exterminating the Jews, and continued this function very efficiently while (somewhat less efficiently) trying to reorder the remainder of the camp regime away from the previous practices of arbitrary brutality against all inmates.[143]

Broadly speaking, the direct complicity of local auxiliaries in genocide in eastern Europe was largely restricted to the territories conquered from June 1941, notably to Belarussians, Ukrainians and citizens of the Baltic states, though this is not to overlook the role of French or Dutch collaborators and police in the west, for instance. In the formerly Soviet territories in the year from the winter of 1941–42, as more police battalions were pulled into military combat, and as simultaneously the 'final solution' gathered steam, the number of natives recruited to serve under the order police in various capacities increased from 33,000 to 300,000.[144] As an absolute minimum, 11,000 Ukrainians were involved with the 'final solution' alone.[145] The main involvement of such collaborators – most volunteers to begin with – was in the bigger, 'second sweep' of killings in the Ukraine and Belarus in the summer and autumn of 1942, completing most of the work started by the Einsatzgruppen the previous year. They served as the much-needed manpower in rounding up Jews and guarding killing sites for the political police, while sometimes also participating directly in the shooting. Then they would search for and kill any Jews who had escaped the massacres, being particularly effective in this regard because many of them knew the local Jews.[146]

Coming at motivation for these men is again highly complex, though antisemitism was frequently present, combining more traditional religious hatred with the Judeo-Bolshevik stereotype. Nevertheless, their killing scope too exceeded Jews alone, for they also targeted some Romanies, POWs, 'partisans' and Russians. Greed could be important, and the desire to gain favour with the occupiers, or promotion within the unit, as also the factors of peer pressure influencing the men of reserve police battalion 101, and, in some cases, alcoholism. There are some analogies too with enrolment in the 'volksdeutsche Selbstschutz' units established for a brief but violent existence, and then disbanded, in Poland in 1939–40. As Black writes, the incentives for these units to collaborate, putting aside for a moment the question of ethnic solidarity, were: 'concern about unemployment or starvation; ... unbearable family relationships; ... perhaps, simple boredom'; and the prospect of 'extra rations, or adventure'. Not least may have been the simple desire of the bully to 'lord it' over other members of the community. (Interestingly, it was not the local ethnic majorities alone who alienated these 'ethnic Germans'; during the occupation years, the Selbstschutz members were also treated with contempt by Germans from the 'Reich'.[147])

Ukrainian, Latvian and Lithuanian 'volunteers' ('*Hilfswillige*'; '*Hiwis*') formed the main body of non-German perpetrators in the Generalgouvernement. From their 'training camp' at Trawniki in Lublin they were assigned both to the Operation Reinhard death camps and to shooting massacres. The savagery with which some of them carried out their duties may be explained in part – but only in part – by the method of their recruitment. They were selected for their anti-communism from Soviet POW camps whence they were otherwise almost certain to perish. Once in their Trawniki units, they were subjected to harsh discipline by their German superiors.[148] Like some of their counterparts to the east, some of these appear to have used alcohol as a means of easing the psychological effects of murder.[149]

Completely different considerations influenced the participation in Nazism's racist crimes of a broad swathe of German industry. Here fear, inherent brutality, reluctance or trepidation were not factors at all, nor were a colonial mindset, wartime barbarisation or rabid racism. How might we account for their decision to use slave labour and to treat it in the most abominable way?

From the turn of 1943–44 the number of concentration camp labourers in the armaments industry increased from around 30,000 to around 500,000,[150] and the total of camp inmates to over 700,000. The moves from the WVHA and the Speer ministry for camp inmate deployment in the armament industry ultimately also affected Jews.[151] The most concerted use of Jewish labour followed on from the deportation of the Hungarian Jews, from May 1944; about 200,000 Hungarian Jews were used for labour in the German or occupied territories, around 126,000 of whom survived the war.[152] After the war, German industrialists protested that they exploited slave labour because they were *forced* to do so.[153] This is not so. The Nazi economy was not a command economy; firms had freedom of movement, and some Nazi initiatives were turned down by companies. There are also recorded rejections of business requests for slaves by the state. Some were refused because the taskmasters were already considered to have sufficient slaves.[154] Moreover it was not true in all or even in most cases that the state took the initiative; and the SS simply did not have the authority to do so. For the majority of firms on which case studies have been conducted, the initial moves were taken by those companies, swayed by the cheapness and availability of slave labour.[155] Besides, though on a smaller scale, the preparedness to use slave labour preceded the panicked and terror-driven final phase of the war. Some German firms had resorted to using Jews up to two years previously, despite the SS's security concerns.[156]

From the point of view of industrialists, there were strong arguments for the use of slave labourers. Many firms were unwilling to make substantial capital investments in 1943–44 in anticipation of Germany losing the war. Expensive military production lines would soon be rendered redundant, they reasoned, thus it was far better to make production labour-intensive, particularly when that labour and its up-keep were cheap. The existence of large labour forces would give the impression of high-tempo production and prevent the dissolution of companies during the war, thus preserving them in the long term.[157] *Capitalist* self-preservation rather than ideological commitment to the Nazi war effort was also behind the involvement of companies such as Daimler-Benz in the dispersal of its most important machinery to the security of the underground factories created by the enslaved miners.[158]

The prospective availability of labour from Auschwitz, for instance, was an important factor in the founding of the nearby IG Farben plant.[159] Around 30,000 human beings lost their lives either on the grounds of a synthetic rubber factory during and after its construction, or in the camp called Monowitz erected to house the inmates, or on return to Auschwitz-Birkenau, when the work overseers considered them to be too exhausted to be of further use, and secured replacements.[160] In the eyes of IG Farben and the SS this procedure was the 'logical' alternative to better provision for a fixed labour force.[161] As Ferencz has pointed out, there is no adequate translation of how people were *verbraucht*, or 'used-up', consumed, spent.[162] The consideration of such cases renders the extent of the pressure on companies to deploy slaves irrelevant. Even if there was a shortage of other labour sources, and though the use of the slaves did carry with it preconditions as well as unspoken assumptions as to their treatment, the incredibly draining work, the inadequate provision of food, accommodation and clothing (by way of cost-cutting), the acceptance of the brutality of the SS guards and their punitive beatings of 'shirkers', and of the 'replacement' scheme, were all choices made by German firms. This evidence is all the more damning given the resources that evidently were available for providing for the German IG Farben employees.[163]

Despite variations,[164] it is a fair generalisation to state that most businessmen who used Jewish and other sources of slave labour were supremely unmoved by the devastation inflicted on their charges. In accounting for the overriding callousness of the industrial usage of slave and forced labour, the evidence suggests that we should look to economic considerations, in the context of an environment of moral tunnel-vision created over years of collusion with the Nazi regime. Profit, efficiency, self-preservation and long-term survival planning were conceived in terms of 'instrumental rationality', that is, irrespective of the human cost.[165] Firms *expected* to get some economic benefit from using slaves;[166] simultaneously they wished to provide the bare minimum in terms of outlay for these people.

With the vast post-1933 economic boom and the destruction of trade unionism Nazism had been good for industry in a way that the Weimar Republic had not. It is possible to generalise about an ethos of attraction to Nazi authoritarianism amongst the managerial and industrialist classes,[167] and over the years a growing association not just with German aggression but with the openly immoral practices of 'Aryanisation' and the exploitation of POW and other forced labour. In light of this complicity, slave-driving was another step down the road of criminality, not a new depar-

151

ture. For the industrial chieftains, those who did not have to get their hands dirty, morality almost certainly conformed to Zygmunt Bauman's 'law of optical perspective'. To them, their decisions only impacted on the lives of the slaves in an abstract way.

Several factors combined to maintain the 'moral' distance between shop-floor representatives of industry and the slaves, even though the physical distance was often negligible. General wartime hardship, and specifically the impact of Allied air bombardments of Germany during the most intensive period of slave-labour deployment, fostered a mentality wherein people became even more exclusively concerned with the well-being of their own. Some German overseers completely accepted the Nazi propaganda about their slaves being the dregs of humanity, the criminals and the 'asocial'[168] – it is nothing new to observe that the degrading Nazi practices of dressing inmates in ill-fitting striped uniforms and removing their hair made these people appear to conform to the degraded image of them projected by the Third Reich – though that is not the reason that industrialists became involved in the labour programmes in the first place.

One upshot of these contrasting case studies is that our understanding of perpetration is inevitably going to be conditioned by whom one studies. There is no emblematic perpetrator or perpetrator group incorporating in a necessary and sufficient way the 'essence' of genocide or the mindset of the genocidaire. Nevertheless, from Arendt through Aly and Heim to Goldhagen this reductive tendency has been in evidence. The key figure of Adolf Eichmann, the best known and arguably the most important middle-ranking perpetrator, has been the subject of great debate both in terms of the person himself and of the wider caste of whom he is held to be representative.

Bureaucracy, 'banality' and modernity

Arendt's famous report of Eichmann's trial in Jerusalem in 1961 painted a picture of a 'banal' bureaucrat, incapable of addressing the bigger moral picture whilst oiling the wheels of the murderous machinery in accordance with a perverted understanding of Immanuel Kant's 'categorical imperative' to lawfulness. She was certainly correct in her criticisms of the Jerusalem court that it made little effort to understand Eichmann. While the prosecution recognised early on that it was dealing with a very specific category of killer, a 'desk-murderer', it never concerned itself with the prospect that his motivation was anything other than antisemitism. Yet Arendt's critique must be seen against the backdrop of her wider comparative interest in the workings of 'totalitarian' systems and their ability to co-opt individuals.[169]

Arendt was wrong about Eichmann the person. He was far from commonplace and unimaginative in his roles as solver of the Jewish question, and his staff were more than a small cog in a big machine. From 1938, in the days when the 'final solution' meant emigration, he had been instrumental in creating the 'Vienna model' of production-line expatriation and expropriation of Jews. With its success he was brought to Berlin to replicate it there. During the war, as head of the RSHA's Jewish desk, he and his subordinates orchestrated or facilitated the deportation of the Jewish communities of southern, western and central Europe, primarily to Auschwitz-Birkenau. In this capacity he was not hidebound by a set of official procedures, but rather had to innovate policy and practice towards the ultimate goal. As Lozowick has recently shown, in findings corroborated elsewhere, the Eichmann staff performed all of these functions with elan, commitment and overt antisemitism.[170]

Yet like Arendt Lozowick is also seeking to make a wider point, this time not about totalitarianism but about the Nazi system, as is shown by his pointed comparison of the German bureaucracy with that of the Italian state, the state with perhaps the best record in the Holocaust of those under German influence.[171] He is not the only scholar to react indignantly to the notion that racism may not have been a primary motive for individual perpetrators and, more, that the perpetrating system as a whole may have developed its peculiar potency from mundane organisational norms inherent to complex modern states. (This reaction may well stem from the perceived threat to the case for 'uniqueness' if the perpetration process is rendered 'banal', or in some way a product of a general modernity.[172]) His response is a more sophisticated form of the reductive ideas of antisemitism – and 'Germanism' – underpinning the scholarship of the intentionalists and of *Hitler's Willing Executioners*. But the explanation cannot account fully for the fact that the RSHA had once pursued Jewish emigration just as hard as it ultimately pursued annihilation; and it itself concedes that Eichmann's staff contained both more and less overtly antisemitic, more and less brutal individuals who nevertheless all acted effectively in unison.[173] And while Arendt's idea of the totalitarian bureaucrat was too schematic, based on inadequate study of the particular characteristics of the Nazi system, she may well still have been nearer the truth as regards other individual and group perpetrators.

As for Eichmann's office, it is unsurprising that one of the nerve centres of the whole apparatus should have fully internalised the regime's goals and even acted as a divining rod for the development of its policies. The WVHA officials confirmed that ideological commitment and technical and bureaucratic efficiency could happily co-exist. From March 1942, as it expanded, the WVHA incorporated the Inspectorate of Concentration Camps (IKL). From August 1938 the bureaucrats at the headquarters of the IKL at Oranienburg had worked in the direct physical vicinity of the Sachsenhausen camp, with easy access to the obscenities that were the outcome of their reign. The IKL also had close personal links with the concentration camp officer corps.[174] Amongst the SS technicians and the leadership of the WVHA itself, many of whom shared the age, educational and ideological profiles of the RSHA men, there was in most cases a fundamental, ideological refusal to ameliorate camp living and supply conditions to maximise workforce productivity, mirroring the perverse logic of the management of the Polish ghetto economies in 1941–42. (Technical changes were made, though, to improve productivity.[175]) But such ideological commitment was not essential across the full spectrum of perpetrators.

To stake its claim in Nazi *Judenpolitik*, the German Foreign Office's department DIII under Martin Luther, containing the Jewish desk, fought successfully in the Nazi turf-war over negotiations with other countries concerning the deportation of their Jewish populations, as well as helping to precipitate the shooting of male Serbian Jews. If Luther was an opportunist, 'an amoral technician of power', 'ruthless and unscrupulous ... unsurpassed in his ambition and energy', the bureaucrats below him were much more straightforward careerists. They were selected randomly from bureaucratic ranks and like so many others bent with the wind, adapting themselves to the increasingly extreme measures, though they themselves exhibited a variety of convictions (or lack thereof) about the Jewish question. When it came to participation in outright murder, the distaste for the policy of three of the four studied by Browning led them to attempt to extricate themselves from the section, but never at the price of damaging their career prospects; indeed, they continued to discharge their responsibilities admirably.[176]

Beyond the existence of specialist Jewish desks such as Eichmann's and Luther's offices and smaller equivalents in police outposts in the east, for many with a hand in the processes of definition, deportation and murder, such functions were only one among many more everyday official duties. This is true for the timetablers of the Reichsbahn, the German railway authorities, but also in a different way for the middle-ranking occupation authorities who inherited the full ambit of normal responsibilities entailed in national administration, for instance labour allocation officials in Eastern Galicia who were effectively involved in selection of 'incapable' Jews for death. Particularly for officials separated from the killing process both spatially and conceptually (by routinisation and compartmentalisation of mundane bureaucratic responsibilities, as in the case, say, of the Reichsbahn timetabler), irrespective of ideological disposition, the 'distance' facilitated participation by reducing its moral dimensions and its impact on individual sensibility.

This brings us in closing to one of the more misunderstood attempts to generalise about the perpetration process, Zygmunt Bauman's theory of the relationship between modernity and the Holocaust. The interpretative confusion lies in part in the critics' understanding of what Bauman means by modernity.[177] Clearly if we equate modernity simply with modern technology, then much of the 'final solution' outside Auschwitz does not fit the picture.[178] Neither can the murder by shooting *in situ* of millions of Polish, Soviet and Serbian Jews be described in any meaningful sense as a modern 'bureaucratic' process.[179] The orchestrated deportations from western Europe to distant killing fields did by necessity have a more bureaucratic character,[180] but we have already seen that the numbers thus murdered were relatively small; it seems that the focus on the bureaucratic side of the 'final solution' owes much to the misleading Holocaust metanarrative and its overriding emphasis on trains to Auschwitz. Besides, it bears repeating that the main perpetrator institutions within the Reich bureaucracy were not 'typical' of bureaucracy generally. But here criticisms of Bauman have tended, unfairly, to lump his work in with Arendt's thesis.

Alongside the technology and technique of genocide, both of which undeniably do occupy him, Bauman has a third and overarching factor in mind in his application of the term 'modernity'. To him, as in the writings of Michel Foucault, modernity is characterised by a post-enlightenment sense of 'order', a sense that mankind has the ability to reshape itself into an image of perfectibility that in a more religious age was regarded as the sole preserve of god. The quintessence of 'modern' genocide is the radical application of this doctrine of perfectibility by one particular section of mankind against debilitating or imperfectible elements within and outside its collective body. That determination to re-order the world found extreme expression in racial genocide and thus provides the broadest of historical contexts for the Nazi project, if not necessarily a blueprint for how it was to be conducted on the ground. Thus for instance it is interesting, given his implicit critique of Bauman's understanding of Nazi bureaucracy, that Allen's analysis of the murderously ideological 'engineers and modern managers' of the SS-WVHA could actually dovetail with Bauman's wider vision of the Holocaust: Allen's subjects evinced an attraction to Nazi authoritarian discipline and vision that was based as much on the re-ordering of populations and internal order and stratification in the concentration camps as on architectural and mechanical achievement.[181]

Cornelia Sorabji has written of the 'ethnic cleansing' in the break-up of the former Yugoslavia that whatever arbitrary horrors individual perpetrators could invent in the process, they were only enabled to do so within an *ordered context*.[182] The same is the case for individual ideological conviction and willing innovation, as for corruption, but also for more 'disinterested' or mechanical contributions to murder. The Nazi machinery of destruction accommodated both planning and direct brutality and got its flavour from the combination: this, not the trope of bureaucratic organisation, is what made the genocide into a genuine state project, incorporating all social and attitudinal levels.

Conclusions: representing the perpetrator

The ostensible simplicity of the concepts of 'dehumanisation', 'racism' or 'antisemitism' harmfully reduces the complexity of perpetrator-hood, the often multi-faceted motivation that each killer or facilitator brought to their task. Each was a peculiar product of complex societies (in a complex continent), experiences, educational and professional institutions, and each travelled a long and 'twisted road' to participation at some point on the broad spectrum of complicity in murder within a state-sponsored framework. The level of attention currently devoted to survivors of the Holocaust and the judiciousness of treatment called for in the first chapter of this book both need to be applied to the study of the perpetrators, however distasteful that might sound. There was no 'ideal type' perpetrator, just as there was no 'ideal type' victim experience, however much the creation of a 'genre' of survivor testimony may suggest there was. Yet amongst the many differences between the methodology that might be used to interrogate the act of perpetration and the testimony of the survivor, one is of paramount importance.

If getting to grips meaningfully with survivor testimony is less a question of asking what it can tell us of the experiences recalled than of the way those experiences have been processed, if expert readings need to focus less on the 'horizontal' axis of shared persecution and more on the 'vertical' axis of the individual life history approach, the opposite can often be true of study of the perpetrator, and particularly the direct perpetrator of atrocity. This in no way contradicts the foregoing call for nuanced and detailed study, but it demands that that study be directed in particular ways. Specifically, the knowledge that there was no ideal type perpetrator limits the value of the biographical or 'psychological' approach to individual killers or groups of killers, potentially focusing on the individual at the expense of the bigger picture. (In any case, historians are not always best equipped to ask the psychological/criminological questions that pertain to participation in discrete murderous acts.)

Since the story of the Holocaust and other genocides is the story of many individuals of different dispositions reaching the same end by different routes, and since also it is perfectly possible to have prejudice and hatred without that being consummated in murder, the immediate context of the killing act takes on the greatest significance of all of the variables (including ideology as formed over the longer term) contributing to participation. In short, a large proportion of all people will become perpetrators in the right (wrong) situation. This has yet to be universally accepted in a historiography which is still in part devoted to restating the importance of the Holocaust and equating its supposed 'uniqueness' with the uniqueness of all of its contingent elements, thus resisting attempts to study either perpetrators or the perpetration process without due acknowledgement of the primacy of murderous antisemitism. Such one-dimensional explanations are of course even more prevalent in the popular sphere.

From the very beginning popular representations of Nazi criminals in Britain and the USA have tended to cast them distinctly in the role of 'other'. Stereotypes of Gestapo and SS sadists or automatons occupy a particular place in the popular consciousness, fed by the creation in 1945 of easily identifiable villains such as Joseph Kramer, the 'beast of Belsen', or Ilse Koch, the 'bitch of Buchenwald', or focusing disproportionately on individual or particularly nauseating acts of depravity, such as medical 'experiments' on concentration camp inmates, rather than on the more orchestrated, much larger-scale campaigns of racial extermination. Though these specific images of atrocity and perpetrator have coexisted with a broadly entrenched cultural anti-Germanism in Britain at least, this has not equated to general awareness of the sheer breadth of German involvement in Nazi criminality, as the enduring belief in the honourable conduct of the Wehrmacht shows.

Engaging with the perpetrator at even the most basic level remains something of a taboo, most notably in the national Holocaust museums, perhaps for fear that understanding will be equated with excusing. Thus the few perpetrators who are personalised in the Holocaust exhibition of the Imperial War Museum appear in the classic guise of the ordinary criminal, namely the mug shot, with no acknowledgement that many of them would have led law-abiding existences in a non-Nazi context. (Conversely, another room contains only a chair and a desk, the latter burdened only with a typewriter and telephone. Engraved into the four walls is an excellent diagram of the machinery of destruction, incorporating all of the main Wehrmacht, SS and police and civilian offices involved in the killing process. This room is superb in transmitting the complexity and integrated nature of the Nazi machine, but on another level it reinforces the stereotype of the faceless bureaucratic perpetrator.)

Echoing Mark Levene, contending that the capacity to become a perpetrator is the norm and not the opposite is not to suggest some acceptance of original sin or of dubious scientific formulae of inherent human aggression. It is based on the empirical evidence provided by a wide variety of societies at different points in their historical development.[183] The evidence is there in genocidal processes from Turkey in 1915 to Nazi Europe to Rwanda and the former Yugoslavia that irrespective of education, socialisation and prior ties with the victim community, and cutting across membership of civil administrations, the military, the paramilitary or just the general public, people will kill under particular circumstances. Knowledge of the quasi-universality of a killing potential should be accepted as the point of departure for enquiry into genocide, and the social contexts in which that potential is promoted and channelled brought more clearly into focus, thereby de-fetishising the killing act and re-humanising the killer. This would replace the current trend which works in reverse fashion, gradually increasing the circle of recognised killers on the basis of documentary revelations, with each new discovery of an implicated group sending ripples through the academic community (or even, as was the case with the travelling German exhibition on the crimes of the Wehrmacht, the public), without the automatic accompaniment of asking what this really tells us.

Incidentally, such discoveries on the breadth of the community of perpetrators do not support the Goldhagen thesis, nor the theory of the uniqueness of the Holocaust. On the contrary, the sheer breadth (and variety of immediate motives) of participation would not be a surprise if Germany's genocidal projects were studied in a comparative context, which in turn is a vital tool in the demystification of the Holocaust. This is not to deny the specificity of the historical events in question, to depict some bland melange of which the Holocaust is an interchangeable ingredient. Nor, of course, is it to advocate throwing up one's hands in despair of humanity and forgoing the task of forensic differentiation. History writing is nothing if not about finding the balance between the general and the particular. The homogenisation of human experiences across the past is just as detrimental to understanding that past as is its opposite, the main manifestation of which in this subject area is the claim to the uniqueness of the Holocaust. Some of the characteristics of the 'final solution' may be 'unique' – in the banal sense of the word – to German history; some to modern European 'civilisation' and warfare; some are peculiar to Judeo-Christian relations; some are specific to none of the above. Antisemitism, on the level both of general causation in the 'final solution' and of individual participation, is obviously far, far too blunt an analytical tool on its own, an idea divorced from its contexts. As the following chapter will show, the same is true in analysing the responses of the liberal democracies to the fate of the Jews.

Notes

1   Ian Kershaw, 'The Persecution of the Jews and German Public Opinion in the Third Reich', *Leo Baeck Institute Yearbook*, vol. 26 (1981), pp. 261–89, covering both the pre- and post-1933 periods.

2   On which subject see Ian Kershaw, *Hitler, 1889 to 1936: Hubris* (London, Allen Lane, 1998) and Peter Longerich, *The Unwritten Order: Hitler's Role in the Final Solution* (Stroud, Tempus, 2002).

3   Saul Friedländer, *Nazi Germany and the Jews: The Years of Persecution 1933–39* (London, Weidenfeld & Nicolson, 1997), pp. 86–90.

4   Peter Pulzer, *The Rise of Political Antisemitism in Germany and Austria* (London, Halban, 1988).

5   Omer Bartov, *Mirrors of Destruction: War, Genocide, and Modern Identity* (Oxford, Oxford University Press, 2000), pp. 96–8.

6   Helen Fein, *Accounting for Genocide: National Responses and Jewish Victimization during the Holocaust* (New York, Free Press, 1980).

7   David Bankier, *The Germans and the Final Solution: Public Opinion under Nazism* (Oxford, Blackwell, 1992), pp. 72, 84, on the increasing indifference of the majority of the population to the Jewish plight.

8   Implicit in Robert Gellately, *Backing Hitler: Consent and Coercion in Nazi Germany* (Oxford, Oxford University Press, 1991). See also Michael Burleigh and Wolfgang Wippermann, *The Racial State: Germany 1933–1945* (Cambridge, Cambridge University Press, 1991) on the integrative effects on the majority of exclusion of minorities.

9   Bankier, *The Germans and the Final Solution*, pp. 101–15.

10   Christopher Browning, *Nazi Policy, Jewish Workers, German Killers* (Cambridge, Cambridge University Press, 2000), pp. 51–6 on the issues of killing German Jews.

11   Frank Bajohr, *'Arisierung' in Hamburg: Die Verdrängung der jüdischer Unternehmer 1933–1945* (Hamburg, Christians, 1997).

12   Peter Longerich, *Die Wannsee-Konferenz vom 20 Januar 1942* (Berlin, Gedenk- und Bildungsstätte Haus der Wannsee-Konferenz, 1988), pp. 42–3.

13   Eric Johnson, *Nazi Terror: The Gestapo, Jews and Ordinary Germans* (London, John Murray, 2000).

14   Burleigh and Wippermann, *The Racial State*.

15   Gellately, *Backing Hitler*, which synthesises a large German literature on the subject.

16   For a short survey of this and other aspects of European thinking on population, see Maria Sophia Quine, *Population Politics in Twentieth Century Europe: Fascist Dictatorships and Liberal Democracies* (London, Routledge, 1996).

17   Stefan Kühl, *The Nazi Connection: Eugenics, American Racism, and German National Socialism* (New York, Oxford University Press, 1994).

18   Henry Friedlander, *The Origins of Nazi Genocide* (Chapel Hill, University of North Carolina Press, 1995).

19   On the Gestapo, Shlomo Aronson, *Reinhard Heydrich und die Frühgeschichte von Gestapo und SD* (Stuttgart, Deutsche Verlags-Anstalt, 1971); on the Kriminalpolizei, Patrick Wagner, *Volksgemeinschaft ohne Verbrecher: Konzeption und Praxis der Kriminalpolizei in der Zeit der Weimarer Republik und des Nationalsozialismus* (Hamburg, Christians, 1996).

20   Ulrich Herbert, *Best: Biographische Studien über Radikalismus, Weltanschauung und Vernunft 1903–1989* (Bonn, Dietz, 1996), pp. 170–7; Michael Wildt, *Generation des Unbedingten: Das Führungskorps des Reichssicherheitshauptamtes* (Hamburg, Hamburger Edition, 2003), pp. 314–21.

21   For example, Michael Zimmermann, *Rassenutopie und Genozid: Die nationalsozialistische 'Lösung der Zigeunerfrage'* (Hamburg, Christians, 1996).

22   Götz Aly and Suzanne Heim, *Vordenker der Vernichtung: Auschwitz und die deutschen Pläne für eine neue europäischen Ordnung* (Frankfurt am Main, Fischer, 1993), particularly the concluding chapter.

23   For a critique of Aly and Heim, see Christopher Browning, *The Path to Genocide: Essays on Launching the Final Solution* (Cambridge, Cambridge University Press, 1992), ch. 5.

24   A point also made by Wagner in *Volksgemeinschaft ohne Verbrecher*, pp. 401–2.

25   Hans Mommsen, *Beamtentum in Dritten Reich* (Stuttgart, Oldenbourg, 1966).

26   Jeremy Noakes and Geoffrey Pridham (eds), *Nazism: A History in Documents and Eyewitness Accounts, 1919–1945, vol. 1* (New York,

Schocken, 1984), pp. 530–41.

27   Ibid., pp. 547–51.

28   Raul Hilberg, *The Destruction of the European Jews*, 3 vols (New York, Holmes and Meier, 1985), vol. 1, p. 95 on 'voluntary' and 'compulsory' Aryanisation.

29   Marion A. Kaplan, *Between Dignity and Despair: Jewish Life in Nazi Germany* (New York, Oxford University Press, 1998).

30   Martin Broszat, *The Hitler State: The Foundation and Development of the Internal Structure of the Third Reich* (London, Longman, 1981), p. 294 and ch. 9 passim.

31   On the SD at this time, Götz Aly, '"Judenumsiedlung": Überlegungen zur politischen Vorgeschichte des Holocaust', in Ulrich Herbert (ed.), *Nationalsozialistische Vernichtungspolitik 1939–1945: Neue Forschungen und Kontroversen* (Frankfurt am Main, Fischer, 1998), pp. 67–97, especially here pp. 69–73; Michael Wildt's document collection *Die Judenpolitik des SD 1935–1938* (Munich, Oldenbourg, 1995). On the security police as well as the SD, Herbert, *Best*, pp. 221–4. On the supposedly 'rational' nature of SD antisemitism, Lutz Hachmeister, *Der Gegnerforscher: Die Karrier des SS-Führers Franz Alfred Six* (Munich, Beck, 1998), p. 184. On the concentration camp incarcerations after Kristallnacht, Detlef Garbe, 'Absonderung, Strafkommandos und spezifischer Terror: Jüdische Gefangene in nationalsozialistischen Konzentrationslagern 1933 bis 1945', in Arno Herzig and Ina Lorenz (eds), *Verdrängung und Vernichtung der Juden unter dem Nationalsozialismus* (Hamburg, Christians, 1992), pp. 173–204, here pp. 195–9.

32   Mark Roseman, *The Villa, the Lake, the Meeting: Wannsee and the Final Solution* (London, Penguin, 2001), pp. 88–9.

33   Edward B. Westermann, '"Ordinary Men" or "Ideological Soldiers"?: Police Battalion 310 in Russia, 1942', *German Studies Review*, vol. 21 (1998), pp. 41–68, here p. 44; Christopher Browning, *Ordinary Men: Reserve Police Battalion 101 and the Final Solution in Poland* (New York, HarperCollins, 1993), pp. 3–4. On the 'Nazification' of the ordinary German police force from 1933, see also Stephan Linck, *Der Ordnung verpflichtet: Deutsche Polizei 1933–1949: Der Fall Flensburg* (Paderborn, Ferdinand Schöningh, 2000), p. 27.

34   Mommsen, *Beamtentum*.

35   Noakes and Pridham (eds), *Nazism, vol. 1*, pp. 221–2.

36   Walter Naasner, *Neue Machtzentren in der deutschen Kriegswirtschaft 1942–45: Die Wirtschaftsorganisation der SS, das Amt des Generalbevollmächtigten für den Arbeitseinsatz und das Reichsministerium für Bewaffnung und Munition/Reichsministerium für Rüstungs- und Kriegsproduktion im nationalsozialistischen Herrschaftssystem* (Boppard am Rhein, Harald Boldt, 1994).

37   For a synthesis of the large literature on this subject, see Bartov, *Mirrors of Destruction*, ch. 1.

38   Peter Hüttenberger, *Die Gauleiter: Studie zum Wandel des Machtgefüges in der NSDAP* (Stuttgart, Deutsche Verlags-Anstalt, 1969), pp. 173–4.

39   Hilberg, *Destruction*, vol. 1, p. 348.

40   Hannes Heer, 'Killing Fields: The Wehrmacht and the Holocaust in Belorussia, 1941–1942', *Holocaust and Genocide Studies*, vol. 11 (1997), pp. 79–101, here p. 89, summarising the work of Bernhard Kroener in particular. See also Manfred Messerschmidt, '"Harte Sühne am Judentum". Befehlswege und Wissen in der deutschen Wehrmacht', in Jörg Wollenberg (ed.), *'Niemand war dabei und keiner hat's gewußt': Die deutsche Öffentlichkeit und die Judenverfolgung 1933–1945* (Munich, Piper, 1989), pp. 113–28. The military generation preceding this one, comprised of more 'traditional' imperialists and authoritarians, moved from staff officers in the First World War to commanding generals in the Second World War.

41   Ruth Bettina Birn, *Die Höheren SS-und Polizeiführer* (Düsseldorf, Droste, 1986), pp. 350–62; cf. Hüttenberger, *Die Gauleiter*, pp. 173–4, where he is correct about the SS elites generally, but incorrect about the HSSPF.

42   Herbert, *Best*, p. 13; part III, ch. 4; Wildt, *Generation des Unbedingten*; Jens Banach, *Heydrichs Elite: Das Führerkorps der Sicherheitspolizei und des SD 1936–1945* (Paderborn, Ferdinand Schöningh, 1998); see also Hachmeister, *Der Gegnerforscher*, ch. 2 on the social background of key RSHA men.

43   Dan Diner, 'Rassistisches Völkerrecht: Elements einer nationalsozialistischen Weltenordnung', *Vierteljahreshefte für Zeitgeschichte*, vol. 37 (1989), pp. 23–56.

44   Herbert, *Best*, esp. ch. III parts 4, 5 and 6; Sebastian Werner, 'Werner Best – Der völkische Ideologe', in Ronald Smelser, Enrico Syring and Rainer Zitelmann (eds), *Die braune Elite 2: 21 weitere biographische Skizzen* (Darmstadt, Wissenschaftliche Buchgesellschaft, 1993), pp. 13–25, here pp. 14, 16, 22. On the radical student milieu from which Best and others emerged, Hachmeister, *Der Gegnerforscher*, ch. 2.

45   Peter Black, *Ernst Kaltenbrunner: Ideological Soldier of the Third Reich* (Princeton, Princeton University Press, 1984). These conclusions match some of those in Michael Mann, 'Were the Perpetrators of Genocide "Ordinary Men" or "Real Nazis"? Results from Fifteen Hundred Biographies', *Holocaust and Genocide Studies* , vol. 14 (2000), pp. 331–66. See also Valdis O. Lumans, *Himmler's Auxiliaries: The Volksdeutsche Mittelstelle and the German National Minorities of Europe, 1933–1945* (Chapel Hill, University of North Carolina Press, 1993).

46 Dieter Pohl, *Von der 'Judenpolitik' zum Judenmord: Der Distrikt Lublin des Generalgouvernements 1939–1944* (Frankfurt am Main, Peter Lang, 1993), p. 37.

47 On Globocnik, Peter Black, 'Odilo Globocnik – Himmlers Vorposten im Osten', in Smelser et al. (eds), *Die braune Elite 2*, pp. 103–15; on Greiser, Ian Kershaw, 'Arthur Greiser – Ein Motor der "Endlösung"', in Smelser et al. (eds), *Die braune Elite 2*, pp. 116–27.

48 Mann, 'Were the Perpetrators of Genocide "Ordinary Men" or "Real Nazis"?'.

49 Noakes and Pridham, *Nazism, vol. 1*, p. 207; and the concluding chapter of Kershaw, *Hitler, 1889–1936*.

50 William Sheridan Allen, *The Nazi Seizure of Power: The Experience of a Single German Town 1930–1935* (New York, New Viewpoints, 1973), p. 274. The book was originally published in 1965.

51 Ian Kershaw, 'Improvised Genocide? The Emergence of the "Final Solution" in the "Warthegau"', *Transactions of the Royal Historical Society*, 6th series, no. 2 (1992).

52 On Müller and Luther, Roseman, *The Villa*, pp. 90–1. For more on Luther, see Christopher Browning, *The Final Solution and the German Foreign Office* (New York, Holmes and Meier, 1978), pp. 28, 181.

53 Peter Hüttenberger, 'Nationalsozialistische Polykratie', *Geschichte und Gesellschaft*, vol. 2 (1976), pp. 417–42. See also Franz Neumann, *Behemoth: The Structure and Practice of National Socialism* (Oxford, Oxford University Press, 1942).

54 Donald Cameron Watt, *Succeeding John Bull: America in Britain's Place* (Cambridge, Cambridge University Press, 1984), p. 7, on imperial Germany, but also on similar aspects, at times, of American 'bureaucratic politics'.

55 Linck, *Der Ordnung verpflichtet*, pp. 23, 28.

56 Hüttenberger, *Die Gauleiter*, pp. 172–3.

57 Gellately, *Backing Hitler*, p. 94.

58 Nikolaus Wachsmann, '"Annihilation through Labour": The Killing of State Prisoners in the Third Reich', *Journal of Modern History*, vol. 71 (1999), pp. 624–59.

59 On the latter appointment, Heer, 'Killing Fields', p. 80. However Himmler never achieved total authority for 'security' policy throughout the occupied USSR: e.g. Peter Witte et al. (eds), *Der Dienstkalendar Heinrich Himmlers 1941/1942* (Hamburg, Christians, 1999), pp. 58–62.

60 On an important victory in the battle with Frank see Richard Breitman, *The Architect of Genocide: Himmler and the Final Solution* (London, Grafton, 1992), p. 235. On the authorities in the Reichskommissariat Ukraine trying to maintain their authority in all spheres, Dieter Pohl, 'Schauplatz Ukraine', in Norbert Frei, Sybille Steinbacher and Bernd C.

Wagner (eds), *Ausbeutung, Vernichtung, Öffentlichkeit* (Munich, Saur, 2000), p. 172.

61 Bernd Wegner, *The Waffen SS: Organization, Ideology and Function* (Oxford, Blackwell, 1990).

62 Roseman, *The Villa*, pp. 37–8, expanding on Eberhard Jäckel, 'On the Purpose of the Wannsee Conference', in James S. Pacy and Alan P. Wertheimer (eds), *Perspectives on the Holocaust: Essays in Honor of Raul Hilberg* (Boulder, Westview Press, 1995), pp. 39–50.

63 On the Race and Settlement Office see Heinemann, '"Another Type of Perpetrator"'.

64 See Black, *Kaltenbrunner*, on his leadership of the RSHA. Wildt, *Generation des Unbedingten*, pp. 693–728, which shows the importance in the fragmentation process of the decentralisation of RSHA structures as allies bombing intensified. On Heydrich's supremacy over Daluege, Caron Cadle, 'Kurt Daluege – Der Prototyp des loyalen Nationalsozialisten', in Smelser et al. (eds), *Die braune Elite 2*, pp. 66–79, here p. 72.

65 Wegner, *Waffen SS*, p. ix.

66 Hüttenberger, *Die Gauleiter*, p. 173, showing the difficulty of co-operation between SS leaders and the *Gauleiter*, the importance of (variable) personal relations between the two classes, and the fact that when cooperation did occur, it was often a temporary, pragmatic partnership against a third party.

67 Pohl, '*Judenpolitik*', pp. 162–3; Thomas Sandkühler, 'Das Zwangsarbeitslager Lemberg-Janowska 1941–1944', in Ulrich Herbert et al. (eds), *Die nationalsozialistischen Konzentrationslager: Entwicklung und Struktur*, 2 vols (Göttingen, Wallstein, 1998), vol. 2, p. 627.

68 Himmler order, 9 October 1942, in Tatiana Berenstein et al. (eds), *Faschismus – Getto – Massenmord: Dokumentation über Ausrottung und Widerstand der Juden in Polen während des zweiten Weltkrieges* (East Berlin, Rütten and Loening, 1960), pp. 446–7; Nuremberg Document NO-1036, Baier to chief, office WVHA WIV, 19 January 1944. On some of the conflicts of interest around this question of Jewish labour see Donald Bloxham, 'Jewish Slave Labour and its Relationship to the "Final Solution"', in John K. Roth and Elizabeth Maxwell (eds), *Remembering for the Future 2000: The Holocaust in an Age of Genocide* (Basingstoke, Macmillan, 2001), vol. 1, pp. 170–1, and Jan Erik Schulte, 'Zwangsarbeit für die SS: Juden in der Ostindustrie GmbH', in Frei, Steinbacher and Wagner (eds), *Ausbeutung, Vernichtung, Öffentlichkeit*, pp. 43–74.

69 Heinz Höhne, *The Order of the Death's Head* (London, Pan, 1972), p. 333; Browning, *The Path to Genocide*, pp. 108–9.

70 Birn, *Die Höheren SS-und Polizeiführer*, pp. 171–2; Pohl, 'Schauplatz Ukraine', p. 140.

71   Dieter Pohl, 'Die Einsatzgruppe C', in Peter Klein (ed.), *Die Einsatzgruppen in der besetzten Sowjetunion 1941/42: Die Tätigkeits- und Lagerberichte des Chefs der Sicherheitspolizei und des SD* (Berlin, Edition Hentrich, 1997), pp. 71–87.

72   Browning, *Ordinary Men*, pp. 10–11.

73   Breitman, *The Architect of Genocide*, pp. 181–4. Cf. Witte et al. (eds), *Der Dienstkalendar Heinrich Himmlers*, pp. 58–62.

74   On the order police: Browning, *Ordinary Men*; Daniel Jonah Goldhagen, *Hitler's Willing Executioners: Ordinary Germans and the Holocaust* (London, Little, Brown & Co., 1996), pp. 181–280; and, more generally in terms of organisation and administration, Heiner Lichtenstein, *Himmler's grüne Helfer: Die Schutz- und Ordnungspolizei im 'Dritten Reich'* (Cologne, Bund, 1990). For the estimates advanced above, see Browning, *Ordinary Men*, pp. 6–11. On the Kommandostab, see Yehoshua Büchler, 'Kommandostab Reichsführer-SS: Himmler's Personal Murder Brigades in 1941', *Holocaust and Genocide Studies*, vol. 1 (1986), pp. 11–25, here pp. 13–14. On Tito's partisans and the situation in Serbia, see Walter Manoschek, *'Serbien ist Judenfrei': Militärische Besatzungspolitik und Judenvernichtung in Serbien 1941/42* (Munich, Oldenbourg, 1993), pp. 12, 122–3.

75   Wendy Lower, '"Anticipatory Obedience" and the Nazi Implementation of the Holocaust in the Ukraine: A Case Study of Central and Peripheral Forces in the Generalbezirk Zhytomyr, 1941–1944', *Holocaust and Genocide Studies*, vol. 16 (2002), pp. 1–22, here p. 5. See also Martin Dean, *Collaboration in the Holocaust: Crimes of the Local Police in Belorussia and Ukraine, 1941–44* (Basingstoke, Macmillan, 2000).

76   The prominence of the Einsatzgruppen in the historiography of the 'final solution' may well be due to the discovery in 1947 of their operational reports, which detailed their litany of murder, and to the ensuing trial at Nuremberg of a number of Einsatzgruppen leaders. See, for example, Ronald Headland, *Messages of Murder* (Cranbury, Associated University Presses, 1992). On the discovery of the reports and the role of this evidence in influencing views of the Nazi murder machinery, see Donald Bloxham, *Genocide on Trial: War Crimes Trials in the Formation of Holocaust History and Memory* (Oxford, Oxford University Press, 2001), ch. 5. The reports from the USSR are reproduced in Klein (ed.), *Die Einsatzgruppen*. The 3,000 number is an approximate figure for the number in the field at any one time. Approximately 6,000 men served in total in the Einsatzgruppen.

77   In Serbia, from September, male Jews were shot *en masse*, particularly by the Wehrmacht, under the official rationalisation of the fight against 'partisans'. See Manoschek, *'Serbien ist Judenfrei'*; Christopher Browning, *Fateful Months: Essays on the Emergence of the Final Solution*

(New York, Holmes and Meier, 1991), ch. 2.

78   Browning, *The Path to Genocide*, p. 56.

79   Browning, *The Final Solution and the German Foreign Office*.

80   A point made in Hannah Arendt, *The Origins of Totalitarianism* (New York, Harcourt, Brace and World, 1966), p. 123. See also Woodruff D. Smith, *The Ideological Origins of Nazi Imperialism* (New York, Oxford University Press, 1986).

81   Jürgen Zimmerer, 'Colonialism and the Holocaust: Towards an Archaeology of Genocide', in A. Dirk Moses (ed.), *Genocide and Settler Society* (New York, Berghahn Books, 2004, forthcoming); Jürgen Zimmerer, 'Wir müssen jetzt krassen Terrorismus üben. Von der Unterdrückung zur Ausrottung: Der Krieg gegen die Herero und Nama in Deutsch-Südwestafrika als Erbe der deutschen Kolonialzeit und die Klage auf Entschädigung', *Frankfurter Allgemeine Zeitung*, 2 November 2002.

82   Christian Gerlach, *Kalkulierte Morde: Die deutsche Wirtschafts- und Vernichtungspolitik im Weißrußland* (Hamburg, Hamburger Edition, 1999), p. 157.

83   Peter Black, 'Rehearsal for "Reinhard"? Odilo Globocnik and the Lublin Selbstschutz', *Central European History*, vol. 25 (1992), pp. 204–26, here p. 205.

84   Alexander B. Rossino, 'Nazi Anti-Jewish Policy during the Polish Campaign: The Case of the Einsatzgruppe von Woyrsch', *German Studies Review*, vol. 24 (2001), pp. 35–53.

85   For the best overview of these early deportation schemes, and their place in the development of the 'final solution', see Browning, *The Path to Genocide*, ch. 1.

86   On Eastern Galicia as 'bridge', see the studies by Pohl and Sandkühler. On German war aims and their frustration, Dieckmann, 'Der Krieg und die Ermordung der litauischen Juden'.

87   Peter Witte, 'Two Decisions Concerning the "Final Solution to the Jewish Question": Deportations to Lodz and Mass Murder in Chelmno', *Holocaust and Genocide Studies*, vol. 9, (1995); Heer, 'Killing Fields', pp. 90–3. See also Uwe Dietrich Adam, *Judenpolitik im dritten Reich* (Düsseldorf, Droste, 1972), pp. 303–12, 355–61; Browning, *Nazi Policy*, pp. 38–9.

88   See above, chapter 2, pp. 70, 73–6, 82.

89   Wildt, *Generation des Unbedingten*, p. 628.

90   Browning, *Nazi Policy*, pp. 51–6.

91   Pohl, 'Judenpolitik', pp. 102, 110.

92   Witte et al. (eds), *Der Dienstkalendar Heinrich Himmlers 1941/1942*. For examples of Hitler's input, Witte, 'Two Decisions'.

93   Pohl, 'Schauplatz Ukraine', p. 143; Lower, '"Anticipatory Obedience"'.

94 Witte, 'Two Decisions', pp. 333–4.

95 Wildt, *Generation des Unbedingten*, pp. 679–93.

96 Ibid., pp. 688–93. For other evidence on Himmler's personal role, Pohl, *'Judenpolitik'*, p. 179; implicit in Sandkühler, 'Lemberg-Janowska', pp. 627–8.

97 Peter Longerich, *Politik der Vernichtung: Eine Gesamtdarstellung der nationalsozialistische Judenverfolgung* (Munich, Piper, 1998), p. 488. See also Christopher Browning, 'A Final Hitler Decision for the "Final Solution"? The Riegner Telegram Reconsidered', *Holocaust and Genocide Studies*, vol. 10 (1996), pp. 3–10, and the discussion by Gerlach of similar issues in *Krieg, Ernährung, Völkermord: Forschungen zur deutschen Vernichtungspolitik im Zweiten Weltkrieg* (Hamburg, Hamburger Edition, 1998), pp. 254–7. For an example of accelerated killing in the eastern territories from the end of May 1942 through July, see Pohl, 'Schauplatz Ukraine', p. 172; Lower '"Anticipatory Obedience"', p. 14.

98 Lower, '"Anticipatory Obedience"'. See also Lower's forthcoming monograph from the University of North Carolina Press on Nazi occupation policy in the Ukraine.

99 Wildt, *Generation des Unbedingten*, pp. 546–53.

100 Michael Thad Allen, 'The Banality of Evil Reconsidered: SS Mid-Level Managers of Extermination Through Work', *Central European History*, vol. 30 (1997), pp. 253–94.

101 Hans Mommsen, 'Kumulative Radikalisieung und Selbstzerstörung des Regimes', in *Meyers Enzyklopädisches Lexikon*, vol. 16 (1976), pp. 785–90.

102 On these contradictions see Walther Naasner, *SS-Wirtschaft und SS-Verwaltung* (Düsseldorf, Droste, 1998) pp. 4–5 and passim; Franciszek Piper, *Arbeitseinsatz der Häftlinge aus dem KL Auschwitz* (Oswiecim, Auschwitz State Museum, 1995), pp. 364–7.

103 Alexandra-Eileen Wenck, *Zwischen Menschenhandel und 'Endlösung': Das Konzentrationslager Bergen-Belsen* (Paderborn, Ferdinand Schöningh, 2000).

104 Browning, *Ordinary Men*, pp. 171–6; Zygmunt Bauman, *Modernity and the Holocaust* (Ithaca, Cornell University Press, 1989), ch. 6.

105 Bloxham, *Genocide on Trial*, p. 1.

106 As Lower points out in '"Anticipatory Obedience"', p. 14.

107 Bloxham, *Genocide on Trial*, ch. 5.

108 See Dieter Pohl, *Nationalsozialistische Judenverfolgung in Ostgalizien 1941–1944: Organisation und Durchführung eines staatlichen Massenverbrechens* (Munich, Oldenbourg, 1997) and his *'Judenpolitik'*.

109 Browning, *Nazi Policy*, ch. 6.

110 On the decimation of the ghettos, Gerlach, *Krieg, Ernährung, Völkermord*, ch. 3. Bogdan Musial, *Deutsche Zivilverwaltung und*

Judenverfolgung im Generalgouvernement: Eine Fallstudie zum Distrikt Lublin 1939–1944 (Leipzig, Harrassowitz, 1999), pp. 193–200, claims significantly greater involvement by Hans Frank's administration in the decision-making process for the murder of the Polish Jews than does Pohl in *'Judenpolitik'*.

111 Dieter Pohl, 'Die Ermordung der Juden im Generalgouvernement', in Herbert (ed.), *Nationalsozialistische Vernichtungspolitik*, p. 113. On the 'first sweep', see Hilberg, *Destruction*, vol. 1, pp. 291–334.

112 Frank Bajohr, *Parvenüs und Profiteure: Korruption in der NS-Zeit* (Frankfurt am Main, S. Fischer, 2001), pp. 75–89.

113 On the participation of different German agencies 'im Rahmen einer pervertierten Amtshilfe' see Pohl, *Nationalsozialistische Judenverfolgung*, pp. 403–4. On Lublin, and the aspects of volunteering for service in the eastern administration, the exclusion of potential administrators on the grounds of their lack of commitment, the poor quality and small number of the personnel see Pohl, *'Judenpolitik'*, pp. 37–41. For a similar but not quite identical picture in Belarus see Gerlach, *Kalkulierte Morde*, pp. 177, 1151–4. On the make-up of the civil administration in the Generalgouvernement in general and the Lublin province in particular see Musial, *Deutsche Zivilverwaltung*, pp. 23–64.

114 Helmut Krausnick and Hans-Heinrich Wilhelm, *Die Truppe des Weltanschauungskrieges: Die Einsatzgruppen der Sicherheitspolizei und des SD 1938–1942* (Stuttgart, Deutsche Verlags-Anstalt, 1981), p. 137 on this new division of power and responsibility.

115 Christian Streit, *Keine Kameraden: Die Wehrmacht und die sowjetischen Kriegsgefangenen 1941–1945* (Bonn, J. H. W. Dietz, 1991); Omer Bartov, *The Eastern Front, 1941–1945: German Troops and the Barbarization of Warfare* (New York, St Martin's Press, 1985); Omer Bartov, *Hitler's Army: Soldiers, Nazis and War in the Third Reich* (Oxford, Oxford University Press, 1992); Krausnick and Wilhelm, *Die Truppe des Weltanschauungskrieges*; Jürgen Förster, 'Das Unternehmen "Barbarossa" als Eroberungs- und Vernichtungskrieg', in Horst Boog (ed.), *Der Angriff auf die Sowjetunion* (Frankfurt am Main, Fischer, 1991). Another more recent crop of literature has gone even further than these classic works, depicting a rank and file in touch to some degree with the ideological priorities of the political regime, and hence receptive to the idea of 'atrocity by policy'. Walther Manoscheck has gone as far as to suggest that criminal orders and criminal acts are part of a *Kriegsalltag* – the 'everyday history' of the Wehrmacht at war in the east. See his 'Verbrecherische Befehle – Verbrecherische Taten', *Mittelweg*, vol. 36 (1992/3), pp. 137–44; also the essays in Hannes Heer and Klaus Naumann (eds), *Vernichtungskrieg: Verbrechen der Wehrmacht 1941 bis 1944*

(Hamburg, HIS, 1995); and Christian Gerlach, 'Verbrechen deutscher Fronttruppen in Weissrussland 1941–1944', in Karl Heinrich Pohl (ed.), *Wehrmacht und Vernichtungspolitik: Militär im nationalsozialistischen System* (Göttingen, Vandenhoeck and Ruprecht, 1999), pp. 89–114.

116 Alexander B. Rossino, 'Destructive Impulses: German Soldiers and the Conquest of Poland', *Holocaust and Genocide Studies*, vol. 11 (1997), pp. 351–65.

117 Breitman, *Architect of Genocide*, pp. 105–15. For a more nuanced picture see Hans Safrian, *Eichmann und seine Gehilfen* (Frankfurt am Main, Fischer, 1995), p. 137.

118 Ulrich Herbert, 'Die deutsche Militärverwaltung in Paris und die Deportation der französischen Juden', in Herbert (ed.), *Nationalsozialistische Vernichtungspolitik*, pp. 170–208.

119 Pohl, 'Judenpolitik', pp. 159–60.

120 Bartov, *Hitler's Army*.

121 Hilberg, *Destruction*, vol. 1, p. 322.

122 Streit, *Keine Kamaraden*.

123 Heer, 'Killing Fields'. Going even further, and suggesting simple outright antisemitism, Walter Manoschek, *'Es gibt nur eines für das Judentum: Vernichtung': Das Judenbild in deutschen Soldatenbriefen 1939–1944* (Hamburg, Hamburger Edition, 1995).

124 On Belarus, Heer, 'Killing Fields'. On Serbia, Manoschek, *'Serbien ist Judenfrei'*; Browning, *Fateful Months*, ch. 2. On Romanies, see the sections on the Second World War in Zimmermann, *Rassenutopie*.

125 On Yugoslavia, Rossino, 'Destructive Impulses', p. 361.

126 James J. Reid, 'Total War, the Annihilation Ethic, and the Armenian Genocide, 1870–1918', in Richard Hovannisian (ed.), *The Armenian Genocide* (Basingstoke, Macmillan, 1992), pp. 21–52; V. G. Kiernan, *Colonial Empires and Armies 1815–1960* (Stroud, Sutton, 1998), ch. 10.

127 On the creation of 'dead zones' in and around Belarus, see Gerlach, *Kalkulierte Morde*, pp. 1010–36.

128 Messerschmidt, '"Harte Sühne am Judentum"', including information on Manstein and the order in question; Erich Kosthorst, *Die Geburt der Tragödie aus dem Geist des Gehorsams* (Bonn, Bouvier, 1998), pp. 178–203, on Manstein's character and motivation.

129 Krausnick and Wilhelm, *Die Truppe des Weltanschauungskrieges*, p. 148 on the SD representation. More generally, Klein's introductory essay in Klein (ed.), *Die Einsatzgruppen*.

130 On Waffen-SS ideology and indoctrination, see Wegner, *Waffen-SS*, parts I and III. Wegner does, however, show the changing character of the Waffen-SS as it expanded rapidly during the Second World War, such that much greater emphasis was ultimately put on military efficiency than ideology. Nevertheless it can be assumed that those Waffen-

SS men used for racial murder at the beginning of the war were fully in tune with the SS ethos. In terms of group ethos generally, Wegner also shows that unlike in the army, where the officer corps formed a very separate social group to the ordinary soldiers, the Waffen-SS itself was the closed community, and much more inclusive within its own ranks.

131 On the radicalism of these occupation SS and police units, Pohl, *'Judenpolitik'*, p. 38. On the need for further research, Pohl, 'Die Ermordung der Juden im Generalgouvernement', p. 111; Jürgen Matthäus, 'What about the "Ordinary Men"?: The German Order Police and the Holocaust in the Occupied Soviet Union', *Holocaust and Genocide Studies*, vol. 10 (1996), pp. 134–50, here p. 137.

132 Westermann, '"Ordinary Men" or "Ideological Soldiers"?', pp. 44–6.

133 Bartov, *The Eastern Front, 1941–1945*, on the effect of this 'barbarization' process on the Wehrmacht.

134 Westermann, '"Ordinary Men" or "Ideological Soldiers"?'. See also Cadle, 'Kurt Daluege', pp. 72–3.

135 Andrej Angrick et al., '"Da hätte man schon ein Tagebuch führen müssen": Das Polizeibataillon 322 und die Judenmorde im Bereich der Heeresgruppe Mitte während des Sommers und Herbstes 1941', in Helge Gräbitz, Klaus Bästlein and Johannes Tuchel (eds), *Die Normalität des Verbrechens* (Berlin, Edition Hentrich, 1994), pp. 325–85, especially pp. 359–62.

136 Dick de Mildt, *In the Name of the People: Perpetrators of Genocide in the Reflection of their Post-War Prosecution in Germany* (The Hague, Martinus Nijhoff, 1996), p. 311.

137 Browning, *Ordinary Men*, passim; Goldhagen, *Hitler's Willing Executioners*, passim. Matthäus, 'What about the "Ordinary Men?"', draws, from the limited evidence available, conclusions that support the thesis of the vital importance of context. He does not, however, distinguish between reserve and regular order police units.

138 Jean Améry, *At the Mind's Limits: Contemplations by a Survivor of Auschwitz and Its Realities* (Bloomington, Indiana University Press, 1980). See the chapter 'Torture'. Also 'On the Necessity and Impossibility of Being a Jew'.

139 On these initiation rituals, Karin Orth, *Die Konzentrationslager-SS: Sozialstrukturelle Analysen und biographische Studien* (Göttingen, Wallstein, 2000), pp. 129–32.

140 De Mildt, *In the Name of the People*, pp. 310–11.

141 Hermann Kaienburg, 'KZ-Haft und Wirtschaftsinteresse', in idem (ed.), *Konzentrationslager und deutsche Wirtschaft 1939–1945* (Opladen, Leske and Budrich, 1996), pp. 29–60, here pp. 31–2. On the formation of the 'Dachau model', see Karin Orth, *Das System der*

The Holocaust

*nationalsozialistischen   Konzentrationslager: Eine   politische
Organisationsgeschichte* (Hamburg, Hamburger Edition, 1999), pp. 27–31.

142   Orth, *Das System*; Orth, *Die Konzentrationslager-SS*, pp. 153–63 on this military service.

143   Orth, *Die Konzentrationslager-SS*, pp. 205–54, including an analysis of Auschwitz.

144   Browning, *Ordinary Men*, p. 24.

145   Pohl, *Nationalsozialistische Judenverfolgung*, p. 407.

146   On these actions generally, see Dean, *Collaboration in the Holocaust*. On the 'second wave', see Hilberg, *Destruction*, vol. 1, pp. 368–90; Jürgen Matthäus, '"Reibungslos und planmäßig": Die zweite Welle der Judenvernichtung im Generalkommissariat Weißruthenien (1942–1944)', *Jahrbuch für Antisemitismusforschung*, vol. 4 (1995), pp. 254–74.

147   Dean, *Collaboration in the Holocaust*, pp. 162–4; Thomas Sandkühler, 'Die Täter des Holocausts', in Pohl (ed.), *Wehrmacht und Vernichtungspolitik*, p. 55; Black, 'Rehearsal for "Reinhard"?', pp. 210, 213, 217, 225.

148   Sandkühler, 'Die Täter des Holocausts', p. 55; Dean, *Collaboration in the Holocaust*, p. 188, note 73.

149   For example, Browning, *Ordinary Men*, pp. 83–5.

150   Precise totals have not been established, but see Piper, *Arbeitseinsatz*, p. 230, footnote, for estimates cited from 400,000 to 600,000.

151   Piper, *Arbeitseinsatz*, p. 220; Ulrich Herbert, 'Von Auschwitz nach Essen: Die Geschichte des KZ-Aussenlagers Humboltstrasse', in *Dachauer Hefte 2: Sklavenarbeit im KZ* (Munich, Deutsche Taschenbuch Verlag, 1986), pp. 13–34, here pp. 18–19.

152   Christian Gerlach and Götz Aly, *Das letzte Kapitel: Der Mord an den ungarischen Juden* (Stuttgart, Deustche Verlags-Anstalt, 2002), pp. 375, 409.

153   See Jonathan Wiesen, 'Overcoming Nazism': Big Business, Public Relations and the Politics of Memory, 1945–1950', *Central European History*, vol. 29, (1997), pp. 201–26.

154   Mark Spoerer, 'Profiteen Unternehmen von KZ-Arbeit?', *Historische Zeitschrift*, vol. 268 (1999), pp. 61–95, here pp. 74–94 contains a schematic presentation of the decision-making process for labour allocation and a tabular summary of whence the initiatives emanated. See Franciszek Piper, 'Industrieunternehmen als Initiatoren des Einsatzes von KZ-Häftlinge: Das Beispiel Auschwitz', in Hamburger Stiftung zur Förderung von Wissenschaft und Kultur (ed.), *'Deutsche Wirtschaft': Zwangsarbeit von KZ-Häftlinge für Industrie und Behörden* (Hamburg, V. S. A. Verlag, 1991), pp. 97–139.

155   On the application for specifically Jewish labour, see Herbert,

172

'Von Auschwitz nach Essen'; Irena Strzelecka and Tadeusz Szymanski, 'Die Nebenlager Tschechowitz', *Hefte von Auschwitz*, vol. 18 (1990), pp. 190–1. On companies bypassing the Speer ministry to contact the SS directly, see Benjamin Ferencz, *Less than Slaves: Jewish Forced Labour and the Quest for Compensation* (Cambridge, Mass., Harvard University Press, 1979), pp. 23–4.

156 On this use of Jews from 1941/2 onwards, see Michael Schmid, '"Unsere Ausländischen Arbeitskräfte"', in Hamburger Stiftung für Sozialgeschichte (ed.), *Das Daimler-Benz Buch* (Nördlingen, Delphi, 1987), pp. 559–91, here p. 585; and also on the Siemens-Bau Union, see Hermann Kaienburg, 'Wie konnte es soweit kommen?', in Kaienburg (ed.), *Konzentrationslager und deutsche Wirtschaft*, p. 267.

157 Ludolf Herbst, *Der Totale Krieg und die Ordnung der Wirtschaft* (Stuttgart, Deutsche Verlags-Anstalt, 1982). Spoerer, 'Profierten Unternehmen von KZ-Arbeit?', pp. 72–3, 89. For a case study of the effect of post-war planning on one large concern, see Neil Gregor, *Daimler-Benz in the Third Reich* (New Haven, Yale University Press, 1998), and also his 'The Normalisation of Barbarism: Daimler-Benz in the "Third Reich"', *Journal of Holocaust Education*, vol. 6, no. 3 (1997), pp. 1–20, p. 15.

158 Gregor, 'The Normalisation of Barbarism', pp. 15–16.

159 Peter Hayes, *Industry and Ideology: I. G. Farben in the Nazi Era* (Cambridge, Cambridge University Press, 1997), p. 358; Deborah Dwork and Robert Jan Van Pelt, *Auschwitz 1270 to the Present* (London, Norton, 1996), p. 197.

160 Piotr Setkiewicz, 'Häftlingsarbeit im KZ Auschwitz III', in Herbert et al. (eds), *Die nationalsozialistischen Konzentrationslager*, vol. 2, pp. 584–605, p. 600; Hayes, *Industry and Ideology*.

161 Michael Zimmermann, 'Kommentierende Bemerkungen', in Herbert et al. (eds), *Die nationalsozialistischen Konzentrationslager*, vol. 2, pp. 730–54, here p. 739.

162 Ferencz, *Less than Slaves*, p. 13.

163 Setkiewicz, 'Häftlingsarbeit im KZ Auschwitz III', pp. 600–1.

164 Bloxham, 'Jewish Slave Labour', p. 186, n. 134.

165 Piper, 'Industrieunternehmen als Initiatoren', p. 104.

166 Spoerer, 'Profitierten', pp. 87–90.

167 See Kaienburg, 'Wie konnte es soweit kommen?', pp. 270–1 on the particular identification of prominent industrialists with Nazism, for example through Himmler's 'circle of friends'. Though it is not in tune with the general thrust of his argument, Karl-Heinz Roth reveals the extent of Nazification at Siemens: 'Zwangsarbeit im Siemens-Konzern', in Kaienburg (ed.), *Konzentrationslager und deutsche Wirtschaft*, pp. 149–67, here p. 165.

168 Kaienburg, 'Wie konnte es soweit kommen?', pp. 275–6.

169   Hannah Arendt, *Eichmann in Jerusalem: A Report on the Banality of Evil* (New York, Viking, 1963). For her wider work, see *The Origins of Totalitarianism*.

170   Yaacov Lozowick, *Hitlers Bürokraten: Eichmann, seine willigen Vollstrecker und die Banalität des Bösen* (Munich, Pendo, 2000). See also Safrian, *Eichmann und seiner Gehilfen* and the case study of one of Eichmann's staff, Claudia Steur, *Theodor Dannecker: Ein Funktionär der 'Endlösung'* (Essen, Klartext, 1997). For a summary of the age and socioeconomic backgrounds of these men, who were even younger than the RSHA leadership, Steur, *Theodor Dannecker*, pp. 158–61.

171   Lozowick, *Hitlers Bürokraten*, pp. 279–80. On the Italian record in comparison with that of Germany, Jonathan Steinberg, *All or Nothing: The Axis and the Holocaust 1941–1943* (London, Routledge, 1990).

172   As for instance with Burleigh and Wippermann, *The Racial State*, in their introduction and concluding chapter; Dan Diner, 'Varieties of Narration: The Holocaust in Historical Memory', in Jonathan Frankel (ed.), *Studies in Contemporary Jewry: The Fate of the European Jews, 1939–1943* (Oxford, Oxford University Press, 1997).

173   With Theodor Dannecker an example of one of the more extreme: e.g. Lozowick, *Hitlers Bürokraten*, p. 48. On Dannecker see also Steur, *Theodor Dannecker*.

174   See Orth, *Die Konzentrationslager-SS*; also Hermann Kaienburg, *'Vernichtung durch Arbeit': Der Fall Neuengamme* (Bonn, J. H. W. Dietz, 1990) pp. 476–7; Michael Thad Allen, 'Engineers and Modern Managers in the SS', Ph. D. thesis (Pennsylvania, 1995), p. 349.

175   On the running and supply of the camps, Kaienburg, *Vernichtung durch Arbeit*; Orth, *Das System*. But cf. Schulte, who disputes Kaienburg's arguments in 'Zwangsarbeit für die SS', pp. 73–4. For a full contextualisation of Schulte's arguments, see his *Zwangsarbeit und Vernichtung: Das Wirtschaftsimperium der SS. Oswald Pohl und das SS-Wirtschafts- und Verwaltungshauptamt 1933–1945* (Paderborn, Ferdinand Schöningh, 2001). The best overall analysis of the WVHA, its organisational and ideological norms and its leadership is Michael Thad Allen, *The Business of Genocide: The SS, Slave Labor, and the Concentration Camps* (Chapel Hill, University of North Carolina Press, 2002), the published version of his aforementioned doctoral thesis 'Engineers and Modern Managers in the SS'.

176   Browning, *The Final Solution and the German Foreign Office*. Quotes from pp. 181, 183.

177   Bauman, *Modernity and the Holocaust*. As criticised implicitly and explicitly from a variety of perspectives including, for instance, Goldhagen, *Hitler's Willing Executioners*; Burleigh and Wippermann, *The Racial State*; Allen, 'The Banality of Evil Reconsidered'; Lozowick, *Hitlers*

Bürokraten; Diner, 'Varieties of Narration', note 18; and in Ulrich Herbert's introductory chapter to *Nationalsozialistische Vernichtungspolitik.*

178 For example, Michael Thad Allen, 'The Devil in the Details: The Gas Chambers of Birkenau, October 1941', *Holocaust and Genocide Studies*, vol. 16 (2002), pp. 189–216, here p. 190, on the primitive nature of the Reinhard gas chambers in contrast to those of Auschwitz.

179 Pohl, *Nationalsozialistische Judenverfolgung*, p. 405, speaks of a 'de-bureaucratisation' of the Holocaust in Eastern Galicia.

180 As Pohl, ibid., note 3, also suggests.

181 Allen, 'Engineers and Modern Managers in the SS'.

182 C. Sorabji, 'A Very Modern War: Terror and Territory in Bosnia-Herzegovina', in R. Hinde and H. E. Watson (eds), *War: A Cruel Necessity? The Bases of Institutionalised Violence* (London, Tauris, 1995), pp. 80–99. Thanks go to Mark Levene for this reference.

183 Mark Levene, 'The Changing Face of Mass Murder: Massacre, Genocide, and Post-Genocide', *International Social Science Journal*, vol. 54 (2002), pp. 447–50.

4

The bystanders: towards a more sophisticated historiography

Those responsible for the United States Holocaust Memorial Museum in Washington highlighted their belief

> that one of the Holocaust's fundamental lessons is that to be a bystander is to share in the guilt. This lesson is applicable to the contemporary problems of society and to the behaviour of individuals. Within any society, groups and individuals are constantly confronted with the destructive potential human beings possess. Only the intervention of the bystander can help society to become more human.[1]

In his important study on the origins of genocide, *The Roots of Evil* (1989), Ervin Staub states that '[b]ecause the potential power of bystanders is great, so is their obligation, an obligation only occasionally fulfilled'. Staub poses the question: 'How can we engage compassion, the awareness of responsibility for other lives, and the feeling of obligation to act?'[2] In a foreword to Victoria Barnett's study of bystanders during the Holocaust, Carol Rittner and John Roth suggest that '[t]heir behavior raises troubling questions about human nature, about the very foundations of human ethics and morality. Did these ordinary people have choices?'[3] Barnett herself writes that 'bystanders are confronted by a wide range of behavioral options, and they bear some responsibility for what happens'. She concludes that

> The loss of each individual life shakes the universe and changes the course of history. In this way, the conscience of each individual has the power to reach far beyond the public realm, and create the

fabric of a progressively greater whole: of family, society, nation, history, and humanity itself.[4]

With the Holocaust as its focal point, it is clear from these examples reflecting a range of academic approaches to the Holocaust, and heritage representation of it, that there is enormous contemporary moral investment in the concept of the 'bystander'. Somewhat disturbingly, however, the historiography on Holocaust bystanders is relatively undeveloped, certainly at a theoretical level.[5] Barnett's is one of the first overviews and was published as late as 1999. Yet as well as becoming emotionally and ethically charged, the term has become a somewhat loosely defined catch-all for those who are 'neither perpetrator nor victims'.[6] It includes, according to Deborah Lipstadt, 'neutral governments and agencies, Jews living in relative safety, occupied countries, ordinary Germans, and above all, the Allied governments'. As David Cesarani and Paul Levine argue, so casual has been the usage that there is now a pressing need 'to restore the distinction between radically different kinds of "bystander"'.[7]

The emphasis on much literature and reflection on the 'bystander' has been the issue of choices facing the ordinary person. Perspective is thus essential: the choice of a Polish non-Jew, for example, in helping a Jew was immensely risky, whereas for an individual in, say, wartime Britain to write a letter to the Foreign Office or to join a protest meeting on behalf of European Jewry, the price was that of a postage stamp or an hour of leisure. The consequences of action were also radically different – in the first case it could be a matter of life of death for both these historical actors whereas in the second the power of the ordinary person to make a difference was remote. Indeed, many of the humanitarian activists became quickly disillusioned, facing the hugeness and remoteness of their task and the seeming indifference and immovability of the only body they could realistically influence – the British government.[8]

It is difficult even to compare directly those in Nazi-occupied or influenced nations; much literature and popular representation in museums and beyond has worked on the moral duality of 'good Danes' as against 'bad Poles'. Steve Paulsson has controversially suggested that the purpose behind mythologising the collective Danish 'rescue' of the Jews, when over 7,000 were ferried across to Sweden in October 1943, is little to do with what the Danes actually did. On the contrary, 'the Danish case stands as an *accusation* against other nations, which could have done the same thing if they only had ... "The Courage to Care"'.[9] The Danes had more choices available and less risk, whereas the Poles, argues Paulsson, hid and helped Jews far more than has been appreciated and at enormous danger to themselves. In Warsaw, for example, he estimates that 28,000 Jews were in hiding with between 70,000–90,000 non-Jewish Poles helping them. This represented a 'secret city', numbering at least 100,000 people, or 10 per cent of non-Jewish Warsaw.[10]

At the other extreme, there was total choice for those Polish non-Jews who in July 1941 decided to murder their Jewish neighbours in the town of Jedwabne. All but seven of the Jews, representing half Jedwabne's population of 3,000, were brutally murdered. Context is crucial as we have seen in the previous chapter – the pogrom cannot be understood (but cannot also be in any way justified) without reference to the brutalisation that occurred through the Soviet occupation of the town and the outbreak of the Russo-German war in June 1941.[11] This was a different world from that of Denmark in 1943 or for that matter Britain in 1942. Britain's wartime responses towards European Jewry can make grim reading but it is worth reflecting that it had a far more open and generous policy towards Jewish refugees during the latter part of the 1930s than did Denmark.[12] Even Leni Yahil, whose 1969 monograph on the rescue of Danish Jewry helped establish the heroic motif, acknowledged that pre-war '[t]he Danish authorities laid down extremely severe criteria for accepting Jewish refugees. Entry permits were given only to those who could prove family relationship with a Danish citizen resident in the country, and whose economic support could be guaranteed in advance.'[13] In bystander studies like has to be compared with like or at least a strong sense of proportion has to be kept and care taken in contrasting reactions and responses in vastly different circumstances. The Polish non-Jews in Jedwabne were at different stages and sometimes simultaneously perpetrators, victims and bystanders. The same cannot be said of those in the western liberal democracies. Rather than spread its net too thinly in the space available, therefore, this chapter will focus on one specific area – that of the western democracies, and more specifically Britain and the USA – which provides both a discrete overview but also a window into the strengths and limitations of bystander studies as a whole.

Discovering the bystander

Hugo Gryn was a teenage Auschwitz survivor who came to Britain in a scheme to help young victims of the Nazi camps recuperate after the war. Subsequently he became a Reform rabbi working in the USA and India before becoming a much-loved religious leader inside and outside the Jewish community in Britain.[14] In his last speech, proclaiming that 'asylum issues are an index of our spiritual and moral civilisation', Hugo Gryn stated that '[h]ow you are with the one to whom you owe nothing, that is a grave test and not only as an index of our tragic past. I always think that the real offenders at the half way mark of the century were the bystanders, all those people who let things happen because it didn't really affect them directly.'[15]

Hugo Gryn particularly had in mind the historical example of the *SS St Louis*, the German cruise ship which set off from Hamburg in the summer of 1939 carrying over one thousand German Jews. The story has subsequently become famous. Those on board held Cuban visas but when they arrived there all but a tiny fraction were refused entry. The captain of the ship deliberately travelled close to the coast of Florida but the American authorities refused to give the passengers permission to land, as did several South American countries. The ship returned to Europe. Britain, Holland, Belgian and France took the majority of the *St Louis* refugees but only a handful outside Britain survived the war, caught up in the whirlwind that was the Holocaust. There were other such ships carrying refugees in the late 1930s and many more refugees were refused entry to a range of countries using old and new regulations against the entry of aliens. The *St Louis*, however, has become one of the most enduring symbols of what is perceived as the failure of rescue before the Second World War and the unwanted status of the Jewish refugees. There have been many journalistic accounts of the journey, a feature length film, *The Voyage of the Damned* (1976), as well as award-winning documentaries.[16] The *St Louis* also occupies a major place in the United States Holocaust Memorial Museum in Washington, DC.[17]

The eventual murder of the majority of the *St Louis* refugees provokes much anger – here were people who could have been taken in by many different countries had they wanted to, including of course the USA: 'Urgent appeals were made to the [US] State Department, which decided not to intervene. The passengers sent a telegram to President Roosevelt. It went unanswered; the White House maintained its silence on refugee issues.'[18] To Hugo Gryn it was an indictment not only of the contemporaries, but also of those who had not learned any lessons from the episode: 'It is a very painful and I have to say this, it is an unacceptable fact, that half a century later, we, and by we I include our political leaders as well, we act as if nothing happened. It's unacceptable.'[19] Much more, it would seem, has been at stake in the case of the *St Louis*, or even of the Jewish refugee crisis during the 1930s, than is normal in confronting the past.

The first starting point in a historiographical overview of Britain, the USA and the Holocaust is that it was far from inevitable that scholarship would develop as extensively as has been the case. There have been, for example, genocides and mass murders as well as larger refugee movements that have received little or no attention from historians and others. Moreover, in relation to the Holocaust as a whole, Britain and the USA, as prominent liberal democracies during the 1930s and, from American entry into the war, the two leading western Allies, are relatively tangential, not of course to the diplomatic and military narrative of war, but to the Nazi genocide that took place within it. Most obviously, they were not the perpetrators: the recent attempt, for example, to connect the massive American computer company IBM to the destruction process has been utterly lacking in historical or ethical balance and proportion.[20] As bystanders Britain and the USA lacked the physical immediacy of the occupied nations, neutrals and non-belligerents to help or otherwise. In relation to the victims of persecution, again both countries were peripheral. Post-1945 in the war crimes trials and within popular culture, a disproportionate space was found for British and American citizens who suffered under the Nazi regime.[21] Whilst it is true that both countries before the war and the USA after it were major places of emigration for refugees and survivors of the Third Reich, it remains that in terms of the victims as a whole the continent of Europe itself was the focal point as a huge killing field. So what is behind the intense and growing interest in British and American responses to the plight of the Jews during the Third Reich?

The escalating fascination in the Holocaust is clearly one necessary but not sufficient reason why the subject matter of Britain, the USA and the Holocaust has developed. As emphasised earlier, at an artistic and cultural level, representations of the Holocaust, especially in film, media, history and literature, have never been so intense and pervasive. More generally, in the western world (and increasingly beyond) the Holocaust is now commonly perceived as one of the key defining moments of the twentieth century, raising essential moral questions about human nature and the nature of modernity.

It is important to remember, however, that the concept of the Holocaust as a particular part of the Second World War or more generally of the Nazi era, involving specifically the planned extermination of European Jewry, took many years to evolve, a process that was uneven and is still perhaps incomplete. One example of this gradual evolution has emerged from one of the recent attempts to achieve compensation not from a perpetrator nation, but a so-called bystander, Britain. Assets from the deposit accounts of continental Jews who placed assets in British banks were confiscated by the government during the war as these belonged to people who were now citizens of enemy nations or enemy occupied countries. After the war, attempts by those who survived or their relatives to claim back the money or property were for the large part turned down by the British government. Being Jewish was not enough to prove that one was a victim of the Nazis rather than an enemy alien. As one British Treasury official put it, 'I do not know how you will distinguish between the Jew who has been persecuted because of his race or religion, and one who has been sent to a concentration camp for committing a criminal offence against the law of his country'.[22] Moreover, experience of slave labour, hiding and the ghettos was not proof of having suffered persecution. The category of victim was limited to some of those who had died or survived the concentration camps, the definition of which was vague but undoubtedly heavily influenced by perceptions of the images of the liberated western camps such as Buchenwald and Belsen.[23]

In similar fashion, in 1945 the British Home Office allowed in on a temporary basis after much campaigning a very small number of child survivors but stipulated that they must not all be Jewish and that they should come from one or two named camps, particularly, again, Belsen. Not enough children could be found from these specific camps, so the scheme was broadened, enabling those like Hugo Gryn to be granted temporary entry.[24] In short, the immediate legacy of the images of 1945 and the subsequent war crimes trials was largely that of essentially undifferentiated Nazi atrocities. There was little interest in the victims and only a short-lived concern to confront and deal with the perpetrators of atrocities. In the new Cold War logic, the latter were soon transformed from the German nation as a whole into very specific parts of it. In essence the higher echelons of the Nazi state structure were blamed, especially the 'criminal' SS who could be labelled as exceptional monsters, mad(wo)men or sadists, unrelated to everyday folk like 'us'.[25] The concept of the bystander was all but lacking at this time, an absence of consideration eased by the American, British, Soviet, French and Polish involvement in the immediate post-1945 war crimes trials. The world was divided between the Nazis and those who had resisted them, even if this meant, particularly in the case of France, creating a national myth that has been so powerful it is still to be fully overcome.[26]

Perceptions over fifty years later have, however, changed remarkably. Rightly, much time and energy have been spent researching the motivations of the murderers, and the estimates of the number of those involved were growing ever larger well before the sensational work of Daniel Goldhagen. We may never ultimately know why so many ordinary people agreed to take part in the 'final solution', but it is clear that choice played a bigger role than was previously acknowledged. The detailed scholarship revealing the sheer scale of those involved and the greater freedom to say no might have further undermined the idea that genocide was carried out by two-dimensional, leather-clad, diabolic beasts. Nevertheless, the huge popular success of Goldhagen's imagery of bloodthirsty Germans acting as 'willing executioners' in contrast to the relatively unknown work of Christopher Browning and his understated portrayal of mundane 'ordinary men' in a police battalion stumbling into mass murder suggests that we still prefer our killers to be presented as evil sadists.[27] More strikingly, the victim, as we have seen in the first chapter of this book, was initially subject to total obscurity, or at most was represented as an object simply there to represent the evils done by the perpetrator. More recently there has been major interest in the victims, even if they still do not quite enter the centre stage. Survivor evidence was largely excluded from the post-war trials,[28] and in many different countries where they settled treatment of the surviving Jews was shabby and even violent; they were often seen as an embarrassment and their stories ignored or silenced.[29] Steven Spielberg's project founded in the 1990s, the 'Survivors of the Shoah Visual History Foundation', which aimed to interview as many survivors as possible, is one illustration of change,[30] although how to incorporate the voices of the victims other than as rather tokenistic illustrations of what the Nazis did remains an unsolved dilemma in historical writing on the Holocaust and in the growing number of museums devoted to the subject.[31] Considerations of gender, age, religious and political background, to name but a few, have started to be addressed, complicating the 'victim' category even when confined to consideration of the Jews. Nevertheless, 'victim' is now firmly established as the second part of the tripartite division of the principal actors of the Holocaust. The third, of course, is the 'bystander', as unquestioned on a popular level today as it was absent from consideration in 1945.

The Goldhagen–Browning debate about the importance or otherwise of antisemitism and/or Germanness in the motivation of the murderers as much as the fraught controversies of the 1950s and 1960s about alleged Jewish passivity and collaboration show the power of Holocaust scholarship to stir up deep-felt emotions regarding perpetrators and victims. But it is, perhaps, the area of the bystander which has caused the greatest soul searching and anger in recent years. Indeed it must be suggested that it is the popular division of the Holocaust into the neat categories of perpetrator–victim–bystander[32] that is fundamental to why it is seen as raising all the essential moral questions of our age.[33] There is no serious doubting of the horror and scale of the crime, no questioning of the impact on the victims, and few exceptions to a general awareness that little or nothing was done to stop it happening by those who stood by. The moral concern about bystanders comes out of the rather complacent assumption that few of us will become perpetrators, and an equal optimism that we won't become victims, while at the same time we are aware that in an age of almost instant global communications, we are all co-presents witnessing, even if only through the media, the genocides, ethnic cleansing and other manifestations of extreme racism and violence that besmirch the contemporary world. Equally, we fail to help, as Hugo Gryn desperately urged, the tens of millions of refugees across the world. However, whereas the ambiguities and contradictions of human nature make the study of bystanders so fascinating, significant, and ultimately relevant to today, there seems to be little desire so far for this to be brought out in studies of the Holocaust.

Put bluntly, we like our bystanders to be as bifurcated as the categories of victim and perpetrator. Given the centrality of the Holocaust in contemporary philosophical and theoretical debates about the nature of humankind in the modern age and beyond, this is a dangerous if understandable development. For rather than nuancing our understanding of the complexity of human responses during the Holocaust, the bystander category is in danger of aiding the tendency to see the subject in manichean terms, as a symbol of mass evil alongside much less prevalent absolute good (with the emphasis put on the latter to enable hope for the future). As Shoshana Felman has written in relation to literary critic Paul de Man and the heated reaction to his exposure as a collaborator in Belgium during the war: '[he] was "Nazi": in denouncing him as one of "them", we believe we place ourselves in a different zone of ethics and of temporality; "we", as opposed to "they", are on the right side of history – a side untouched, untainted by the evil of the Holocaust'.[34] Even Zygmunt Bauman in his *Modernity and the Holocaust*, which throughout strips away the power of individual agency, concludes by praising those people who 'chose moral duty over the rationality of self-preservation ... Evil is not all-powerful. It can be resisted.'[35] Returning again to the *St Louis*, the dangers of treating it as a simplistic morality story are never far from the surface.

The fact that the real villains are essentially off stage – the Nazis are responsible for the desire to escape but are rarely part of the main storyline once the ship has left Hamburg – enables others to take their place as the 'baddies' who are contrasted to the hero of the narrative in the self-contained world of the *St Louis*. In the words of Hugo Gryn: 'The only decent person in the whole story is the German captain of the ship. He tries whatever he can. He negotiates with the United States, with Columbia, with Chile, with Paraguay, with Argentina – but nothing comes of it. So the ship recrosses the Atlantic and comes back to Europe.'[36] The power of the emotional and ethical engagement with the Holocaust has led, as will emerge, to ongoing difficulties within historiography, especially in developing an approach that is neither accusatory nor defensive nor simplistic in outlining motives for action or inaction. The specific historiography itself, however, developed slowly and unevenly in Britain and the USA.

The historiography of Anglo-America and the Holocaust

During the war a group of dedicated campaigners in Britain, especially the MP Eleanor Rathbone and the publisher Victor Gollancz, attempted to mobilise public opinion in Britain to force the government and international bodies to recognise and publicise the plight of European Jewry and from there to take whatever action was possible to help and rescue the 'victims of Nazi terror'. Their campaigns and proposals for action were influential on Jewish and non-Jewish activists in the USA.[37] Although these campaigners on both sides of the Atlantic were prolific, their work and writings were largely forgotten in the immediate post-war period; they themselves rarely referred to such activities. Outside Zionist circles inside and outside of Palestine for whom Britain was now 'enemy number one', there was no mention of the campaigners and the embarrassing issues they had raised in the war. In the newly independent state of Israel the indifference and antipathy of the Anglo-American world to the fate of the Jews became part of national mythology. Prime Minister David Ben-Gurion's response to the call for restraint from leading left-wingers in Britain at the time of the Suez crisis in 1956 makes this clear: 'We still recall that there were leaders of the Labour Party who did not take seriously Hitler's threat physically to exterminate the Jewish race until it was too late. Six million Jews perished in the gas chambers of the Nazi dictator. I am sorry that you do not see the danger of the Fascist dictator of Egypt.'[38]

In contrast, in Britain and the USA, a more comfortable counter-mythology developed that nothing was known and that only with liberation of the camps did knowledge become available.

Ironically, the liberation of the western camps, rather than prompting questions of what could have been done to stop them, was more often than not used to show the moral certainty of the British and American war effort. Images from the camps were 'proof positive' that it had indeed been a 'just war', most famously summarised by the remarks of General Dwight Eisenhower when entering Ohrdruf concentration camp on 12 April 1945: 'We are told that the American soldier does not know what he was fighting for. Now, at least he will know what he is fighting against.' These words are given prominence at the United States Holocaust Memorial Museum accompanying images of the camp liberations – indeed, Philip Gourevitch has commented that 'Ike's remarks could serve as the museum's motto'.[39]

In the early historiography of the Holocaust in works such as Gerald Reitlinger's *The Final Solution* (1953) the only major mention of the western allies was in the form of camp liberators and even then, showing a rather parochial approach, focusing on the British army's liberation of Belsen. Only two paragraphs were devoted to the responses of the Anglo-American states to the Holocaust. Reitlinger acknowledged the State Department's 'positive obstruction' of rescue measures during the war but he rejected the possibility that the Foreign Office was equally uncooperative.[40] The only major rival in the early 1950s to Reitlinger's narrative of the Holocaust was Leon Poliakov's *Harvest of Hate* published originally in 1951. Poliakov acknowledged that Allied responses to the persecution of the Jews would be revealing 'though they constitute one of the least known aspects of the history of World War II'.[41]

The contesting of this mythology – Anglo-America as liberators or indifferent bystanders – has taken a long time to gather momentum and is still far from complete, although half a century on from Poliakov a case could be made for it being one of the better researched areas of the Second World War. Both the United States Holocaust Museum in Washington and the Imperial War Museum Holocaust Gallery in London start or end with the respective American and British soldiers liberating western concentration camps in the spring of 1945. Nevertheless, beyond these initial images they both have critiques of the American/British responses to the Jewish plight during the Nazi era, especially the Washington museum with its focus on the *St Louis*. There is still a problem, however, with the prism through which they confront the role of these particular bystanders, which in turn reflects a continuing problem in the historiography.[42]

In both Britain and the USA the first books on western Allied responses to the Holocaust were crude, semi-journalistic and angry in tenor.[43] By the early 1960s the comforting myth of ignorance had grown to create a reassuringly safe cocoon against self-reflection at the time when the concept of the Holocaust as a separate entity, largely through the Eichmann trial, was starting to emerge. In a polemical way the Eichmann trial had raised the particular issues of the Allied failure to bomb Auschwitz as well as the possibility of negotiating with the Nazis over Hungarian Jewry in 1944. In similar tone, books such as those by Arthur Morse and to a lesser extent David Wyman in the United States and Andrew Sharf in Britain attempted to shatter the illusion that nothing was known or that nothing could have been done.[44] The mood of complacency marked by Reitlinger gave way to one of accusation. If Reitlinger, an assimilated British Jew, was very much part of the establishment, some of the literature emerging in the late 1960s and early 1970s was marked by a growing ethnic pride and self-confidence on behalf of American Jewry in which it was possible to attack the memory of political icons such as Roosevelt and to challenge the myth of American exceptionalism with regard to antisemitism. It was aided by the release of government papers, speedier in the United States than in Britain, which outlined reactions and responses to the plight of the Jews during the 1930s and the Second World War. Morse's book especially, written by an investigative journalist, was marketed in a sensational way. It was the 'untold and shocking account of the apathy shown, and the deliberate obstructions placed by the USA and Britain in the way of attempts to save the Jewish people from Hitler's "final solution"'.[45] Yet the tendency towards condemnation, which was understandable as the emotional subject was 'rediscovered' during the 1960s, has still, several decades later, not disappeared. Indeed the anger has revived more recently with campaigns for legal redress evidenced by the successful lobbying of the Holocaust Education Trust in Britain and in the USA by its much more powerful equivalents in the world of organised American Jewry. The moral outrage has been reinforced in the former case by the willingness of the media to give attention to material released from these countries' respective national archives, the details of which, particularly relating to state knowledge of the Holocaust during the war, including within the intelligence world, has often already been reported.[46]

Nevertheless, in Britain through the 1970s and 1980s more detailed scholarship emerged, even if it was less intensive because of the slow release of government papers and also the limited interest in the Holocaust across society and culture as a whole. In the USA the first sophisticated analysis was provided in *The Politics of Rescue* (1970) by Henry Feingold, who, in contrast to Morse, wished to 'move beyond the moral aspect to examine the political context in which America's response was conceived'.[47] The first serious work on Britain, tellingly by an American (in fact, an American Jew), was A. J. Sherman's *Island Refuge* covering British refugee policy from 1933 to the outbreak of war. Using what was still a relatively limited range of government papers available in the public domain, Sherman provided a solid narrative of official responses to the Jewish refugee crisis. Yet even in Sherman's self-conscious desire to concentrate on description, it is telling that his conclusion is entitled 'A Balance Sheet'. Indeed, in his much-quoted final paragraph Sherman states that when 'Great Britain's refugee policy [of the 1930s is] compared with that of other countries it emerges ... as comparatively compassionate, even generous'.[48]

It is the 'balance sheet' approach that has continued to dominate the historiography since Sherman's book was published in 1973. Sherman in particular compared Britain to the USA – for example, setting the failure of the Wagner-Rogers bill to bring 20,000 refugee children to the USA in 1939 against the success of the Kindertransports which brought 10,000 children to Britain before the outbreak of war. He therefore rejected the charge 'of indifference to the fate of refugees from the Nazi regime'.[49] Subsequently little genuine national comparative work has been carried out either on the 1930s or on the Second World War with regard to the liberal democracies. Instead the balance sheet metaphor has been applied within individual nation-states in relation to what was done, and not done, for the Jews persecuted by the Nazis. Returning to museum representation of the Holocaust in the Anglo-American world, anti-refugee sentiment, including within the state structure, is included in the two national museums but is done in a self-conscious desire to show fairness alongside the help offered to the persecuted. Indeed, the Imperial War Museum convened an emergency meeting when finalising its text and display, to debate whether the exhibition was either too critical or too uncritical of British responses.[50]

Reviewing the literature in 1987, Michael Marrus stated that 'there is a strong tendency in historical writing on bystanders to the Holocaust to condemn, rather than to explain'. He adds that '[h]istorians have quite properly combed the seamy underside of Allied and Jewish policy, searching through records sometimes deliberately hidden from view. But they should take care in using such material, to give contemporaries a fair hearing.'[51] The key is to understand why they reacted and responded in the way they did, not avoiding the moral issues raised, but doing so by exploring the possibilities of choice that were available to contemporaries, inside and outside of government.

The early work on Allied responses to the plight of the Jews was marred not just by its accusatory nature but by its lack of any wider sense of context. There was little awareness of either the dynamics of the bystander nation or the chronological development and confused nature of Nazi antisemitic policy. Morse's book, for example, maintained 'that both the State Department and the Foreign Office were well aware of Hitler's intentions [to exterminate the Jews] long before the war'.[52] In contrast, the more detailed research that has taken place in the last twenty-five years has had greater success in dealing with questions of *Realpolitik* – the other concerns of government departments and Jewish organisations in the Nazi era. Even more fruitful has been the longer-term approach to the mentality of governments and their state and legal apparatus, especially involving immigrants and refugees – showing how they had evolved *before* the Nazi rise to power and the continuity or otherwise after 1933. In this respect the pioneer work was that of Richard Breitman and Alan Kraut (1987) which revealed the continuity of alien policies in the United States after the First World War and throughout the Nazi era.[53] Even more sophisticated in its understanding of the state apparatus has been Louise London's *Whitehall and the Jews*. Feingold's pioneer work had shown the importance of debates within the American state structure. By painstaking analysis of the material available at what was then the Public Record Office,

London's research in the British case went much further. A whole range of departments are examined, and not simply obvious ones such as the Foreign Office and Home Office. Divisions within as well as between departments, and the role of key individual civil servants, are highlighted throughout in this work. London's book is successful because it understands the complexity of bureaucratic history and the necessity of placing it in political context.[54]

It is significant that both Breitman and Kraut and London have extended chronologies – London continuing the story beyond the end of the war. Only through a longer-term perspective can the practices and mentalities of the state apparatus be outlined and changes from normal procedures become apparent. It is still the case, however, that far less progress has been made with understanding the cultural, societal and ideological underpinnings of either state or society's responses to the plight of the persecuted Jews in the liberal democratic and other bystander nations. In this respect, one of the greatest barriers to progress is the use or avoidance of the term 'antisemitism'.

Michael Marrus, in his survey of literature on bystanders, states that '[g]enerally speaking, few historians believe antisemitism to have been decisive in blocking aid to the Jews' – a view from which he does not seem to dissent.[55] Although early scholarship in the United States by authors such as David Wyman and Saul Friedman had placed emphasis on official antisemitism, even they had placed it alongside other factors.[56] Bernard Wasserstein in his follow-up to Sherman's account of British government responses, taking the story through the Second World War, provides what is still the dominant analysis, blaming 'bureaucratic indifference' for the fact that there was 'little to celebrate in [his] account of British policy towards the Jews of Europe between 1939 and 1945'. Wasserstein, whilst not ignoring what he called 'the tinge of anti-Semitism in the words of some British officials and politicians', states bluntly that 'anti-Semitism does not by itself explain British conduct ... conscious anti-Semitism should not be regarded as an adequate explanation of official behaviour'.[57]

The problem here is one of context and definition. The list of self-identifying antisemites in twentieth-century Anglo-America would hardly enter the hundreds.[58] What do we mean by antisemitism in a liberal democratic context? The easiest answer is to concentrate on the extreme – for example fascists such as

Oswald Mosley in Britain or Father Coughlin in the United States who could be seen to be obsessed by the Jewish peril. Racism in Britain particularly has been and continues to be blamed on such extremists, helping to avoid confrontation with a wider problem. Ultimately such nazis and neo-nazis can be seen to be merely imitating those on the diseased continent; indeed they can be seen as not really English at all. Similarly, it has been argued that the Holocaust Museum in Washington, DC, distances rather than bridges the gulf between the United States and Europe, the former being a place of refuge and the latter a place of persecution.[59]

Throughout the discourse of government officials reproduced by Sherman, Wasserstein and others it is apparent that the Jewishness of the victims of Nazism mattered in their position as potential refugees to Britain, elsewhere in the empire and Palestine, or as other recipients of British support. The same is true of the work of Breitman and Kraut in the case of the United States and their treatment of senior State Department officials such as Breckinridge Long. But neither Sherman, who rejected the term 'indifference', nor Breitman and Kraut and Wasserstein, who embraced it, were comfortable analysing the implications of that contemporary bureaucratic confrontation with Jewishness. In *The Holocaust and the Liberal Imagination* (1994), Kushner attempted to explore this question through the prism of the dominant ideology and culture of Britain and the USA in the Nazi era and beyond. Antisemitism, or other forms of racism, have often been explained as due to the absence or relative weakness of liberalism. But the situation in Britain, the USA and many other liberal democracies during the 1930s and 1940s was more complex. Assimilation was still seen as the dominant solution to the so-called 'Jewish question' in liberal thinking. If antisemitism persisted in the modern, enlightened world, it was because Jews insisted on retaining their difference, or rather went beyond a religious identity that was perceived as being compatible with national belonging. The more different the Jews, the more dangerous – hence the hostility of British and many other officials to Jews from eastern Europe, one which often went alongside praising the much more integrated Jewish communities of western Europe.[60]

In short, a fundamental ambivalence existed: genuine anguish at the violence of Nazi antisemitism but a failure to confront why it was happening and a tendency to blame the victims if not support the severity of the 'punishment'; belief in Britain and the United States as genuinely tolerant societies that prided themselves on the help they had offered refugees in the past, but a fear of letting in other than carefully selected individual Jews, or individual groups of Jews, lest they bring antisemitism with them.[61] As Long put it: 'We have been generous – but there are limitations'.[62] Henry Feingold, in his analysis of the United States and the Holocaust, suggested perceptively that '[t]he villain of the piece, in the last analysis, may not be the State Department or even certain officials but the nature of the nation-state itself'.[63] The problem for ethnic minorities throughout the twentieth century and beyond was how the nation-state would deal with difference. Jewish difference, especially in the first half of the twentieth century, was perceived as particularly problematic by both politicians and state bureaucracies.

What is fascinating in both countries is how at particular moments more generous policies could emerge. At the now infamous international conferences on refugees at Evian (July 1938) and Bermuda (1943) neither Britain nor the United States were willing either to highlight publicly the specific plight of the Jews or to fundamentally change their procedures of entry. At other times, however, politicians and civil servants came up with initiatives that enabled major rescue and relief. In Britain, for example, between 1933 and 1938 highly selective immigration policies dominated. The policy was in the words of a Ministry of Labour official 'not to vary the aliens administration in favour of or against the refugees'.[64] In the twelve months before war, however, entry was opened up through procedural changes, with some 40,000 Jews allowed entry. Nevertheless, this was followed by a policy of almost total restrictionism to be adherred to during the conflict and the years that followed.[65]

How do we explain this relatively large number admitted in the last months of peace? Undoubtedly British guilt after Munich, especially after the moral integrity of appeasement was totally destroyed in the light of Kristallnacht,[66] alongside the closing of the doors to Palestine, explain why procedures were eased by the government. But other factors were at work enabling the movement to be defended on liberal grounds. First, almost all those allowed entry to Britain were on temporary visas – that way they would not create a permanent Jewish 'problem'. Second, they would be spread out and re-trained so as to normalise them – whether as trainee agricultural workers, domestic servants or nurses. It is no accident that Ernest Bevin, who as Foreign Secretary in the 1940s was to exclude Jews from Britain, was very positive, as General Secretary of the world's largest trade union during the 1930s, towards the entry of several thousand German Jewish youngsters who were to be trained in agricultural techniques in the British countryside with the hope that they would practice their new skills in Palestine or elsewhere.[67]

Bevin is worth a little more attention in order to tease out further the problems of utilising the term 'antisemitism' in a context of a liberal democratic world. After the war Bevin became a great hate figure in large parts of the Jewish world, especially in the United States. His opposition to Jewish immigration to Palestine and insensitivity to the survivors helped lead to him being perceived as motivated 'by a personal hatred of Jews'. As Alan Bullock, Bevin's biographer, comments, '[f]rom this sprang the stereotype of him as the latest in the long series of persecutors of the Jews beginning with Titus and Haman and continuing down to Hitler and Himmler'. Subsequently, 'pop' psychology has been employed to explain Bevin's alleged hatred of Jews as coming out of his troubled childhood. His crudity and insensitivity are undoubted – he simply made no attempt to empathise with the horrors inflicted so recently on the Jewish people.[68]

What *is* remarkable about Bevin is that he stubbornly stuck to a classic liberal position on the Jews. Such analysis of Bevin, however, has been regarded as 'untenable' and 'far-fetched'. If 'liberal' is seen *per se* as an absolute good, then the surprise at the label attached to Bevin can be understood.[69] But what Bevin wanted was for the Jews to return to their various 'homelands' rather than attempting to escape their countries of citizenship, or former citizenship, and in so doing jump to 'the head of the queue' to leave the continent of Europe (his public irritation with Jewish displaced persons mirroring that expressed privately by American President Harry S. Truman, as referred to in the introduction). Jews, believed Bevin, should return 'home' and become once again good Germans and Poles and so on. In 1945 and 1946 as Foreign Secretary he allowed a small number of young Jews to come to Britain as long as the men would go on the land and the women become nurses. He wanted them to become useful and to stop an 'undesirable concentration of them in towns'. When this failed to happen, unsurprisingly given their physical state, the Jewish survivors were kept out whilst at the same time the British government enabled hundreds of thousands of continental non-Jews, some of whom had been Nazi collaborators, to enter because they were seen as desirable, assimilable immigrants.[70]

Bevin's policies, however, followed on from those of his rival and fellow Labour cabinet minister Herbert Morrison, who had been Home Secretary from 1940 to the end of the Second World War. Both men were sincere anti-Nazis at home and abroad, and Morrison on a personal level was surrounded by Jewish friends and work colleagues.[71] On the one hand, the label antisemite does not seem to help other than to provide a neat but ultimately superficial explanation of their policies. On the other, to reject the possibility that Jewishness had anything to do with official thinking avoids confronting the contemporary obsession with the subject.[72] Indeed, the almost total restrictionism against Jewish refugees from September 1939 to 1950 carried out by the British government has to be explained, and this can only be done so successfully by analysing how liberal ambivalence, especially the idea that Jews bring antisemitism with them, was taken to its logical extreme, becoming in itself ingrained into bureaucratic mentality and practice.[73]

The reality is that most responses from government, state and public in Britain and the United States were marked by a fundamental ambivalence to Jews and Jewish suffering. Not only is ambivalence difficult to pigeon-hole, but it was fluid and dynamic, able to respond to different impulses and demands in an unpredictable manner. During the war and in contrast to the pre-war months, British officials learned to deal with calls to aid Jews in the most universal way possible (that is to win the war and to reject the idea that Jews particularly were being singled out for persecution). In the United States, however, pressure from Jewish and non-Jewish campaigners outside Congress, and from within the state structure in the Treasury Department, led to the formation of the War Refugee Board (WRB) in January 1944. Although the word 'Jew' was not incorporated in its title, the major function of the WRB was to save Jewish lives. Indeed, it has been claimed that through its work over 100,000 Jews were helped, especially through relief work in Hungary such as providing food, accommodation, money, protective visas and safe houses. A recent account has attempted to demolish the idea that the efforts of the WRB saved Jewish lives.[74] Such a critique is simplistic and reflects a general lacuna in the existing historiography that '[i]n discussions about the Allied response to the Holocaust, scholars have underplayed the relief question in favour of focusing on the question of immigration and rescue'.[75] The WRB was relatively marginal within the American government's state apparatus and most of its resources came from Jewish sources. Nevertheless, its aim was particularistic; it focused on the persecuted and not, as was the official policy of both the British and American governments, on the overall war effort and 'winning the war first'.[76]

Before the war public pressure in Britain, especially after the Kristallnacht pogrom, had helped open up entry. Tens of thousands of ordinary people were involved in refugee work in Britain during 1939, many in relation to the child refugees. Not surprisingly, however, given the previous hostility, the treatment refugees received on entering Britain was mixed. Not all could confront their own ambiguities about Jews, but it did not stop them demanding that the persecuted be allowed entry.[77] Liberal ambivalence within the state and the public enabled both restrictionism and generous rescue policies to succeed within bystander nations at different times and different places.

It is also through what Bryan Cheyette has called a 'semitic discourse' operating in liberal culture that news of the persecution of the Jews was responded to.[78] The first major account of western Allied knowledge of the Holocaust was provided by the right-wing Zionist scholar Andrew Sharf in his 1964 book on the British press and the Holocaust. Sharf's work was part of the accusatory literature of the 1960s. He argued that the press 'knew well and printed accurately exactly what was happening' but that nothing was done with that knowledge. His explanation was 'an inveterate British inability to grasp imaginatively what could happen on the continent of Europe', which in turn was due to an antipathy towards Jews and the 'psychological commonplace that, with the best will in the world, it is hard to grasp the meaning of suffering wholly outside one's immediate experience'.[79]

A more detailed analysis covering both Britain and the United States was not produced until Walter Laqueur's study published in 1980. Laqueur, following Sharf, placed emphasis on psychological factors hindering understanding, posing the question of 'what is the meaning of "to know" and "to believe"'.[80] Psychological factors cannot be dismissed, but they have been highlighted at the expense of a wider cultural context. If, for example, contemporary discourse regarded 'Jews' as powerful, untrustworthy and alien, it becomes less surprising that news of their persecution might be rejected as propaganda or seen to be irrelevant to the concerns of those fighting total war. Instead, a somewhat mystical approach has been developed in the historiography of contemporary Anglo-American understanding of the Holocaust with titles such as 'The Terrible Secret' or 'Beyond Belief'.[81] Anglo-American knowledge of Auschwitz particularly has been subject to ahistorical and incomplete research, overstating its role in the 'final solution' at the expense of camps such as Treblinka, Sobibor, Belzec and Chelmno in 1942 and ignoring what was known about it through Polish and other sources.[82] Too much research in this area of knowledge and understanding has taken place in a contextual vacuum. In relation to official sources it has ignored the type of records such information came in. In relation to the press, some have utilised extensive cuttings collections that inevitably fail to place such news in the wider setting of the individual newspaper as a whole. On the level of popular understanding, preliminary work based on extensive scrutiny of contemporary diaries and other such sources emanating from ordinary people, which has enabled a social history perspective, has not been developed.[83] Instead, attention has focused on the information made available only to a tiny number of people through Anglo-American intelligence intercepts of German signals relating particularly to the killings in the east after the invasion of the Soviet Union. The debate about knowledge has closed in rather than expanded. It requires a social and cultural history perspective if a less newsworthy but more intellectually productive historiography is to develop.

Since *The Holocaust and the Liberal Imagination* was published, the failure in much scholarship on Britain and the United States to confront the nature of liberalism and the importance of ambivalence is itself revealing. Some reviewers have engaged in the central argument and quite rightly called for more detailed work to explore much further the nature of liberalism and its relation to nationalism and ethnic difference.[84] A more common response, however, has been to assume that this is yet another accusatory text that sees 'antisemitism' as the answer to why so little was done, or, paradoxically, to condemn the book for not reaching that conclusion. A similar reception has greeted Louise London's *Whitehall and the Jews*. The desire for black or white explanations is telling. Ambivalent figures are not welcome and there has been an increasing tendency to seek out the moral giants in the by-stander worlds whose actions either confirm the weakness of those around them or confirm that ordinary mortals could have done little to help. In 1999 alone, Frank Foley, senior Passport Control Officer in the British embassy in Berlin, *and* Nicholas Winton, a businessman who helped bring refugee children to Britain from Czechoslovakia in 1939, were labelled as 'Britain's Schindler'. In both cases market research (accurate as it happens) revealed that this is what the public wanted to hear and read. Crudely constructed renderings of the work of Winton and Foley, as Anne Karpf suggests, 'function as the happy endings of the Holocaust that we impossibly crave'.[85]

Such tendencies, which seem to be growing in Holocaust com-memoration, have many problems associated with them. First, they highlight the role of the major figure in the process, as is the case with Raoul Wallenberg, ignoring the very many ordinary people who enabled their actions to have their spectacular suc-cess.[86] Second, they make saints or angels, both words used to describe Foley, out of these figures, often ignoring their more complex nature and their reasons for engaging in rescue and re-lief.[87] We need, in David Cesarani's words, to work towards 'a tax-onomy of rescuers' in countries like Britain and the United States.[88] Third, they allow self-congratulation to become domi-nant – as illustrated in Britain in 1999 with the plaque unveiled in the House of Commons 'in deep gratitude to the people and Par-liament of the United Kingdom for saving the lives of 10,000 Jew-ish and other children who fled to this country from Nazi persecution on the Kindertransport 1938–1939'.[89] There is no mention, of course, of the parents who were excluded from this refugee movement. Was this generous in the circumstances or fundamentally inhumane? The question is unanswerable – no balance sheet approach can take away the heartache of separation from the gratitude of life-saving asylum and come up with a meaningful answer.[90]

But the increasing emphasis on gratitude and the help that was provided by the exceptional few has helped enable the success of a revisionism, led in the Anglo-American cases by William Rubinstein in *The Myth of Rescue* (1997). This work argues that during the 1930s, given the circumstances, all that could have been done was done and that in the Second World War itself not one single Jew could have been rescued by the Allies.[91] Although most academic responses to Rubinstein have so far been critical, popular reviews, especially it has to be said from non-Jews, have been very favourable. Clearly Rubinstein's work has appealed at an emotional level to many: for those anxious about the moral integrity of the British and American war memory, *The Myth of Rescue* removes any nasty tarnish that in their minds has unfairly developed in recent years. Furthermore, it negates the need for further self-reflection.[92] Indeed, a detailed survey of attitudes carried out in 2000 revealed that most believed that Britain had been very generous in helping the Jews of Europe during the Nazi era, with a minority of respondents equally simplistically arguing that nothing had been done to help.[93] This brings me to my final point in relation to *The Myth of Rescue*: Rubinstein lets the reader off from any consideration of the dilemmas facing bystanders, and his book's success suggests that he has struck a popular chord. It might be added that Rubinstein's Jewishness has perhaps removed any restraint about saying the 'wrong thing'. As Norman Stone, praising what he saw as 'a very good book', stated: 'For the rest of us, common sense and decency make it extremely difficult to offend elderly survivors by suggesting that the picture needs to be amended'.[94]

But choices *were* there in the British and American worlds. Of course these need to be placed in their specific contexts, recognising their own particular specific limitations, throughout the Nazi era. Yet there is a danger that rather than confronting the ambivalence, contradictions and ambiguities of contemporaries, we increasingly take refuge in the creation of plaster saints or retreat, as with the obsessive interest in the western intelligence world and its knowledge of the Holocaust, into the comfortable fiction that only the privileged few knew of its existence during the war or that nothing at all could be done to stop mass murder.[95] The possibility of bombing Auschwitz in 1944, prominently featured in the

United States Holocaust Memorial Museum, has become a particularly futile area of research with historians analysing whether or not it could have been carried out successfully. The only major context considered in the Auschwitz bombing debate has been the military.[96] There is a great need to move beyond the elite world of politicians and the state apparatus and to explore how ordinary people and grassroots organisations responded in the Anglo-American world to the plight of the persecuted (including groups that have so far been ignored such as the Sinti and Roma, and those deemed physically and mentally unfit). There is very little information, for example, on local refugee organisations which were so crucial in rescuing refugees and helping them integrate.

The historiography of the Anglo-American world and the Holocaust, which started tentatively, has taken off in the past thirty years. Reviewing a book on United States immigration procedures published in 2001, one of the pioneers of such work, Henry Feingold, commented that he was surprised that there was anything left still to say. At the end of his review, however, Feingold acknowledged that the book in question on United States' Consuls and the Jews did indeed show a continuing justification for such research.[97] Even state responses in Britain and the United States need teasing out further, as exemplified by the research of Louise London. By employing a wide-ranging chronology that goes well before and after the Nazi era it is possible to chart continuity and change in alien and refugee policy and to avoid the tendency towards ahistorical and emotionally driven work. Such vertical comparisons need to be placed alongside the horizontal – what was the contemporary response of the Anglo-American world to other crises during the Nazi era? Meridith Hindley, for example, has made important observations comparing responses to the Holocaust and the European hunger crisis during the war.[98] Through such broadening contexts a genuinely productive historiography could emerge rather than the simplistic pseudo-debate created by William Rubinstein. Away from political and state responses we are still at an early stage in understanding how ordinary people in Britain and the United States, including the Jewish minority, responded to the plight of the persecuted. There is also need to develop further some of the excellent work that has recently emerged on literary, cultural and artistic responses to the Holocaust in the 'free world' both at the time and subsequently.[99] Again, by taking a long time span, the complex processes of history and memory can be analysed, revealing much about the making and re-making of British and American identities. Such fresh work, if carried out subtly and away from the accusatory–defensive oppositional that has dominated the specific subject matter for too long, may tell us little about the specific history of the Holocaust. It will, however, continue to provide important and unique insights into the workings and dynamics of liberal democratic politics, culture and society.

Returning to the general theme of this chapter, the detailed analysis of the historiographical trends in Anglo-American reactions and responses to the Holocaust reveals the critical importance of context. In particular, it has focused on the construction and re-construction of Britishness (or more specifically, Englishness) and Americanness, just as a different geographical bystander focus would have revealed much about Danishness, Dutchness, Hungarianness and so on. Ultimately it has to be remembered that the relationship with the enemy or the occupying forces and the freedoms that were possible were of crucial importance during the war in determining the responses of bystanders. Yet national, local and other traditions and discourses were also of deep significance, without which, for example, the pogrom in Jedwabne could never have taken place.

Broadening the geographical and conceptual scope further, H. R. Kedward, in a 1998 lecture on 'Resiting French Resistance', has emphasised the crucial importance of specific circumstances and how acceptance of such local contextualisation has begun to transform studies of resistance: 'it is only recently that [the] question of what resistance had to offer to certain places and people has come to supplement the previously dominant question of what places and people had to offer to resistance'.[100] It is worth pausing on the example of France and to question further the helpfulness of labels such as 'resister', 'collaborator' and 'bystander' in understanding wartime responses.

In what has been called the 'Vichy syndrome', the politics of memory has played a critical role in post-liberation France. Soon after 1945, as Philippe Burrin argues, '[t]hanks to the cold war, the myth of an entire people committed to resistance logically enough soon led to an amnesty designed to bring peace through the integration of a handful of traitors'.[101] It has taken many decades in a still ongoing process for French society and politics to come to terms with the collaboration that took place with the German authorities, most notoriously relating to the 70,000 Jews who were deported, mostly to their death, to Auschwitz. As with Kedward's approach to resistance, we need to ask what collaboration had to offer to places and people as well as the other way round. Not surprisingly, adopting a more complex approach hinders the possibility of labelling individuals as one thing or another, let alone a whole nation. In his excellent overview of the 'dark years' in France, Julian Jackson concludes that the '[o]ccupation should be written not in black and white but in shades of grey … The Resistance was never monolithic, and the lines dividing it from Vichy were not always well defined.' The ambiguities of Vichy are neatly summarised by Jackson in his list of unexpected figures that emerged in his study:

> A pro-Petainist resister; a pro-British and anti-German Petainist; a pro-Jewish Petainist; two anti-Semitic resisters … They reveal the complexity of reactions to the Occupation and the extent to which antagonists might share as many assumptions with their enemies as with those on their own side. People who made different choices often did so in defence of similar values.[102]

In less extreme circumstances than the Poles or other 'racially inferior' peoples occupied by the Nazis, the French could still be simultaneously collaborator, resister, bystander and victim. As ever, the wheres and the whens, especially the local context, are vital in situating and explaining the often ambivalent responses of individuals, particularly in the understandably emotive issue of the fate of the Jews.

Once the context and *spécificité* are taken into account, one is left with the role of the individual as moral agent, and the choices, however limited, that were put before him or her. It is these choices that make the study of the bystander so compelling, but given the complexity of the modern world, we should be cautious not to overstate the bystander's responsibility and power, thereby ignoring those who are the real perpetrators and their determination to carry out genocide, or forgetting, in our moral indignation, those who are the persecutors' victims. In this respect, when these limitations are recognised, the case of Danish Jewry does have significance. Even when the relative ease of the operation and the fortuitous circumstances of high and low level Nazi confusion over what to do about Danish Jewry is taken into account, as well as the ambivalence towards Jewish refugees, something remarkable remains as an example of collective and spontaneous humanitarianism.[103] And lest it give the impression that, in terms of the saving of the Jews, there was nothing like a Dane, the example of Steve Paulsson's 'secret city' of Warsaw, in which many Jews were hidden for a long period of time, should be kept in mind. Lacking the spectacular quality of the 'rescue' of Danish Jewry, the 'secret city' led to three times the number of Jews being protected.[104]

Finally, the Danish case has a wider importance in showing again the danger of bifurcating the bystander into categories of saints or sinners. The 'rescue' was only possible because it was clear that the neutral Swedish government (partly for pragmatic reasons of distancing itself from the Nazis, given the turning fortunes of the war) was prepared to take in the Jews of Denmark. Prominent in this process was Gosta Engzell, head of the Legal Division of the Swedish Foreign Office which was responsible for visa and immigration issues. Engzell's language during the 1930s and at least the early years of the Second World War indicated 'a general distrust of, and unwillingness to help Jews'. Yet in 1942 Engzell and his division played an instrumental role in helping Norwegian Jews. In 1943 the Legal Division was equally important in the rescue of Danish Jews and in 1944 it was at the heart of the Swedish efforts to save the lives of Hungarian Jews. In short, from 1942 to 1944 Engzell helped Sweden rescue Jews who in the former year were closely connected to its own Jewish community and in the latter year had no links with it whatsoever.[105] Engzell's earlier ambivalent attitudes and responses towards Jewish refugees resembled those of Morrison and Bevin outlined earlier. In 1944, when the possibility of mass rescue of Hungarian Jewry was being raised by the War Refugee Board in America and activists in Britain, Morrison responded to his civil servants that it was 'essential that we do nothing at all which involves the risk that the further reception of refugees here might be the ultimate outcome'.[106] Faced with a similar possibility, Engzell led his division with the assumption that it was, in his words, 'better to save too many rather than too few'. As Paul Levine concludes, Engzell and his colleagues *'chose* to help Jews' whereas many other similar bureaucrats and politicians in the liberal democracies did not.[107] Ultimately, as with Levine's and London's work on state bureaucracies in Sweden and Britain respectively, or Kushner's study of Anglo-American culture and society, successful studies of Holocaust bystanders should inform us not only about responses to the fate of the Jews, but also, and of equal and perhaps greater importance, about the competing ideologies and identities of such countries.

Notes

1 Jeshajahu Weinberg and Rina Elieli, *The Holocaust Museum in Washington* (New York, Rizzoli, 1995), p. 18.

2 Ervin Staub, *The Roots of Evil: The Origins of Genocide and Other Group Violence* (Cambridge, Cambridge University Press, 1989), p. 169.

3 Carol Rittner and John Roth, 'Foreword', in Victorial Barnett, *Bystanders: Conscience and Complicity During the Holocaust* (Westport, Ct., Greenwood Press, 1999), p. x.

4 Barnett, *Bystanders*, pp. 10, 175.

5 See the comments of David Cesarani and Paul Levine, 'Introduction', in idem (eds), *'Bystanders' to the Holocaust: A Re-evaluation* (London, Frank Cass, 2002), pp. 1–3.

6 Rittner and Roth, 'Foreword', p. x.

7 Cesarani and Levine, 'Introduction', p. 3.

8 G. S. Paulsson, *Secret City: The Hidden Jews of Warsaw 1940–1945* (New Haven and London, Yale University Press, 2002), pp. 128–9; Tony Kushner, *The Holocaust and the Liberal Imagination: A Social and Cultural History* (Oxford, Blackwell, 1994), pp. 183–7.

9 G. S. Paulsson, 'The Bridge over the Oresund: The Historiography on the Expulsion of the Jews from Nazi-occupied Denmark', *Journal of Contemporary History*, vol. 30 (July 1995), p. 431.

10 Paulsson, *Secret City*, p. 231.

11 Jan Gross, *Neighbors: The Destruction of the Jewish Community in Jedwabne, Poland* (Princeton, Princeton University Press, 2001).

12 Tony Kushner and Katharine Knox, *Refugees in an Age of Genocide: Global, National and Local Perspectives during the Twentieth Century* (London, Frank Cass, 1999), ch. 5.

13 Leni Yahil, *The Rescue of Danish Jewry: Test of a Democracy* (Philadelphia, Jewish Publication Society of America, 1969), p. 19.

14 Hugo Gryn with Naomi Gryn, *Chasing Shadows* (London and New York, Viking, 2000); obituaries in the national British press, 20 August 1996.

15   Rabbi Hugo Gryn, 'A Moral and Spiritual Index' (London, Refugeee Council, 1996).

16   The film was directed by Stuart Rosenberg and was based on Gordon Thomas and Max Morgan-Witts, *Voyage of the Damned* (London, Hodder and Stoughton, 1974). In 1996 an award-winning documentary, *The Voyage of the St Louis*, was directed by Maziar Bahari.

17   Michael Berenbaum, *The World Must Know: The History of the Holocaust as Told in the United States Holocaust Memorial Museum* (Boston, Little, Brown & Co., 1993), p. 59.

18   Ibid., p. 58.

19   Gryn, ' A Spiritual and Moral Index'.

20   Edwin Black, *IBM and the Holocaust: The Strategic Alliance Between Nazi Germany and America's Most Powerful Corporation* (London, Little, Brown & Co., 2001).

21   See Donald Bloxham, *Genocide on Trial: War Crimes Trials in the Formation of Holocaust History and Memory* (Oxford, Oxford University Press, 2001).

22   R. R. Whitty of the Custodian of Enemy Property Office, to Gregory of the Trading with the Enemy Department, 9 October 1947, Public Record Office (PRO) T 236/4312, quoted in Gill Bennett et al., *History Notes: British Policy Towards Enemy Property During and After the Second World War* (London, Foreign & Commonwealth Office, 1998), p. 37. For a more critical appraisal, see The Holocaust Educational Trust, *'Ex-Enemy Jews': The Fate of the Assets in Britain of Holocaust Victims and Survivors* (London, Holocaust Educational Trust, 1997).

23   Ibid.

24   H. Prestige memorandum, 21 September 1945, in PRO HO 213/618 E409.

25   Bloxham, *Genocide on Trial*.

26   Kushner, *The Holocaust and the Liberal Imagination*; Henry Rousso, *The Vichy Syndrome: History and Memory in France since 1944* (Cambridge, Mass. and London, Harvard University Press, 1991).

27   Ernst Klee, Willi Dressen and Volker Piess, *'Those were the Days': The Holocaust through the Eyes of the Perpetrators and Bystanders* (London, Hamish Hamilton, 1991); Christopher Browning, *Ordinary Men: Reserve Police Battalion 101 and the Final Solution in Poland* (New York, HarperCollins, 1992); Daniel Goldhagen, *Hitler's Willing Executioners: Ordinary Germans and the Holocaust* (Boston, Little, Brown & Co., 1996).

28   Bloxham, *Genocide on Trial*.

29   Kushner, *The Holocaust and the Liberal Imagination*, introduction and ch. 7; idem, 'Holocaust Survivors in Britain: An Overview and Research Agenda', *Journal of Holocaust Education*, vol. 4, no. 2 (Winter 1995), pp. 147–66.

30 See, for example, its *The Last Days* (London, Weidenfeld & Nicolson, 1999).

31 Amongst the limited literature examining the nature of Holocaust testimony from ordinary survivors, mainly relating to the Fortunoff Video Archive for Holocaust Testimonies at Yale University, see Geoffrey Hartman, 'Learning from Survivors: The Yale Testimony Project', *Holocaust and Genocide Studies*, vol. 9, no. 2 (Fall 1995), pp. 192–207; Lawrence Langer, *Holocaust Testimonies: The Ruins of Memory* (New Haven, Yale University Press, 1991); and Shoshana Felman and Dori Laub, *Testimony: Crises of Witnessing in Literature, Psychoanalysis and History* (New York and London, Routledge, 1992). A less systematic but much more dynamic and sensitive account is provided by Henry Greenspan, *On Listening to Holocaust Survivors: Recounting and Life History* (Westport, Ct., Praeger, 1998).

32 Raul Hilberg, *Perpetrators Victims Bystanders: The Jewish Catastrophe 1933–1945* (New York, HarperCollins, 1992), although it should be added that Hilberg does explore the complexity of and slippage between all these categories.

33 An early example was Hannah Arendt, *Eichmann in Jerusalem: A Report on the Banality of Evil* (New York, Viking Press, 1963). From the late 1980s there has been an immense flood of books using the Holocaust to explore the nature of humanity and morality in the modern world written by those with both expertise and little knowledge of the subject matter. See, for example, Rainer Baum, 'Holocaust: Moral Indifference as *the* Form of Modern Evil', in A. Rosenberg and G. Meyers (eds), *Echoes from the Holocaust: Philosophical Reflections on a Dark Time* (Philadelphia, Temple University Press, 1988), pp. 53–90; Zygmunt Bauman, *Modernity and the Holocaust* (Oxford, Polity Press, 1989); Berel Lang, *Act and Idea in the Nazi Genocide* (Chicago and London, University of Chicago Press, 1990); Saul Friedländer, *Memory, History and the Extermination of the Jews of Europe* (Bloomington and Indianapolis, Indiana University Press, 1993); Omer Bartov, *Murder in our Midst: The Holocaust, Industrial Killing, and Representation* (New York and Oxford, Oxford University Press, 1996); Michael Burleigh, *Ethics and Extermination: Reflections of Nazi Genocide* (Cambridge, Cambridge University Press, 1997); Norman Geras, *The Contract of Mutual Indifference: Political Philosophy after the Holocaust* (London, Verso, 1998); Jonathan Glover, *Humanity: A Moral History of the Twentieth Century* (London, Jonathan Cape, 1999); and David Blumenthal, *The Banality of Good and Evil: Moral Lessons from the Shoah and the Jewish Tradition* (Washington, Georgetown University Press, 1999).

34 Felman and Laub, *Testimony: Crises of Witnessing*, p. 122.

35 Bauman, *Modernity and the Holocaust*, p. 207.

36 Gryn, 'A Spiritual and Moral Index'.

37   Eleanor Rathbone, *Rescue the Perishing* (London, National Committee for Rescue from Nazi Terror, 1943); Victor Gollancz, *Let My People Go* (London, Gollancz, 1943). See Kushner, *The Holocaust and the Liberal Imagination*, part II, and Kushner and Knox, *Refugees in an Age of Genocide*, ch. 6, for an analysis of these activists, their writings and their impact on state and society.

38   Ben-Gurion quoted by Jad Adams, *Tony Benn* (London, Macmillan, 1992), p. 122.

39   Tony Kushner, 'The Memory of Belsen', in Joanne Reilly et al. (eds), *Belsen in History and Memory* (London, Frank Cass, 1997), pp. 181–205; Edward Linenthal, *Preserving Memory: The Struggle to Create America's Holocaust Museum* (London and New York, Viking, 1995), pp. 90–1; Berenbaum, *The World Must Know*, pp. 8–9; Philip Gourevitch, 'Nightmare on 15th Street', *Guardian*, 4 December 1999.

40   Gerald Reitlinger, *The Final Solution* (London, Vallentine Mitchell, 1953), pp. 406–7, 463–9.

41   Leon Poliakov, *Harvest of Hate* (London, Elek Books, 1956 [orig. in French, 1951]), p. 245.

42   Linenthal, *Preserving Memory*, p. 193; Berenbaum, *The World Must Know*; Gourevitch, 'Nightmare on 15th Street'; on the Imperial War Museum see Donald Bloxham and Tony Kushner, 'Exhibiting Racism: Cultural Imperialism, Genocide and Representation', *Rethinking History*, vol. 2, no. 3 (1998), pp. 353–6, and Tony Kushner, 'Oral History at the Extremes of Human Experience: Holocaust Testimony in a Museum Setting', *Oral History*, vol. 29, no. 2 (Autumn 2001).

43   For example, Arthur Morse, *While Six Million Died* (New York, Random House, 1968) and Andrew Sharf, *The British Press and Jews under Nazi Rule* (London, Institute of Race Relations/Oxford University Press, 1964).

44   David Wyman, *Paper Walls: America and the Refugee Crisis 1938–1941* (Amherst, University of Massachusetts Press, 1968) represented the first account based on detailed, scholarly research; Sharf, *The British Press and Jews Under Nazi Rule*.

45   Arthur Morse, *While Six Million Died* (London, Secker & Warburg, 1968), front cover.

46   For recent British press coverage see the following: Denis Staunton, 'Whitehall Sat on 1942 Goebbels Genocide Speech', *Observer*, 21 November 1993; Michael Dynes, 'Nazis Wanted British Troops as Guards at Death Camps', *The Times*, 27 November 1993, which partly relates to the release of material in PRO HW 1/929; Tim Rayment, 'Britain Barred Rescue Plan for Doomed Jews', *Sunday Times*, 8 May 1994; *The Times*, 23 and 30 January 1995 has articles on French Jewish orphans and the British government in 1942 which relate to Public Record Office papers released many years before 1995; on release of records relating to news of the 'final solution' see Bernard Josephs, 'War Papers Show Britain Knew of Mass Slaughter', *Jewish Chronicle*, 15 November 1996; Richard Norton-Taylor, 'Code Breakers Reported Slaughter of Jews in 1941', *Guardian*, 20 May 1997 and similar reports in the national press on the same day; Richard Norton-Taylor, 'Britain Stymied Help for Jews in Nazi Camps', *Guardian*, 21 July 1999; Barbara Rogers, 'Aushwitz and the British', *History Today*, vol. 49, no. 10 (October 1999), pp. 2–3.

47 Henry Feingold, *The Politics of Rescue: The Roosevelt Administration and the Holocaust 1938–1945*, 2nd edn (New York, Holocaust Library, 1980), p. ix.

48 A. J. Sherman, *Island Refuge: Britain and Refugees from the Third Reich 1933–1939* (Berkeley and Los Angeles, University of California Press, 1973), p. 267.

49 Ibid., pp. 264–5. See also Sherman's comments on later historiography in the new edition of his book (London, Frank Cass, 1994), pp. 1–8.

50 Linenthal, *Preserving Memory*, pp. 216–28; private information concerning the Imperial War Museum. The public controversies that were such a feature of the Washington Museum, which whilst creating difficulties also made its planning more democratic and openly accountable, have been almost totally absent in the case of the Imperial War Museum.

51 Michael Marrus, *The Holocaust in History* (London, Weidenfeld & Nicolson, 1988), p. 157.

52 Morse, *While Six Million Died*, inside cover.

53 Richard Breitman and Alan Kraut, *American Refugee Policy and European Jewry, 1933–1945* (Bloomington and Indianapolis, Indiana University Press, 1987).

54 Louise London, *Whitehall and the Jews 1933–1948: British Immigration Policy and the Holocaust* (Cambridge, Cambridge University Press, 2000).

55 Marrus, *The Holocaust in History*, p. 166.

56 Saul Friedman, *No Haven for the Oppressed: United States Policy Towards Jewish Refugees, 1938–1945* (Detroit, Wayne State University Press, 1970); Wyman, *Paper Walls*.

57 Bernard Wasserstein, *Britain and the Jews of Europe 1939–1945* (Oxford, Oxford University Press/Institute of Jewish Affairs, 1979), pp. 344, 350–2.

58 See Colin Holmes, *Anti-Semitism in British Society 1876–1939* (London, Edward Arnold, 1979).

59 Tony Kushner, 'The Fascist as "Other"? Racism and Neo-Nazism in Contemporary Britain', *Patterns of Prejudice*, vol. 28, no. 1 (January

1994), pp. 27–45; Paul Gilroy, *There Ain't No Black in the Union Jack: The Cultural Politics of Race and Nation* (London, Hutchinson, 1987); Peter Novick, *The Holocaust in American Life* (New York, Houghton Mifflin, 2000).

60 More generally see Bill Williams, 'The Anti-Semitism of Tolerance: Middle-Class Manchester and the Jews, 1870–1900', in A. J. Kidd and K. W. Roberts (eds), *City, Class and Culture* (Manchester, Manchester University Press, 1985), pp. 74–102.

61 Kushner, *The Holocaust and the Liberal Imagination*, passim.

62 Fred Israel (ed.), *The War Diary of Breckinridge Long: Selections from the Years 1939–1944* (Lincoln, University of Nebraska Press, 1966), p. 128 diary entry for 9 September 1940.

63 Feingold, *The Politics of Rescue*, p. xiii.

64 Humbert Wolfe minute, 5 March 1935, PRO LAB 8/78.

65 Kushner, *The Holocaust and the Liberal Imagination*, parts I and II.

66 N. J. Crowson, *Facing Fascism: The Conservative Party and the European Dictators 1935–1940* (London, Routledge, 1997), pp. 32–3.

67 Kushner, *The Holocaust and the Liberal Imagination*, chs 2 and 3.

68 Ibid., pp. 233–5; Alan Bullock, *Ernest Bevin: Foreign Secretary 1945–1951* (London, Heinemann, 1983), p. 164. See also pp. 165, 182, 277–8. Allen Podet, 'The Unwilling Midwife: Ernest Bevin and the Birth of Israel', *European Judaism*, vol. 11, no. 2 (1977), pp. 35–42 and esp. p. 38 dismisses the charge of antisemitism as 'a spurious issue'. More nuanced is Joseph Gorny, *The British Labour Movement and Zionism, 1917–1948* (London, Frank Cass, 1983), p. 219, who in analysing Bevin and Attlee concludes that: 'If we take antisemitism to imply denial of the rights of Jews to live as equal citizens in non-Jewish society, they were not antisemitic. But if we are speaking of prejudices against Jewish culture, conduct, economic acumen and social "pushiness", they were not innocent.' Nevertheless, Gorny still wants to analyse their 'cool malice' through the prism of the term. Ian Mikardo, a Jewish Labour MP who confronted Bevin in 1947 over Palestine, believed that the Foreign Secretary was a straightforward antisemite and that it related to earlier episodes in his life: Ian Mikardo, *Back-Bencher* (London, Weidenfeld & Nicolson, 1988), pp. 97–9.

69 Melvin Shefftz in *AJS Review*, vol. 21, no. 2 (1996), pp. 421–3, and Anthony Glees in *Journal of Holocaust Education*, vol. 6, no. 1 (Summer 1997), pp. 112–14. For an alternative perspective on the thesis of the book, see Steven Beller, '"Your Mark is Our Disgrace": Liberalism and the Holocaust', *Contemporary European History*, vol. 4, no. 2 (1995), pp. 209–21.

70 Bevins' comments are in PRO LAB 8/99; David Cesarani, *Justice Delayed: How Britain Became a Refuge for Nazi War Criminals* (London,

Heinemann, 1992).

71   Bernard Donoughie and G. W. Jones, *Herbert Morrison: Portrait of a Politician* (London, Weidenfeld & Nicolson, 1973).

72   Bryan Cheyette, *Constructions of 'the Jew' in English Literature and Society: Racial Representations, 1875–1945* (Cambridge, Cambridge University Press, 1993) and more generally Geoff Dench, *Minorities in the Open Society: Prisoners of Ambivalence* (London, Routledge & Kegan Paul, 1986). For an insistence on an 'either for or against us' approach to British attitudes towards Jews, limiting antisemitism to extremists, see William Rubinstein, *A History of the Jews in the English-Speaking World: Great Britain* (Basingstoke, Macmillan, 1996).

73   Kushner, *The Holocaust and the Liberal Imagination*, chs 5–7; Kushner and Knox, *Refugees in an Age of Genocide*, ch. 6.

74   William Rubinstein, *The Myth of Rescue: Why the Democracies Could Not Have Saved More Jews from the Nazis* (London, Routledge, 1997).

75   Meredith Hindley, 'Constructing Allied Humanitarian Policy', in Cesarani and Levine (eds), *'Bystanders' to the Holocaust: A Re-evaluation*, p. 86.

76   Breitman and Kraut, *American Refugee Policy*, chs 9 and 10 provide a positive assessment of the Board. See also David Wyman, *The Abandonment of the Jews: America and the Holocaust 1941–1945* (New York, Pantheon, 1985), part IV, and Feingold, *The Politics of Rescue*, ch. 9.

77   Kushner and Knox, *Refugees in an Age of Genocide*, ch. 5.

78   Cheyette, *Constructions of 'the Jew'*.

79   Sharf, *The British Press and Jews Under Nazi Rule*, pp. 113, 194, 209.

80   Walter Laqueur, *The Terrible Secret* (London, Weidenfeld & Nicolson, 1980), pp. 3, 197, and 'Hitler's Holocaust: Who Knew What, When and How?', *Encounter*, vol. 55 (July 1980), p. 24.

81   Laqueur, *The Terrible Secret*; Deborah Lipstadt, *Beyond Belief: The American Press and the Coming of the Holocaust 1933–1945* (New York, Free Press, 1986). For an alternative approach, see Kushner, *The Holocaust and the Liberal Imagination*, ch. 4.

82   Martin Gilbert, *Auschwitz and the Allies* (London, Michael Joseph, 1981) and the television documentary version directed by Rex Bloomstein in 1982 stress the elusive nature of Auschwitz, and Barbara Rogers, 'Auschwitz and the British' continues this tradition. For a critique see David Engel, *In the Shadow of Auschwitz: The Polish Government-in-Exile and the Jews, 1939–1942* (Chapel Hill, University of North Carolina Press, 1987).

83   Sharf and Lipstadt, for example, relied on press cuttings. For a social history approach, see Tony Kushner, 'Different Worlds: British Perceptions of the Final Solution during the Second World War', in David Cesarani (ed.), *The Final Solution: Origins and Implementation* (London,

Routledge, 1994), pp. 246–67.

84 Beller, '"Your Mark is Our Disgrace"', pp. 218–21; Michael Burleigh, 'Synonymous with Murder', *Times Literary Supplement*, 3 March 1995.

85 Michael Smith, *Foley: The Spy Who Saved 10,000 Jews* (London, Hodder & Stoughton, 1999), the paperback edition of which announced that it was 'the book that uncovered Britain's Schindler'. The phrase was used earlier on *Today*, BBC Radio 4, 26 February 1999. On the book's immense success see *Jewish Chronicle*, 23 July and 19 November 1999. Foley was later granted status by Yad Vashem as a 'Righteous Among Nations'. See *Jewish Chronicle*, 22 October 1999. On Nicholas Winton, see *Britain's Schindler*, Radio 4, 7 June 1999, written and presented by myself (Kushner). Both the producer and myself objected to the title but were over-ruled by the BBC. The account of Winton and of British refugee policy was more complex than the title suggested; Anne Karpf, 'The Future Prospects for Remembering the Past', *Jewish Chronicle*, 2 July 1999. Winton was subsequently knighted. See *Guardian*, 1 January 2003.

86 Paul Levine, *From Indifference to Activisism: Swedish Diplomacy and the Holocaust, 1938–1944* (Uppsala, Studia Historica Uppsaliensia, 1998), passim.

87 Smith, *Foley*, pp. vi, 169; *Jewish Chronicle*, 23 July 1999: 'The Saintly Spy of Berlin'.

88 David Cesarani, 'Mad Dogs and Englishmen: Towards a Taxonomy of Rescuers in a "Bystander" Country – Britain 1933–45', in Cesarani and Levine (eds), *'Bystanders' to the Holocaust*, pp. 28–56.

89 *Jewish Chronicle*, 18 June 1999.

90 Kushner and Knox, *Refugees in an Age of Genocide*, pp. 154–7.

91 Rubinstein, *The Myth of Rescue*.

92 In the new introduction to the paperback edition (London, Routledge, 1999, p. 1) Rubinstein comments himself how '[i]t sharply divided critics, and I became used to reading reviews consisting of either fulsome praise or venomous hostility'. David Cesarani has commented on the division representing also those who have and have not carried out archive work on the subject. On *Lateline*, Australian Broadcasting Corporation, 20 July 1997.

93 Mass-Observation Archive, University of Sussex: Summer Directive 2000, 'Coming to Britain'.

94 Norman Stone, 'Could the Allies Have Saved Them?', *Guardian*, 3 July 1997.

95 For the increasing fascination in relation to the historiography of the Allies and the Holocaust, see Richard Breitman, *Official Secrets: What the Nazis Planned, What the British and Americans Knew* (New York, Hill and Wang, 1998), a book that has received widespread attention and popular success. See also the second edition of Wasserstein, *Britain and the Jews of Europe* (London, Leicester University Press, 1999), which includes newly available intelligence material.

96 Michael Neufeld and Michael Berenbaum (eds), *The Bombing of Auschwitz: Should the Allies Have Attempted It?* (New York, St Martin's Press, 2000).

97 Bat-Ami Zucker, *In Search of Refuge: Jews and US Consuls in Nazi Germany 1933–1941* (London, Vallentine Mitchell, 2001), reviewed by Feingold in *Holocaust and Genocide Studies*, vol. 16, no. 2 (2002), pp. 296–8.

98 Hindley, 'Constructing Allied Humanitarian Policy', pp. 77–102.

99 See, for example, Jeffrey Shandler, *While America Watches: Televising the Holocaust* (New York, Oxford University Press, 1999); Judith Doneson, *The Holocaust in American Film* (Philadelphia, Jewish Publication Society, 1987).

100 H. R. Kedward, 'Resiting French Resistance', *Transactions of the Royal Historical Society*, vol. 9 (1999), p. 272.

101 Philippe Burrin, *France Under the Germans: Collaboration and Compromise* (New York, New Press, 1996), p. 2.

102 Julian Jackson, *France: The Dark Years 1940–1944* (Oxford, Oxford University Press, 2001), pp. 2–4.

103 Hans Kirchhoff, 'Denmark: A Light in the Darkness of the Holocaust? A Reply to Gunnar S. Paulsson', *Journal of Contemporary History*, vol. 30 (July 1995), p. 477.

104 Paulsson, *Secret City*, p. 230 for statistical comparisons between Poland and Denmark.

105 Paul Levine, 'Attitudes and Action: Comparing the Responses of Mid-level Bureaucrats to the Holocaust', in Cesarani and Levine (eds), *'Bystanders' to the Holocaust*, pp. 212–36, and idem, *From Indifference to Activism*.

106 Morrison, 1 July 1944, quoted by Yehuda Bauer, *Jews for Sale? Nazi–Jewish Negotiations, 1933–1945* (New Haven, Yale University Press, 1994), p. 188.

107 Levine, 'Attitudes and Action', pp. 226, 234.

Conclusion

It may ultimately prove an impossible task to produce a cohesive narrative of the Holocaust that does justice both to its chronology and to its players. Even when confined to the perpetrators, the chronology is complex and often contradictory. Increasingly detailed research, alongside more sophisticated understandings of the Third Reich, has already revealed the multi-layered nature of the decision-making process, the connections of the 'final solution' to other contemporary policies, as well as the importance of local initiatives in the 'radicalisation' process. The beginnings of a critical engagement with the testimony of the victims is leading, though not without controversy, to an acceptance that the Holocaust was experienced differently by men and women, children and adults, the religious and the secular, eastern and western European Jews, rich and poor, intellectuals and non-intellectuals, and so on. There are still gaps and biases.

Feminist scholars have rightly pointed out that for many years the experiences of men in the Holocaust were taken as typical of the total Jewish experience of persecution. Subsequently they have tried to restore the balance and have explored women's experience in the Holocaust and gender relations within it. In the late 1980s and early 1990s, when the first serious efforts were made to 'take women into account' within Holocaust studies, there were those such as the critic Cynthia Ozick who argued that the 'wrong' question was being asked: 'a *morally* wrong question, a question that leads us still further down the road of eradicating Jews from history'. Some still argue from the same perspective, but the quality of recent scholarship on women's experience and on gender issues works against the idea that such approaches and interests will inevitably weaken the idea that all Jews were victims or lead to a league table of suffering.[1] Yet how men experienced the Holocaust *as men* and the impact of it on their sense of masculinity remains to be studied. Similarly, whilst historians such as Deborah Dwork are right to point out the absence of analysis of children during the Holocaust, some 1.5 million of whom were murdered, there is no literature that breaks up the experience for adults, whether young, middle-aged or elderly.[2] The situation in relation to non-Jewish victims of the Nazis is even less satisfactory. Historians and others are somewhat belatedly beginning the work of recording their experiences and have thus not yet had the possibility of more subtle analysis of it. A collection of 'eyewitness accounts' representing a 'century of genocide', for example, relies in its section on disabled peoples in the Third Reich on the testimony of those who observed the euthanasia programme. The possibility of testimony from those who were labelled mentally or physically unfit is curiously discounted by its author.[3]

There are some who view the breaking down of victims into categories such as sex and age as somehow sacrilegious, undermining the importance of the six million as a collectivity and inevitably leading to a hierarchy of suffering. But accepting differences of experience within the overarching persecution does not imply the Holocaust was worse for one person than another. As Lenore Weitzmann and Dalia Offer argue in relation to their work on women and the Holocaust, 'questions of gender lead us to a richer and more finely nuanced understanding of the Holocaust. They help us envision the specificity of everyday life and the different ways in which men and women responded to the Nazi onslaught.'[4] It is, however, crucial to avoid simplistic categories in which to place the persecuted. As Mary Lagerwey suggests, some attempts at gendered reading have 'ignored survivors' attempts in Auschwitz and in their writings to maintain or re-establish multiple identities for themselves. The stories of Auschwitz are too complex to fit neatly into gender stereotypes.'[5] If such complexity is accepted, however, it becomes increasingly difficult to incorporate the experiences and voices of the victims as a coherent whole, let alone integrate them within an overall narrative of the Holocaust other than as tokenistic soundbites of testimony. The use of life story in recording survivors restores some semblance of individuality to the victims. At the same time, it poses immensely complicated dilemmas in the writing of Holocaust history and the representation of the Holocaust more generally, but this is to be welcomed. Indeed, we should be wary of versions of the Holocaust that do not challenge our everyday sense of time and place. As Claude Lanzmann said of his epic documentary film *Shoah* (1985), an oral history of the Holocaust, 'it is an investigation into the scars left by a past on places and on people's minds that are still so fresh and unhealed that this past gives the strange impression of being outside of time'.[6]

Early histories of the Holocaust not only excluded the victims but also the more recently coined category of the 'bystander'. Subsequently, the most successful works on bystanders have as one of their central themes the role of the individual nation-state, and the cultural and political ideologies working within it (and the construction and re-construction of national identities), in helping to determine reactions and responses to the Nazis' victims. The relationship of the nation-state to Nazi Germany (or within the Third Reich, the relationship between the state and the populace) is obviously of central importance in determining the freedom to act: league tables showing the percentage of Jews murdered in each occupied country are thus on their own no clear indication of antipathy or indifference to the Jewish plight.[7] Neutral Sweden's cumulative rescue of the Jews from 1942 onwards, for example, was at one level linked to its growing distance from the Nazis,[8] and the same can be said of Italy during the latter stages of the war.[9] And yet in both cases it took the work of many individuals, often taking risks, to make a difference. National and individual pride, basic humanitarianism and the overcoming of earlier ambivalent attitudes towards Jews came into play. For some, the realisation of the enormity of the crime being committed by the Nazis sprung them into action. For others, the majority of the bystanders, the Jews remained other to their concerns.

The task still remaining for historians of the bystanders is to explain rather than the easier option of to condemn. What is clear, however, after two or three decades of solid research, is that most of the details of the Holocaust, far from being hidden in a 'secret universe', were known to contemporaries not just in the places of destruction but in the 'free world' as well. Contemporary engagement with that information was less profound, but the processes by which it was either disbelieved or more commonly ignored and marginalised were far from simple.[10] The bystanders' engagement with the Holocaust thus varied geographically, chronologically and in intensity.

The macro-level determinants of national 'bystander' action have analogies on the micro-level of the individual perpetrator. Any examination of 'ordinary' German executors of Nazi Jewish policy must begin with the recognition that they were working within an extraordinary national framework of institutionalised racism and violence. Embracing these tenets was a way to advancement within the Nazi system, whether or not the perpetrators in question had previously subscribed to them, though many of course had. And given the premium within the 'social Darwinist' Nazi system on radicalism, energy and initiative, the ascendancy of the most effective elements, notably the SS, further enforced the racist consensus and forced it in more extreme directions. For the remainder of the perpetrators, tolerating the violent expression of racism and participating in it to varying extents became the socially and professionally enforced norm, not an aberrance.

The effect of war, noted by G. F. Hegel amongst others, in strengthening and more tightly circumscribing the national community, and in entrenching the perception of Germany's enemies, is important in explaining the extent of participation in genocide, particularly for Germans operating within the theatres of combat. War is vital too in understanding the very escalation of Nazi Jewish policy from 1939 and again 1941. Then, also, the occupation of the newly conquered lands, and the cultural associations entrenched in the German psyche about 'the east' (not to mention 'eastern Jews'), were conducive to behaviour that elsewhere might have seemed transgressive. Beyond those larger contextual generalisations and the imponderables of individual character and 'human nature', in explaining types of participation (or non-participation) we have to address the significance of certain cohorts of age and life-experience, as well as specific institutional norms. In short, though, a complete picture can only be achieved by examining the full gamut of characteristics that shape the behaviour of the individual within any social context anywhere.

This study has sought to problematise the three categories of perpetrator, victim and bystander. The desire is not to demolish the appropriateness of these categories but to reveal the dangers of oversimplifying them so that the Holocaust becomes a basic morality story with two-dimensional victims, onlookers, villains and processes. The book has no magic formula for the integration of the different categories into a smooth historical narrative or any other form of representation. On the contrary, it suggests that the Holocaust, as global and catastrophic history, is hard to contain within any straightforward chronological or organisational structure. Recognising the scale and complexity of the Holocaust, however, does not imply any support for those who attempt to mystify the subject, one version of which has been the deeply unhelpful and divisive debate about its uniqueness. This notion has done much to discourage the understanding of Nazi Jewish policy as it developed, and from the point of view of the perpetrators themselves. It also carries faulty assumptions about the internal dynamics of the perpetrator system and extricates to an untenable degree the 'final solution' from other Nazi occupation, economic, population and genocidal policies.

As Alan Rosenbaum has argued, in his introduction to a collection of essays on the uniqueness debate,

> The time has come to fix the place of the Nazi-engineered Holocaust against the Jews, Gypsies and millions of others so that it may be accurately integrated into the mainstream of recorded history ... Normalizing the Holocaust in this manner recognizes both its continuities and discontinuities with the past. It is not an attempt to marginalize or dilute its horror but rather to point out that a social phenomenon that is treated as external to history and literally beyond the reach of human understanding (which it may be to those who endured and suffered its ravages) will undoubtedly be seen quite differently from the perspectives of future generations.[11]

Alongside the more common case studies in 'comparative genocide' – the Armenians, the Romanies, and the Stalinist terror – Rosenbaum includes an essay by Seymour Drescher on the Atlantic slave trade as another example of 'historical instances of mass death'.[12] Is the comparison with slavery a helpful one, and if not, what are the implications for wider contextualisation of the Holocaust?

According to Drescher, the points of similarity are few and far between. One evolved over many centuries whilst the other was envisaged as a rapid solution to a 'real' problem. Slavery was driven to a lesser or greater extent by economics and the market whereas the murder of the Jews was driven by ideology. It is true, argues Drescher, that both were justified by 'race' arguments. He concludes, however, that 'if racism undergirded the African slave trade, it was an effect rather than the cause of that system ... Racism fulfilled a different systematic function during the Holocaust ... The [Nazi] regime intended that one precisely designated group would, one way or another, disappear.'[13]

Drescher still believes the comparison is helpful for the light it sheds on both subjects – 'even if the differences remain overwhelming' – and he is surely right to point out that comparative history is not necessarily about showing similarities.[14] Nevertheless, it seems that he misses out a key context in which the Holocaust might be placed, that of the centrality of 'race thinking' within modernity.

Jeshajahu Weinberg, the founding director of the United States Holocaust Memorial Museum, related how the Museum 'consciously avoided including in its permanent exhibition or its Learning Center genocidal events other than those that occurred in the framework of the Holocaust of 1933–1945'. He added that he and the other planners of the Museum were well aware 'of the strong intellectual and moral relevance of many such events to the Holocaust', but they had a mandate to build a Holocaust exhibition and not a museum of genocide. Nevertheless, this 'thematic distinction' did not preclude the inclusion of materials pertaining to other genocidal events, such as the Middle Passage of African slaves, the Armenian genocide in 1915, or the Cambodian genocide after the Vietnam war 'in the museum's library and archives or in its educational activities'.[15]

Are we left then with only the humanistic and moral urge to compare? 'What could be more encouraging than to see the recent surge of historical interest in the Holocaust as a model for calling attention to other human catastrophes?', as Drescher remarks.[16] Are the Holocaust and the Atlantic slave trade only alike in their horror and mass death? Paul Gilroy argues otherwise, situating race thinking, or what he calls 'raciology', at the heart of modernity with its emphasis on rationality and categorisation, 'order', 'progress' and (western) human perfectibility. 'Although "race" thinking certainly existed in earlier periods, modernity transformed the ways "race" was understood and acted upon.' The racialisation of the nineteenth-century nation-state, he suggests, enabled the destructive potential of nationalism to be realised, whether articulated in imperialism, slavery or antisemitism. This potential was certainly realised from the late nineteenth century in the central European milieu from which Nazism emerged, and in which more or less radical 'solutions' to demographic 'problems' had by 1933 become commonplace. Any sense of human universalism – other than white, Nordic, Europeanness (with extensions into American whiteness) – was lost. Gilroy calls for more work in 'approaching the relationship between modernity and enlightenment, which becomes pivotal at this point in the history of anti-semitisms and other racisms'.[17] The ongoing processes of racialisation, the major focus of which in Britain today are the vilified 'asylum seekers', link together victim groups across history *not* in an act of well-meaning liberal anti-racist solidarity, but as one of the crucial factors explaining why the twentieth century and beyond has become the age of genocide.

Notes

1   Joan Ringelheim, 'The Holocaust: Taking Women into Account', *Jewish Quarterly*, no. 147 (Autumn 1992), pp. 19–23, pp. 20–1 for the Ozick quote; Dalia Offer and Lenore Weitzmann (eds), *Women in the Holocaust* (New Haven, Yale University Press, 1998); Judith Tydor Baumel, *Double Jeopardy: Gender and the Holocaust* (London, Vallentine Mitchell, 1998); S. L. Kremer, *Women's Holocaust Writing: Memory and Imagination* (Lincoln, University of Nebraska Press, 1999); and Elizabeth Baer and Myrna Goldenberg (eds), *Experience and Expression: Women, the Nazis, and the Holocaust* (Detroit, Wayne State University Press, 2003).

2   Deborak Dwork, *Children With a Star: Jewish Youth in Europe* (New Haven, Yale University Press, 1991).

3   Hugh Gregory Gallagher, 'Holocaust: Disabled Peoples', in Samuel Totten, William Parsons and Israel Charny (eds), *Century of Genocide: Eyewitness Accounts and Critical Views* (New York, Garland, 1997), p. 220. For a more open approach to producing the history of disability through the testimony of those affected, see Steve Humphries and Pamela Gordon, *Out of Sight: The Experience of Disability 1900–1950* (Plymouth, Northcote House, 1992). Michael Burleigh's documentary film,

Selling Murder (London, Domino Films, 1991), includes moving testimony from disabled survivors. Sybil Milton, 'Holocaust: The Gypsies', in Parsons and Charny (eds), *Century of Genocide*, pp. 171–207 provides analysis and snippets of testimony. More extensive in analysis is Claudia Schoppmann, *Days of Masquerade: Life Stories of Lesbians during the Third Reich* (New York, Columbia University Press, 1996).

4 Lenore Weitzmann and Dalia Offer, 'The Role of Gender in the Holocaust', in idem (eds), *Women in the Holocaust*, p. 1.

5 Mary Lagerwey, *Reading Auschwitz* (London, Sage, 1998), p. 104.

6 Claude Lanzmann, 'Shoah as Counter-Myth', *Jewish Quarterly*, vol. 33 (Spring 1986), p. 12.

7 See Helen Fein, *Accounting for Genocide: National Responses and Jewish Victimization during the Holocaust* (New York, Free Press, 1980).

8 Paul Levine, *From Indifference to Activism: Swedish Diplomacy and the Holocaust, 1938–1944* (Uppsala, Studia Historica Uppsaliensia, 1998).

9 Jonathan Steinberg, *All or Nothing: The Axis and the Holocaust, 1941–1943* (London, Routledge, 1990).

10 The first major study of knowledge was by Walter Laqueur, *The Terrible Secret* (London, Weidenfeld & Nicolson, 1980). See Tony Kushner, *The Holocaust and the Liberal Imagination: A Social and Cultural History* (Oxford, Blackwell, 1994), chs 1 and 4 for an analysis on a broader level of society.

11 Alan Rosenbaum, 'Introduction', in idem (ed.), *Is the Holocaust Unique? Perspectives on Comparative Genocide* (Boulder, Col., Westview Press, 1998), p. 1.

12 Ibid., p. 4.

13 Seymour Drescher, 'The Atlantic Slave Trade and the Holocaust: A Comparative Analysis', in Rosenbaum (ed.), *Is the Holocaust Unique?*, pp. 65–85, esp. pp. 77–9.

14 Ibid., p. 67.

15 Jeshajahu Weinberg, 'From the Director', in Michael Berenbaum, *The World Must Know: The History of Holocaust as told in the United States Holocaust Memorial Museum* (Boston, Little, Brown & Co., 1993), p. xv.

16 Drescher, 'The Atlantic Slave Trade', p. 79.

17 Paul Gilroy, *Between Camps: Nations, Cultures and the Allure of Race* (London, Allen Lane, 2000), pp. 57, 94.

Select bibliography

Victims

Ball-Kaduri, K., 'Evidence of Witnesses, its Value and Limitations', *Yad Washem Studies*, vol. 3 (1959)

Bertaux, Daniel (ed.), *Biography and Society: The Life Story Approach in the Social Sciences* (Beverly Hills, Calif., Sage, 1981)

Boder, David, *I Did Not Interview the Dead* (Urbana, University of Illinois Press, 1949)

Chamberlain, Mary, and Paul Thompson (eds), *Narrative and Genre* (London, Routledge, 1998)

Cohen, Nathan, 'Diaries of the *Sonderkommandos* in Auschwitz: Coping with Fate and Reality', *Yad Vashem Studies*, vol. 20 (1990)

Corni, Gustavo, *Hitler's Ghettos: Voices from a Beleaguered Society 1939–1944* (London, Arnold, 2002)

Des Pres, Terence, *The Survivor: An Anatomy of Life in the Death Camps* (Oxford, Oxford University Press, 1976)

Dwork, Deborah, *Children with a Star: Jewish Youth in Europe* (New Haven, Yale University Press, 1991)

Enzer, Hyman, and Sandra Solotaroff-Enzer (eds), *Anne Frank: Reflections on Her Life and Legacy* (Urbana and Chicago, University of Illinois Press, 2000)

Eskin, Blake, *A Life in Pieces* (London, Aurum Press, 2002)

Felman, Shoshana, and Dori Laub, *Testimony: Crises of Witnessing in Literature, Psychoanalysis and History* (London and New York, Routledge, 1992)

Frank, Anne, *The Diary of a Young Girl* (London, Penguin Books, 2000)

Friedländer, Saul, *Nazi Germany and the Jews: The Years of Persecution 1933–39* (London, Weidenfeld & Nicolson, 1997)

Seleect bibliography

Gilbert, Martin, *The Holocaust: The Jewish Tragedy* (Collins, Glasgow, 1986)

Gordon, Robert, *Primo Levi's Ordinary Virtues: From Testimony to Ethics* (Oxford, Oxford University Press, 2001)

Gray, Martin, *For Those I Loved* (New York, Signet, 1974)

Greenspan, Henry, *On Listening to Holocaust Survivors: Recounting and Life History* (New York, Praeger, 1998)

Hartman, Geoffrey, *The Longest Shadow: In the Aftermath of the Holocaust* (Bloomington, Indiana University Press, 1996)

Hartman, Geoffrey, 'Memory.com: Tele-Suffering and Testimony in the Dot Com Era', *Raritan*, vol. 19, no. 3 (Winter 2000)

Hilberg, Raul, *Perpetrators Victims Bystanders: The Jewish Catastrophe 1933–1945* (New York, HarperCollins, 1992)

Hilberg, Raul, Stanislaw Staron and Josef Kermisz (eds), *The Warsaw Diary of Adam Czerniakow* (New York, Stein and Day, 1979)

Katsch, Abraham (ed.), *Scroll of Agony: The Warsaw Diary of Chaim A. Kaplan* (London, Hamish Hamilton, 1966)

Kermish, Joseph (ed.), *To Live with Honor and Die With Honor* (Jerusalem, Yad Vashem, 1986)

Klemperer, Victor, *The Klemperer Diaries 1933–1945* (London, Orion, 2000)

Korczak, Janusz, *Ghetto Diary* (New York, Holocaust Library, 1978)

Kushner, Tony, 'Oral History at the Extremes of Human Experience: Holocaust Testimony in a Museum Setting', *Oral History*, vol. 29, no. 2 (Autumn 2001)

Lagerwey, Mary, *Reading Auschwitz* (London, Sage, 1998)

Langer, Lawrence, *Holocaust Testimonies: The Ruins of Memory* (New Haven, Yale University Press, 1991)

Lanzmann, Claude, *Shoah: An Oral History of the Holocaust* (New York, Pantheon Books, 1985)

Lejeune, Philippe, *On Autobiography* (Minneapolis, University of Minnesota Press, 1989)

Lang, Berel (ed.), *Writing and the Holocaust* (New York, Holmes & Meier, 1988)

Levi, Primo, *The Drowned and the Saved* (London, Michael Joseph, 1988)

Nussbaum, Felicity, 'Towards Conceptualizing the Diary', in James Olney (ed.), *Studies in Autobiography* (New York, Oxford University Press, 1988)

Offer, Dalia, and Lenore Weitzmann (eds), *Women in the Holocaust* (New Haven, Yale University Press, 1998)

Okely, Judith, and Helen Calloway (eds), *Anthropology and Autobiography* (London, Routledge, 1992)

Polonsky, Antony (ed.), *A Cup of Tears: A Diary of the Warsaw Ghetto* (Oxford: Blackwell, 1988)

Reiter, Andrea, *Narrating the Holocaust* (London, Continuum, 2000)

Select bibliography

Rose, Jonathan (ed.), *The Holocaust and the Book: Destruction and Preservation* (Amherst, University of Massachusetts Press, 2001)

Roseman, Mark, 'Surviving Memory: Truth and Inaccuracy on Holocaust Testimony', *Journal of Holocaust Education*, vol. 8, no. 1 (Summer 1999)

Roseman, Mark, *The Past in Hiding* (London, Allen Lane, 2000)

Roskies, David, 'The Library of Jewish Catastrophe', in Geoffrey Hartman (ed.), *Holocaust Remembrance: The Shapes of Memory* (London, Blackwell, 1994)

Rozett, Robert, 'The Scribes of Memory', *Yad Vashem Magazine*, vol. 10 (Summer 1998)

Samuel, Raphael, and Paul Thompson (eds), *The Myths We Live By* (London, Routledge, 1990)

Shapiro, Robert Moses (ed.), *Holocaust Chronicles: Individualizing the Holocaust Through Diaries and Other Contemporaneous Personal Accounts* (Hoboken, N.J., KTAV, 1999)

Sloan, Jacob (ed.), *Notes from the Warsaw Ghetto: The Journal of Emmanuel Ringelblum* (New York, McGraw-Hill, 1951)

Spielberg, Steven, and Survivors of the Shoah Visual History Foundation, *The Last Days* (London, Weidenfeld & Nicolson, 1999)

Spivak, Gayatri, 'Can the Subaltern Speak?', in G. Nelson (ed.), *Marxism and the Interpretation of Culture* (Basingstoke, Macmillan, 1988)

Thompson, Paul, *The Voice of the Past: Oral History*, 3rd edn (Oxford, Oxford University Press, 2000)

Totten, Samuel, William Parsons and Israel Charny (eds), *Century of Genocide: Eyewitness Accounts and Critical Views* (New York, Garland, 1997)

Wiesel, Elie, *From the Kingdom of Memory: Reminiscences* (New York, Schocken, 1990)

Wilkormirski, Binjamin, *Fragments* (Basingstoke, Picador, 1996)

Young, James, *Writing and Rewriting the Holocaust: Narrative and the Consequences of Interpretation* (Bloomington, Indiana University Press, 1988)

Perpetrators and perpetration

Allen, Michael Thad, *The Business of Genocide: The SS, Slave Labor, and the Concentration Camps* (Chapel Hill, University of North Carolina Press, 2002)

Aly, Götz, *'Final Solution': Nazi Population Policy and the Murder of the European Jews* (London, Arnold, 1999).

Aly, Götz, and Susanne Heim, 'The Economics of the Final Solution: A Case Study from the General Government', *Simon Wiesenthal Center Annual*, vol. 5 (1988)

Seleect bibliography

Aly, Götz, and Suzanne Heim, *Vordenker der Vernichtung: Auschwitz und die deutschen Pläne für eine neue europäischen Ordnung* (Frankfurt am Main, Fischer, 1993), translated as *Architechts of Annihilation* (London, Weidenfeld & Nicolson, 2002)

Arendt, Hannah, *Eichmann in Jerusalem: A Report on the Banality of Evil* (New York, Viking, 1963)

Bajohr, Frank, *'Arisierung' in Hamburg: Die Verdrängung der jüdischer Unternehmer 1933–1945* (Hamburg, Christians, 1997)

Bankier, David, *The Germans and the Final Solution: Public Opinion under Nazism* (Oxford, Blackwell, 1992)

Bartov, Omer, *Hitler's Army: Soldiers, Nazis and War in the Third Reich* (Oxford, Oxford University Press, 1992)

Bartov, Omer, *Mirrors of Destruction: War, Genocide, and Modern Identity* (Oxford, Oxford University Press, 2000)

Bartusevicius, Vincas, Joachim Tauber and Wolfram Wette (eds), *Holocaust in Litauen: Krieg, Judenmorde und Kollaboration im Jahre 1941* (Cologne, Böhlau, 2003)

Bauman, Zygmunt, *Modernity and the Holocaust* (Ithaca, Cornell University Press, 1989)

Berenbaum, Michael (ed.), *A Mosaic of Victims: Non-Jews Persecuted and Murdered by the Nazis* (London, Tauris, 1990)

Berenbaum, Michael, and Abraham Peck (eds), *The Holocaust and History: The Known, the Unknown, the Disputed and the Reexamined* (Bloomington, Indiana University Press, 1998)

Birn, Ruth Bettina, *Die Höheren SS-und Polizeiführer* (Düsseldorf, Droste, 1986)

Bloxham, Donald, 'Jewish Slave Labour and its Relationship to the "Final Solution"', in John K. Roth and Elizabeth Maxwell (eds) *Remembering for the Future 2000: The Holocaust in an Age of Genocide* (Basingstoke, Macmillan, 2001), vol. 1

Bloxham, Donald, 'The Armenian Genocide of 1915–16: Cumulative Radicalisation and the Development of a Destruction Policy', *Past and Present*, vol. 183, no. 1 (November 2003)

Braham, Randolph L., *The Politics of Genocide: The Holocaust in Hungary* (Detroit, Wayne State University Press, 2000)

Brechtken, Magnus, *'Madagaskar für die Juden': Antisemitische Idee und politische Praxis 1885–1945* (Munich, Oldenbourg, 1997)

Breitman, Richard, *The Architect of Genocide: Himmler and the Final Solution* (London, Grafton, 1992)

Broszat, Martin, *The Hitler State: The Foundation and Development of the Internal Structure of the Third Reich* (London, Longman, 1981)

Browning, Christopher, *The Final Solution and the German Foreign Office* (New York, Holmes and Meier, 1978)

Select bibliography

Browning, Christopher, *Fateful Months: Essays on the Emergence of the Final Solution* (New York, Holmes and Meier, 1991)

Browning, Christopher, *The Path to Genocide: Essays on Launching the Final Solution* (Cambridge, Cambridge University Press, 1992)

Browning, Christopher, *Ordinary Men: Reserve Police Battalion 101 and the Final Solution in Poland* (New York, HarperCollins, 1993)

Browning, Christopher, *Nazi Policy, Jewish Workers, German Killers* (Cambridge, Cambridge University Press, 2000)

Buchler, Yehoshua, 'Himmler's Personal Murder Brigades in 1941', *Holocaust and Genocide Studies*, vol. 1, no. 1 (1986)

Burleigh, Michael, *Death and Deliverance: 'Euthanasia' in Germany, 1900–1945* (Cambridge, Cambridge University Press, 1994)

Burleigh, Michael, and Wolfgang Wippermann, *The Racial State: Germany 1933–1945* (Cambridge, Cambridge University Press, 1991)

Cesarani, David (ed.), *The Final Solution: Origins and Implementation* (London, Routledge, 1994)

Cesarani, David (ed.), *Genocide and Rescue: The Holocaust in Hungary 1944* (Oxford, Berg, 1997)

Crew, David F. (ed.), *Nazism and German Society, 1933–1945* (London, Routledge, 1994)

Dean, Martin, *Collaboration in the Holocaust: Crimes of the Local Police in Belorussia and Ukraine, 1941–44* (Basingstoke, Macmillan, 2000)

Dieckmann, Christoph, Christian Gerlach, Wolf Gruner et al. (eds), *Kooperation und Verbrechen: Formen der Kollaboration im östlichen Europa 1939–1945* (Göttingen, Wallstein, 2003)

Dwork, Deborah, and Robert Jan Van Pelt, *Auschwitz 1270 to the Present* (London, Norton, 1996)

Ezergailis, Andrew, *The Holocaust in Latvia 1941–1944: The Missing Center* (Riga, Historical Institute of Latvia, 1996).

Frei, Norbert, Sybille Steinbacher and Bernd C. Wagner, *Ausbeutung, Vernichtung, Öffentlichkeit* (Munich, Saur, 2000)

Friedländer, Saul, *Nazi Germany and the Jews: The Years of Persecution, 1933–1939* (New York, HarperCollins, 1997)

Gellately, Robert, *Backing Hitler: Consent and Coercion in Nazi Germany* (Oxford: Oxford University Press, 1991)

Gerlach, Christian, 'Failure of Plans for an SS Extermination Camp in Mogilev, Belorussia', *Holocaust and Genocide Studies*, vol. 11 (1997)

Gerlach, Christian, 'The Wannsee Conference, the Fate of German Jews, and Hitler's Decision in Principle to Exterminate all European Jews', *Journal of Modern History*, vol. 70 (1998)

Gerlach, Christian, *Krieg, Ernährung, Völkermord: Forschungen zur deutschen Vernichtungspolitik im Zweiten Weltkrieg* (Hamburg, Hamburger Edition, 1998)

Gerlach, Christian, *Kalkulierte Morde: Die deutsche Wirtschafts- und Vernichtungspolitik im Weißrußland* (Hamburg, Hamburger Edition, 1999)

Gerlach, Christian, and Götz Aly, *Das letzte Kapitel: Der Mord an den ungarischen Juden* (Stuttgart, Deustche Verlags-Anstalt, 2002)

Gräbitz, Helge, Klaus Bästlein and Johannes Tuchel (ed.), *Die Normalität des Verbrechens* (Berlin, Edition Hentrich, 1994)

Gross, Jan T., *Polish Society under German Occupation: The Generalgouvernement, 1939–44* (Princeton, Princeton University Press, 1979)

Gutman, Yisrael, and Michael Berenbaum (eds), *Anatomy of the Auschwitz Death Camp* (Bloomington, University of Indiana Press, 1994)

Hachmeister, Lutz, *Der Gegnerforscher: Die Karrier des SS-Führers Franz Alfred Six* (Munich, Beck, 1998)

Hartog, L. J., *Der Befehl zum Judenmord: Hitler, Amerika und die Juden* (Bodenheim, Syndikat Buchgesellschaft, 1997)

Hayes, Peter, *Industry and Ideology: I. G. Farben in the Nazi era* (Cambridge, Cambridge University Press, 1997)

Heer, Hannes, 'Killing Fields: The Wehrmacht and the Holocaust in Belorussia, 1941–1942', *Holocaust and Genocide Studies*, vol. 11 (1997)

Heer, Hannes, and Klaus Naumann (eds), *Vernichtungskrieg: Verbrechen der Wehrmacht 1941 bis 1944* (Hamburg, HIS, 1995)

Herbert, Ulrich, 'Labour and Extermination: Economic Interest and the Primacy of Weltanschauung in National Socialism', *Past and Present*, vol. 138 (1993)

Herbert, Ulrich, *Best: Biographische Studien über Radikalismus, Weltanschauung und Vernunft 1903–1989* (Bonn, Dietz, 1996)

Herbert, Ulrich (ed.), *Nationalsozialistische Vernichtungspolitik 1939–1945: Neue Forschungen und Kontroversen* (Frankfurt am Main, Fischer, 1998), translated as *National Socialist Extermination Policies: Contemporary German Perspectives and Controversies* (Oxford, Berghahn, 2000).

Herbert, Ulrich et al. (eds), *Die nationalsozialistischen Konzentrationslager Entwicklung und Struktur*, 2 vols (Göttingen, Wallstein, 1998)

Hilberg, Raul, *The Destruction of the European Jews*, 3 vols (New York, Holmes and Meier, 1985)

Hilberg, Raul, *Perpetrators, Victims, Bystanders* (London, Lime Tree, 1993)

Höhne, Heinz, *The Order of the Death's Head* (London, Pan, 1972)

Ioanid, Radu, *The Holocaust in Romania: The Destruction of Jews and Gypsies Under the Antonescu Regime, 1940–1944* (Chicago, Ivan R. Dee, 2000)

Kaienburg, Hermann (ed.), *Konzentrationslager und deutsche Wirtschaft 1939–1945* (Opladen, Leske and Budrich, 1996)

Kershaw, Ian, *The Nazi Dictatorship* (London, Edward Arnold, 1989)

Kershaw, Ian, 'Improvised Genocide? The Emergence of the "Final Solution" in the "Warthegau"', *Transactions of the Royal Historical Society*, 6th series, no. 2 (1992)

Kershaw, Ian, *Hitler, 1889–1936: Hubris* (London, Allen Lane, 1998)

Kershaw, Ian, *Hitler, 1936–1945: Nemesis* (London, Allen Lane, 2000)

Klein, Peter (ed.), *Die Einsatzgruppen in der besetzten Sowjetunion 1941/42: Die Tätigkeits- und Lagerberichte des Chefs der Sicherheitspolizei und des SD* (Berlin, Edition Hentrich, 1997)

Koehl, Robert L., *German Resettlement and Population Policy, 1939–45* (Cambridge, Mass., Harvard University Press, 1957)

Krausnick, Helmut, and Hans-Heinrich Wilhelm, *Die Truppe des Weltanschauungskrieges: Die Einsatzgruppen der Sicherheitspolizei und des SD 1938–1942* (Stuttgart, Deutsche Verlags-Anstalt, 1981)

Kühl, Stefan, *The Nazi Connection: Eugenics, American Racism, and German National Socialism* (New York, Oxford University Press, 1994)

Longerich, Peter, *Die Wannsee-Konferenz vom 20 Januar 1942* (Berlin, Gedenk- und Bildungsstätte Haus der Wannsee-Konferenz, 1988)

Longerich, Peter, *Politik der Vernichtung: Eine Gesamtdarstellung der nationalsozialistische Judenverfolgung* (Munich, Piper, 1998)

Longerich, Peter, *The Unwritten Order: Hitler's Role in the Final Solution* (Stroud, Tempus, 2002)

Lower, Wendy, '"Anticipatory Obedience" and the Nazi Implementation of the Holocaust in the Ukraine: A Case Study of Central and Peripheral Forces in the Generalbezirk Zhytomyr, 1941–1944', *Holocaust and Genocide Studies*, vol. 16 (2002)

Lozowick, Yaacov, *Hitlers Bürokraten: Eichmann, seine willigen Vollstrecker und die Banalität des Bösen* (Munich, Pendo, 2000)

Lumans, Valdis O., *Himmler's Auxiliaries: The Volksdeutsche Mittelstelle and the German National Minorities of Europe, 1933–1945* (Chapel Hill, University of North Carolina Press, 1993)

Manoschek, Walter, *'Serbien ist Judenfrei': Militärische Besatzungspolitik und Judenvernichtungin Serbien 1941/42* (Munich, Oldenbourg, 1993)

Marrus, Michael R., and Robert O. Paxton, *Vichy France and the Jews* (New York, Basic Books, 1981)

Matthäus, Jürgen, 'What about the "Ordinary Men"?: The German Order Police and the Holocaust in the Occupied Soviet Union', *Holocaust and Genocide Studies*, vol. 10 (1996)

Michman, Dan (ed.), *Belgium and the Holocaust: Jews, Belgians, Germans* (Jerusalem, Yad Vashem, 1998)

Mierzejewski, Alfred C., 'A Public Enterprise in the Service of Mass Murder: The Deutsche Reichsbahn and the Holocaust', *Holocaust and Genocide Studies*, vol. 15 (2001)

Mommsen, Hans, 'The Realisation of the Unthinkable: The "Final Solution of the Jewish Question" in the Third Reich', in Gerhard

Seleect bibliography

Hirschfeld (ed.), *The Policies of Genocide* (London, German Historical Institute, 1986)

Moore, Bob, *Victims and Survivors: The Nazi Persecution of the Jews in the Netherlands 1940–45* (London, Arnold, 1997)

Musial, Bogdan, *Deutsche Zivilverwaltung und Judenverfolgung im Generalgouvernement: Eine Fallstudie zum Distrikt Lublin 1939–1944* (Leipzig, Harrassowitz, 1999)

Naimark, Norman M., *Fires of Hatred: Ethnic Cleansing in Twentieth-Century Europe* (Cambridge, Mass., Harvard University Press, 2001)

Ogorreck, Ralf, *Die Einsatzgruppen und die 'Genesis der Endlösung'* (Berlin, Metropol, 1996)

Orth, Karin, *Das System der nationalsozialistischen Konzentrationslager: Eine politische Organisationsgeschichte* (Hamburg, Hamburger Edition, 1999)

Orth, Karin, *Die Konzentrationslager-SS: Sozialstrukturelle Analysen und biographische Studien* (Göttingen, Wallstein, 2000)

Pohl, Dieter, *Von der 'Judenpolitik' zum Judenmord: Der Distrikt Lublin des Generalgouvernements 1939–1944* (Frankfurt am Main, Peter Lang, 1993)

Pohl, Dieter, *Nationalsozialistische Judenverfolgung in Ostgalizien 1941–1944: Organisation und Durchführung eines staatlichen Massenverbrechens* (Munich, Oldenbourg, 1997)

Röhr, Werner (ed.), *Okkupation und Kollaboration (1938–1945): Beiträge zu Konzepten und Praxis der Kollaboration in der deutschen Okkupationspolitik* (Berlin, Hüthig, 1994).

Roseman, Mark, *The Villa, the Lake, the Meeting: Wannsee and the Final Solution* (London, Penguin, 2001)

Safrian, Hans, *Eichmann und seine Gehilfen* (Frankfurt am Main, Fischer, 1995)

Sandkühler, Thomas, *'Endlösung' in Galizien: Der Judenmord in Ostpolen und die Rettungsinitiativen von Berthold Beitz 1941–1944* (Bonn, J. H. W. Dietz, 1996)

Smelser, Ronald, Enrico Syring and Rainer Zitelmann (eds), *Die braune Elite 2: 21 weitere biographische Skizzen* (Darmstadt, Wissenschaftliche Buchgesellschaft, 1993)

Steinbacher, Sybille, *'Musterstadt' Auschwitz: Germanisierungspolitik und Judenmord in Oberschlesien* (Munich, K. G. Saur, 2000)

Steinberg, Jonathan, *All or Nothing: The Axis and the Holocaust, 1941–1943* (London, Routledge, 1990)

Steur, Claudia, *Theodor Dannecker: Ein Funktionär der 'Endlösung'* (Essen, Klartext, 1997)

Streit, Christian, *Keine Kameraden: Die Wehrmacht und die sowjetischen Kriegsgefangenen 1941–1945* (Bonn, J. H. W. Dietz, 1991)

Wagner, Patrick, *Volksgemeinschaft ohne Verbrecher: Konzeption und Praxis*

Select bibliography

der Kriminalpolizei in der Zeit der Weimarer Republik und des Nationalsozialismus (Hamburg, Christians, 1996)

Weindling, Paul, *Epidemics and Genocide in Eastern Europe, 1890–1945* (Oxford, Oxford University Press, 2000)

Wenck, Alexandra-Eileen, *Zwischen Menschenhandel und 'Endlösung': Das Konzentrationslager Bergen-Belsen* (Paderborn, Ferdinand Schöningh, 2000)

Westermann, Edward B., '"Ordinary Men" or "Ideological Soldiers"?: Police Battalion 310 in Russia, 1942', *German Studies Review*, vol. 21 (1998)

Wildt, Michael, *Generation des Unbedingten: Das Führungskorps des Reichssicherheitshauptamtes* (Hamburg, Hamburger Edition, 2003)

Wildt, Michael (ed.), *Die Judenpolitik des SD 1935–1938* (Munich, Oldenbourg, 1995)

Witte, Peter, 'Two Decisions Concerning the "Final Solution to the Jewish Question": Deportations to Lodz and Mass Murder in Chelmno', *Holocaust and Genocide Studies*, vol. 9 (1995)

Witte, Peter, et al. (eds), *Der Dienstkalendar Heinrich Himmlers 1941/1942* (Hamburg, Christians, 1999)

Zimmermann, Michael, *Rassenutopie und Genozid: Die nationalsozialistische 'Lösung der Zigeunerfrage'* (Hamburg, Christians, 1996)

Zuccotti, Susan, *The Holocaust, the French and the Jews* (New York, Basic Books, 1993)

Bystanders

Barnett, Victoria, *Bystanders: Conscience and Complicity During the Holocaust* (Westport, Ct., Greenwood Press, 1999)

Bauer, Yehuda, *Jews for Sale? Nazi–Jewish Negotiations, 1933–1945* (New Haven, Yale University Press, 1994)

Bloxham, Donald, *Genocide on Trial: War Crimes Trials in the Formation of Holocaust History and Memory* (Oxford, Oxford University Press, 2001)

Breitman, Richard, *Official Secrets: What the Nazis Planned, What the British and Americans Knew* (New York, Hill and Wang, 1998)

Breitman, Richard, and Alan Kraut, *American Refugee Policy and European Jewry, 1933–1945* (Bloomington and Indianaopolis, Indiana University Press, 1987)

Burrin, Philippe, *France Under the Germans: Collaboration and Compromise* (New York, New Press, 1996)

Cesarani, David, and Paul Levine (eds), *'Bystanders' to the Holocaust: A Reevaluation* (London, Frank Cass, 2002)

Fein, Helen, *Accounting for Genocide: National Responses and Jewish Victimi-*

zation during the Holocaust (New York, Free Press, 1980)

Feingold, Henry, *The Politics of Rescue: The Roosevelt Administration and the Holocaust 1938–1945*, 2nd edn (New York, Holocaust Library, 1980)

Friedman, Saul, *No Haven for the Oppressed: United States Policy Towards Jewish Refugees, 1938–1945* (Detroit, Wayne State University Press, 1970)

Gilbert, Martin, *Auschwitz and the Allies* (London, Michael Joseph, 1981)

Gollancz, Victor, *Let My People Go* (London, Gollancz, 1943)

Gross, Jan, *Neighbors: The Destruction of the Jewish Community in Jedwabne, Poland* (Princeton, Princeton University Press, 2001)

Jackson, Julian, *France: The Dark Years 1940–1944* (Oxford, Oxford University Press, 2001)

Kedward, H.R., 'Resiting French Resistance', *Transactions of the Royal Historical Society*, vol. 9 (1999)

Kirchhoff, Hans, 'Denmark: A Light in the Darkness of the Holocaust?', *Journal of Contemporary History*, vol. 30 (July 1995)

Kushner, Tony, *The Holocaust and the Liberal Imagination: A Social and Cultural History* (Oxford, Blackwell, 1994)

Kushner, Tony, and Katharine Knox, *Refugees in an Age of Genocide: Global, National and Local Perspectives during the Twentieth Century* (London, Frank Cass, 1999)

Laqueur, Walter, *The Terrible Secret* (London, Weidenfeld & Nicolson, 1980)

Levine, Paul, *From Indifference to Activism: Swedish Diplomacy and the Holocaust, 1938–1944* (Uppsala, Studia Historica Uppsaliensis, 1998)

Lipstadt, Deborah, *Beyond Belief: The American Press and the Coming of the Holocaust 1933–1945* (New York, Free Press, 1986)

London, Louise, *Whitehall and the Jews 1933–1948: British Immigration Policy and the Holocaust* (Cambridge, Cambridge University Press, 2000)

Morse, Arthur, *While Six Million Died* (New York, Random House, 1968)

Neufeld, Michael, and Michael Berenbaum (eds), *The Bombing of Auschwitz: Should the Allies Have Attempted It?* (New York, St Martin's Press, 2000)

Paulsson, G. S., 'The Bridge over the Oresund: The Historiography on the Expulsion of the Jews from Nazi-occupied Denmark', *Journal of Contemporary History*, vol. 30 (July 1995)

Paulsson, G. S., *Secret City: The Hidden Jews of Warsaw 1940–1945* (New Haven and London, Yale University Press, 2002)

Rathbone, Eleanor, *Rescue the Perishing* (London, National Committee for Rescue from Nazi Terror, 1943)

Rubinstein, W. D., *The Myth of Rescue: Why the Democracies Could Not Have Saved More Jews from the Nazis* (London, Routledge, 1997)

Select bibliography

Sharf, Andrew, *The British Press and Jews under Nazi Rule* (London, Institute for Race Relations, 1964)

Sherman, A. J., *Island Refuge: Britain and Refugees from the Third Reich 1933–1939* (Berkeley, University of California Press, 1973)

Staub, Ervin, *The Roots of Evil: The Origins of Genocide and Other Group Violence* (Cambridge, Cambridge University Press, 1989)

Steinberg, Jonathan, *All or Nothing: The Axis and the Holocaust, 1941–1943* (London, Routledge, 1990)

Wasserstein, Bernard, *Britain and the Jews of Europe 1939–1945*, 2nd edn (London, Leicester University Press, 1999)

Wyman, David, *Paper Walls: America and the Refugee Crisis 1938–1941* (Amherst, University of Massachusetts Press, 1968)

Wyman, David, *The Abandonment of the Jews: America and the Holocaust, 1941–1945* (New York, Pantheon, 1984)

Yahil, Leni, *The Rescue of Danish Jewry: Test of a Democracy* (Philadelphia, Jewish Publication Society of America, 1969)

Zucker, Bat-Ami, *In Search of Refuge: Jews and US Consuls in Nazi Germany 1933–1941* (London, Vallentine Mitchell, 2001)

Memory and representation

Baldwin, Peter (ed.), *Reworking the Past: Hitler, the Holocaust and the Historians' Debate* (Boston, Beacon Press, 1990)

Bauer, Yehuda, *The Holocaust in Historical Perspective* (London, Sheldon Press, 1978)

Berenbaum, Michael, *The World Must Know: The History of the Holocaust as Told in the United States Holocaust Memorial Museum* (Boston, Little, Brown & Co., 1993)

Binet, Helene, *Jewish Museum Berlin: Architect Daniel Libeskind* (Berlin, G + B Arts International, 1999)

Bloxham, Donald, *Genocide on Trial: War Crimes Trials and the Formation of Holocaust History and Memory* (Oxford, Oxford University Press, 2001)

Doneson, Judith, *The Holocaust in American Film* (Philadelphia, Jewish Publication Society, 1987)

Douglas, Lawrence, *The Memory of Judgment: Making Law and History in the Trials of the Holocaust* (New Haven, Yale University Press, 2001)

Gilroy, Paul, *Between Camps: Nations, Culture and the Allure of Race* (London, Allen Lane, 2000)

Friedländer, Saul, *Memory, History and the Extermination of the Jews of Europe* (Bloomington and Indianapolis, Indiana University Press, 1993)

Friedländer, Saul (ed.), *Probing the Limits of Representation: Nazism and the 'Final Solution'* (Cambridge, Mass., Harvard University Press, 1992)

Hartman, Geoffrey (ed.), *Holocaust Remembrance: The Shapes of Memory*

(London, Blackwell, 1994)

Imperial War Museum, *The Holocaust: The Holocaust Exhibition at the Imperial War Museum* (London, Imperial War Museum, 2000)

Imperial War Museum, *Imperial War Museum North* (London, Imperial War Museum, 2002)

Langer, Lawrence, *Admitting the Holocaust* (New York, Oxford University Press, 1995)

Lanzmann, Claude, 'Shoah as Counter-Myth', *Jewish Quarterly*, no. 121 (Spring 1986)

Linenthal, Edward, *Preserving Memory: The Struggle to Create America's Holocaust Museum* (New York, Viking, 1995)

Maier, Charles, *The Unmasterable Past: History, Holocaust, and German National Identity* (Cambridge, Mass., Harvard University Press, 1988)

Mintz, Alan, *Popular Culture and the Shaping of Holocaust Memory in America* (Seattle, University of Washington Press, 2001)

Novick, Peter, *The Holocaust and Collective Memory* (London, Bloomsbury, 2000)

Reilly, Jo, et al. (eds), *Belsen in History and Memory* (London, Frank Cass, 1997)

Rosenbaum, Alan (ed.), *Is the Holocaust Unique? Perspectives on Comparative Genocide* (Boulder, Col., Westview Press, 1998)

Rousso, Henry, *The Vichy Syndrome: History and Memory in France since 1944* (Cambridge, Mass., Harvard University Press, 1991)

Shandler, Jeffrey, *While America Watches: Televising the Holocaust* (New York, Oxford University Press, 1999)

Vice, Sue (ed.), *Representing the Holocaust* (London, Frank Cass, 2003)

Vidal-Naquet, Pierre, *The Assassins of Memory: Essays on the Denial of the Holocaust* (New York, Columbia University Press, 1992)

Weinberg, Jeshajahu, and Rina Elieli, *The Holocaust Museum in Washington* (New York, Rizzoli, 1995)

Wollaston, Isabel, *A War Against Memory? The Future of Holocaust Remembrance* (London, SPCK, 1996)

Wood, Marcus, *Blind Memory: Visual Representations of Slavery in England and America 1780–1865* (Manchester, Manchester University Press, 2000)

Young, James, *The Texture of Memory: Holocaust Memorials and Meanings* (New Haven Yale University Press, 1993)

Zelizer, Barbie, *Remembering to Forget: Holocaust Memory Through the Camera's Eye* (Chicago, University of Chicago Press, 1988)

Index